STUDY GUIDE

John A. Ward
Miami University

Development Across the Life Span

FOURTH EDITION

Robert S. Feldman
University of Massachusetts at Amherst

PEARSON

Prentice
Hall

Upper Saddle River, New Jersey 07458

Copyright © 2006 by Pearson Education, Inc.
Upper Saddle River, New Jersey 07458
All rights reserved

Printed in the United States of America
10 9 8 7 6 5 4 3 2

ISBN 0-13-192541-5

Table of Contents

Preface

Your Time Is Valuable

Invest your study time so you get the greatest benefit!

The following techniques have been shown to increase a student's mastery of new information:

Use as many of your senses and abilities as possible—writing, reading, hearing, speaking, drawing, etc.

Organize information so it is meaningful to you

Study with other people whenever possible

Have FUN. We remember what we enjoy.

How to Use This Study Guide

1. Learning Objectives

After you have read and studied each chapter, you should be able to complete the learning objectives listed at the beginning of each chapter in this Study Guide.

2. Multiple Choice Questions (Pretest and Post Tests)

Practice tests are an important way to check your progress. There is a pretest at the start of each chapter and a post test at the end of each chapter in this Study Guide. These tests measure your progress toward your goal of mastering the material. Your scores on the post tests should be higher than your scores on the pretests if you have studied the programmed review.

3. Key Names

Different theorists often have conflicting views. And research results may not always agree. Therefore, it is important to know who the major researchers and theorists are.

4. Key Vocabulary Terms

It is important to learn the definitions of terms as they are used in the field of psychology, so you should complete all the exercises related to definitions.

5. Programmed Review

The programmed review will help you learn the major points in each chapter. Try to fill in what you can on your own, but don't hesitate to look up in the text what you don't remember. The act of looking up the material will reinforce your learning of it.

6. Critical Thinking Questions

Many college courses are designed to help you develop your writing skills so completing short essay questions can be useful. This is especially true if your psychology course will include essay exams. Some of the questions you find in each of these chapters are from the chapters in your text.

Study Tips

1. Make material meaningful to you by creating associations with what you already know.
2. Learn the material actively.
    a. Imagine vivid pictures.
    b. Recite out loud.
    c. Tell someone about what you have learned.
1. Study in a quiet environment by reducing noise and interruptions.
2. Be aware of your attitude toward information.
3. Study at spaced intervals—studying the material in manageable blocks as opposed to "cramming" will improve your retention.
4. Remember related information when you are having trouble recalling something.
5. Use mnemonic devices (rhymes or words created from material).

When and How to Study

1. Plan two hours of study time for every hour you spend in class.
2. Study difficult or boring subjects first.
3. Avoid long study sessions.
4. Be aware of your best time of day.
5. Use a regular study area.
6. Don't get too comfortable.
7. Use a library.
8. Take at least one 10-minute break for every 50 minutes of study time.
9. Avoid noise distractions.

Study in Groups

Research has shown that one of the most effective ways to learn is to study with other students. Your grades on exams will be better and you will have a lot more fun doing it.

How to Form a Group

1. Look for dedicated students who share some of your academic goals and challenges.
2. Only study in a group after you have studied individually and this is the same for your other group members.
3. Ask your instructor for help in recruiting group members.
4. Limit groups to fewer than six people.
5. Test the group by planning a one-time-only session. If that session works, plan another.

Possible Activities for a Study Group

1. Compare notes.
2. Have discussions and debates about the material.
3. Test each other with questions brought to the group meeting by each member.
4. Practice teaching each other.
5. Brainstorm possible test questions.
6. Share suggestions for problems in the area of finances, transportation, child care, time scheduling, or other barriers.

Better Test Taking

1. Ask your instructor to describe the test format—how long it will be, and what kind of questions to expect.

2. Have a section in your notebook labeled "Test Questions" and add several questions to this section after every lecture and after reading the text. Record topics that the instructor repeats several times or goes back to in subsequent lectures. Write down questions the instructor poses to students.

3. Know the rules for taking the test so you do not create the impression of cheating.

4. Scan the whole test immediately. Budget your time based on how many points each section is worth.

5. Read the directions slowly. Then reread them.

6. Answer easiest, shortest questions first. This gives you the experience of success, stimulates associations, and prepares your mind for more difficult questions.

7. Use memory techniques when you are stuck. If your recall on something is blocked, remember something else that's related.

8. Look for answers in other test questions. A term, name, date, or other fact that you can't remember might appear in the test itself.

9. Don't change an answer unless you are sure because your first instinct is usually best.

Reading for Remembering

1. Skim the entire chapter.
2. Read the outline at the front of the chapter in the text.
3. Read the material.
4. Highlight the most important information.
5. Recite the key points when you finish an assignment.
6. Plan your first review within 24 hours.
7. Reread the chapter summary.
8. Weekly reviews are important. Go over your notes. Read the highlighted parts of your text. Recite the more complicated points.

More about Review

You can do short reviews anytime, anywhere, if you are prepared. If you don't have time to read a whole assignment, review last week's assignment. Conduct 5 minute reviews regularly. Three-by-five note cards work well for review. Write ideas and facts on cards and carry them with you. These short review periods can be effortless.

Effective Note-Taking During Class

1. Review the text book chapter before class. Instructors often design a lecture based on the assumption that you have read the chapter before class. You can take notes more easily if you already have some idea of the material.

2. Bring your favorite note-taking tools to class.

3. Sit as close to the instructor as possible so that you have fewer distractions.

4. Arrive to class early. Relax and review your notes from the previous class.

5. Focus on understanding what the instructor is saying because that is what you will find on the test. When you hear something you disagree with, make a note about it and ask the instructor for clarification during office hours or after class.

6. Be active in class. Volunteer for demonstrations. Join in class discussions.

7. Relate the topic to an interest of yours. We remember things we are most interested in.

8. Watch for clues of what is important such as repetition, summary statements, information written on the board, information that interests the instructor, information the instructor takes directly from notes.

Chapter 1

An Introduction to Lifespan Development

CHAPTER OUTLINE

- An Orientation to Lifespan Development
  - Characterizing Lifespan Development: The Scope of the Field
  - The Context of Development: Taking a Broad Perspective

- Key Issues and Questions: Determining the Nature—and Nurture—of Lifespan Development

- Theoretical Perspectives
  - The Psychodynamic Perspective: Focusing on the Inner Person
  - The Behavioral Perspective: Focusing on Observable Behavior
  - The Cognitive Perspective: Examining the Roots of Understanding
  - The Humanistic Perspective: Concentrating on the Unique Qualities of Human Beings
  - Evolutionary Perspectives: Our Ancestors' Contributions to Behavior
  - Why "Which Approach is Right?" Is the Wrong Question

- Research Methods
  - Theories and Hypotheses: Posing Developmental Questions
  - Choosing a Research Strategy: Answering Questions
  - Correlational Studies
  - Experiments: Determining Cause and Effect
  - Theoretical and Applied Research: Complimentary Approaches
  - Measuring Developmental Change
  - Ethics and Research

LEARNING OBJECTIVES

After you have read and studied this chapter, you should be able to answer the following questions.

1. What is lifespan development, and what are some of the basic influences on human development?
2. What are the key issues in the field of development?
3. Which theoretical perspectives have guided lifespan development?
4. What role do theories and hypotheses play in the study of development?
5. How are developmental research studies conducted?

PRACTICE TEST - PRETEST

Circle the correct answer for each multiple choice question and check your answers with the Answer Key at the end of the chapter.

1. A research developmentalist is focusing her investigations on physical development in infants. In which of the following would she be most interested?
    a. memory   c. crawling
    b. language   d. emotions

2   A developmentalist who studies how memory changes over the life span specializes in
    a. social development.   c. cognitive development.
    b. physical development.   d. personality development.

3. What is the average age range for young adulthood?
    a. 12-19 years of age   c. 20-30 years of age
    b. 18-21 years of age   d. 20-40 years of age

4. Bronfenbrenner labeled our larger cultural environment as the
    a. microsystem.   c. mesosystem.
    b. macrosystem.   d. exosystem.

5. Race is a _____ concept.
    a. cognitive   c. biological
    b. cultural   d. social

6. Jennifer is experiencing symptoms of menopause. Her monthly menstrual cycle has stopped and she has had some hot flashes. What she is experiencing could be labeled as a
    a. nonnormative life event.
    b. age-graded influence.
    c. history-graded influence.
    d. sociocultural-graded influence.

7. Freud theorized that when we are born we function totally from our
    a. id.   c. superego.
    b. ego.   d. libido.

8. Erikson's stages of development focus on
    a. a hierarchy of needs.
    b. pleasurable erogenous zones.
    c. conflicts throughout the life span.
    d. infancy and childhood developmental needs.

9. A developmental psychologist who believes that only observable behavior is the key to understanding development advocates the
    a. cognitive perspective.   c. psychodynamic perspective.
    b. behavioral perspective.   d. information-processing perspective.

10. Sociocultural theory is discussed by
    a. Skinner.   c. Vygotsky.
    b. Watson.   d. Freud.

11. Which of the following is an advocate of the humanistic perspective?
    a. Rogers   c. Piaget
    b. Freud   d. Watson

12. Evolutionary theory would suggest that behavior is a result of genetic inheritance from our
    a. animals.   c. free will.
    b. ancestors.   d. current society.

13. According to the social learning theory, behavior is learned through
    a. observation.   c. fixation.
    b. trial and error.   d. self-actualization.

14. A researcher conducts in-depth interviews with a small group of children who are thought to have psychic abilities. What type of study is she conducting?
    a. survey   c. field study
    b. case study   d. experiment

15. Michael is the son of a woman with schizophrenia. Annually for the last 10 years he has received a questionnaire from scientists researching whether schizophrenia is an inherited disorder. He is participating in a
    a. longitudinal study.   c. cross-sectional study.
    b. cross-cultural study.   d. sequential study.

16. A primary proponent of the psychodynamic perspective is
    a. Skinner.   c. Watson.
    b. Lorenz.   d. Freud.

17. Which correlation is strongest?
    a. -.86   c. -.15
    b. +.63   d. +.42

18. Which of the following approaches is NOT associated with behavioral theory?
    a. cognitive neuroscience   c. classical conditioning
    b. social-cognitive learning theory   d. operant conditioning

19. Requiring that participants understand the research in which they participate satisfies the ethical guideline concerning
    a. freedom from harm.   c. maintenance of privacy.
    b. informed consent.   d. use of deception.

20. The variable manipulated by the researchers is the _____ variable.
    a. dependent   c. control
    b. independent   d. correlational

KEY NAMES

Match the following names with the appropriate description and check your answers with the Answer Key at the end of this chapter.

1. ___ Paul Baltes   a. behavioral approach

2. ___ Albert Bandura   b. cognitive development

3. ___ Urie Bronfenbrenner   c. bioecological approach

4. ___ Charles Darwin   d. ethology

5. ___ Erik Erikson   e. evolution

6. ___ Sigmund Freud   f. longitudinal research

7. ___ Konrad Lorenz   g. operant conditioning

8. ___ Abraham Maslow   h. positive regard

9. ___ Jean Piaget   i. psychosexual theory

10. ___ Carl Rogers   j. psychosocial theory

11. ___ B. F. Skinner   k. self-actualization

12. ___ Lewis Terman   l. social-cognitive learning theory

13. ___ Lev Vygotsky   m. sociocultural theory

14. ___ John B. Watson   n. lifespan approach

KEY VOCABULARY TERMS

Look up the definition and give a specific example of each of the following types of development.

1. Physical development   4. Social development
2. Cognitive development   5. Psychosexual development
3. Personality development   6. Psychosocial development

Label each definition and give a specific example of each.

7. Biological and environmental influences associated with a particular historical moment.

8. Biological and environmental influences that are similar for individuals in a particular age group, regardless of when or where they are raised.

9. The impact of social and cultural factors present at a particular time for a particular individual depending on such variables as ethnicity, social class, and subcultural membership.

10. Specific, atypical events that occur in a particular person's life at a time when they do not happen to most people.

Match the definition with the correct perspective, theory, or approach listed below.

a. Behavioral perspective   e. Humanistic perspective
b. Cognitive neuroscience perspective   f. Information-processing approaches
c. Cognitive perspective   g. Social-cognitive learning theory
d. Evolutionary perspective   h. Sociocultural theory

11. Learning by observing the behavior of another person, called a model.

12. The approach that focuses on the processes that allows people to know, understand, and think about the world.

13. The model that seeks to identify the ways individuals take in, use, and store information.

4

14. The approach that emphasizes how cognitive development proceeds as a result of social interactions between members of a culture.

15. The theory that contends that people have a natural capacity to make decisions about their lives and control their behavior.

16. The theory that seeks to identify behavior that is a result of our genetic inheritance from our ancestors.

17. The approach that suggests that the keys to understanding development are observable behavior and outside stimuli in the environment.

18. The approach that examines cognitive development through the lens of brain processes.

Explain the difference between the following sets of terms.

19. Continuous change; Discontinuous change
20. Critical period; Sensitive period
21. Classical conditioning; Operant conditioning
22. Treatment group; Control group
23. Independent variable; Dependent variable
24. Theoretical research; Applied research

Give a brief example of each of the following types of research.

25. Experimental research
26. Correlational research
27. Case studies
28. Survey research
29. Cross-sectional research
30. Sequential studies

Fill in the term matching the definition. The first letters of each term from top to bottom will spell the term for the definition at the bottom of the puzzle.

31. _ _ _ _ _ _ _ _   According to Freud, the aspect of personality that represents a person's conscience.

    _ _ _ _ _ _ _ _ _ _ _   The process in which people understand an experience in terms of their current stage of cognitive development.

    _ _ _ _ _ _ _ _ _   The predetermined unfolding of genetic information.

    _ _ _ _ _ _ _ _ _ _ _   The approach that states behavior is motivated by inner forces, memories, and conflicts that are generally beyond people's awareness or control.

    _ _ _ _ _ _ _ _ _ _   Research in which the behavior of one or more participants in a study is measured as they age.

    _ _ _   According to Freud, the part of the personality that is rational and reasonable.

The group of participants chosen for an experiment. _ _ _ _ _ _

32. _ _ _ _ _ _ _ _ _   A study in which research is conducted in a controlled setting explicitly designed to hold events constant.

5

_ _	According to Freud, the raw, unorganized, inborn part of personality present at birth, that represents primitive drives related to hunger, sex, aggression, and irrational impulses.
_ _ _ _ _ _ _ _ _ _	A research investigation carried out in a naturally occurring setting.
_ _ _ _ _ _ _ _ _ _ _	The perspective that seeks to identify behavior that is a result of our genetic inheritance from our ancestors.
_ _ _ _ _ _ _ _ _ _	The method of posing and answering questions using careful, controlled techniques that include systematic, orderly observation and the collection of data.
_ _ _ _ _ _ _ _ _ _ _ _ _	The theory proposed by Freud that suggests that unconscious forces act to determine personality and behavior.
_ _ _ _ _ _ _ _ _ _ _ _	The process that changes existing ways of thinking in response to encounters with new stimuli or events.
_ _ _ _ _ _ _ _ _ _	A type of observational study in which naturally occurring behavior is observed without intervention.

The field of study that examines patterns of growth, change, and stability in behavior that occur from prenatal development through death is _ _ _ _ _ _ _ _ development.

Write out the definitions to the following terms and give a specific example of each.

33. Behavior modification
34. Cohort
35. Experiment
36. Hypothesis
37. Sequential study
38. Theories

PROGRAMMED REVIEW

Fill in the blanks in the following programmed review. Then check your answers with the Answer Key at the end of the chapter.

An Orientation to Lifespan Development

1. Lifespan development is the field of study that examines patterns of growth, _____, and stability in behavior that occur throughout the entire life span. This field takes a _____ approach and focuses on _____ development.

Characterizing Lifespan Development: The Scope of the Field

2. Some developmentalists focus on _____ development, examining the ways in which the body's makeup helps determine behavior. Others examine _____ development, seeking to understand how growth and change in intellectual capabilities influence a person's behavior. _____ development is the study of stability and change in the enduring characteristics that differentiate one person from another over the life span. _____ development is the way in which individuals' interactions with others and their social relationships grow, change, and remain stable over the course of life.

3. The life span is usually divided into the _____ period from conception to birth, _____ and _____ from birth to age 3, the _____ period from age 3 to 6, _____ childhood from age 6 to 12, _____ from age 12 to 20, _____ adulthood from age 20 to 40, _____ adulthood from age 40 to 60, and _____ adulthood from age 60 to death.

4. It is important to keep in mind that these broad age ranges are _____ and there are substantial _____ in the timing of events in people's lives.

<u>The Context of Development: Taking a Broad Perspective</u>

5. Bronfenbrenner proposed the _____ approach that suggests there are four levels of the environment that simultaneously influence individuals. The _____ is the everyday, immediate environment in which people lead their daily lives; the _____ provides connections between the various aspects of the microsystem; the _____ represents broader influences, encompassing societal institutions; the _____ represents the larger cultural influences on an individual; finally, the _____ underlies each of the previous systems. This approach emphasizes the _____ of the influences on development.

6. The dominant Western philosophy is _____, emphasizing personal identity, uniqueness, freedom, and the worth of the individual. Asian cultures value _____, the notion that the well-being of the group is more important than that of the individual.

7. _____ is a biological concept; whereas _____ or _____ refers to cultural background, nationality, religion, and language.

8. Each person belongs to a particular _____, a group of people born at around the same time in the same place. _____ provide an example of _____ influences which are biological and environmental influences associated with a particular historical moment. In contrast, _____ influences are similar for individuals in a particular age group. Development is also affected by, _____ the social and cultural factors present at a particular time for a particular individual. _____ life events are specific, atypical events that occur in a particular person's life at a time when such events do not happen to most people.

Key Issues and Questions: Determining the Nature—and Nurture—of Lifespan Development

9. In _____ change, development is gradual; in _____ change, development occurs in distinct stages. A _____ period is a specific time during development when a particular event has its greatest consequences; _____ periods are times when an organism is particularly susceptible to certain kinds of stimuli in the environment.

10. _____ refers to traits, abilities, and capacities that are inherited from one's parents. The predetermined unfolding of genetic information is a process known as _____. _____ refers to the environmental influences that shape behavior.

Theoretical Perspectives

11. Explanations and predictions concerning phenomena of interest are _____.

<u>The Psychodynamic Perspective: Focusing on the Inner Person</u>

12. Proponents of the _____ perspective believe that behavior is motivated by unconscious forces, memories, and conflicts of which a person has little awareness or control. In Freud's _____ theory, the _____ is a part of the personality about which a person is unaware. Freud stated that the personality has _____ aspects. The _____ is the raw, unorganized, inborn part of the personality present at birth, representing primitive _____, and operating according to the _____ principle. The _____ is the part of the personality that is rational and reasonable and operates on the _____ principle. The _____ represents a person's _____, incorporating distinctions between right and wrong and developing around age _____.

13. Freud argued that _____ development occurs as children pass through a series of stages. Pleasure shifts from the mouth (the _____ stage) to the anus (the _____ stage), and eventually to the genitals (the _____ stage and the _____ stage). _____ reflecting an earlier stage of development is due to an unresolved conflict.

14. Erikson's theory of _____ development encompasses changes in interactions with and understanding of one another as well as knowledge and understanding of ourselves as members of society. There are _____ distinct stages, each presenting a _____ or conflict that the individual must resolve.

The Behavioral Perspective: Focusing on Observable Behavior

15. The behavioral perspective suggests that the keys to understanding development are observable _____ and outside stimuli in the _____. The first American psychologist to advocate the behavioral approach was _____.

16. In _____ conditioning, an organism learns to respond in a particular way to a neutral stimulus that normally does not evoke that type of response. In _____ conditioning as described by _____, a voluntary response is strengthened or weakened by association with positive or negative consequences. The process by which a stimulus is provided that increases the probability that a preceding behavior will be repeated is _____; whereas _____ is the introduction of an unpleasant or punitive stimulus or the removal of a desirable stimulus to decrease the probability that a preceding behavior will occur in the future. Behavior that receives no reinforcement or is punished becomes _____. Principles of operant conditioning are used in behavior _____, a formal technique for promoting the frequency of desirable behaviors and decreasing the incidence of unwanted ones.

17. According to Bandura, a significant amount of learning is explained by _____ learning theory, an approach that emphasizes learning by observing the behavior of another person called a _____. Bandura suggests that social-cognitive learning proceeds in _____ steps. First an observer must pay _____ and perceive the most critical features of a model's behavior, then successfully _____ the behavior, _____ the behavior accurately, and be _____ to learn and carry out the behavior.

The Cognitive Perspective: Examining the Roots of Understanding

18. The cognitive perspective focuses on the processes that allow people to know, _____, and think about the world and emphasizes how people _____ represent and think about the world. Piaget suggested that human thinking is arranged into _____, organized patterns that represent behaviors and actions. Children's understanding of the world can be explained by the basic principle of _____, the process in which people understand experiences in terms of their current stage of cognitive development, and _____, changes in existing ways of thinking in response to encounters with new stimuli or events.

19. _____ approaches to cognitive development seek to identify the ways individuals take in, use, and store information. Piaget's view is that thinking undergoes _____ advances as children age; whereas information-processing approaches assume that development is marked more by _____ changes.

20. Vygotsky's _____ theory emphasizes how cognitive development proceeds as a result of social _____ between members of a culture. This theory also emphasizes that development is a _____ transaction between the people in a child's environment and the child.

21. _____ approaches examine cognitive development though the lens of brain processes.

The Humanistic Perspective: Concentrating on the Unique Qualities of Human Beings

22. The humanistic perspective contends that people have a natural capacity to make _____ about their lives and _____ their behavior. It emphasizes _____, the ability of humans to make choices and come to decisions about their lives. Rogers suggested that all people have a need for _____ regard that results from an underlying wish to be loved and respected. Maslow suggested that _____ is the primary goal in life.

Evolutionary Perspectives: Our Ancestors' Contributions to Behavior

23. The evolutionary perspective seeks to identify behavior that is the result of our _____ inheritance from our ancestors. Evolutionary approaches grow out of the work of _____ and draw heavily on the field of _____ which examines the ways in which our biological makeup influences our behavior. Behavioral _____ studies the effects of heredity on behavior.

Research Methods

Theories and Hypotheses: Posing Developmental Questions

24. The _____ method is the process of posing and answering questions using careful, controlled techniques that include systematic, orderly observation and the collection of data. A _____ is a prediction stated in a way that permits it to be tested.

Choosing a Research Strategy: Answering Questions

25. _____ research seeks to identify whether an association or relationship between two factors exists, but cannot be used to determine whether one factor _____ changes in the other. _____ research is designed to discover causal relationships.

Correlational Studies

26. The strength and direction of a relationship between two factors is represented by a correlation _____ that ranges from +1.0 to -1.0. A _____ correlation indicates that the two factors increase or decrease together; a _____ correlation indicates that increases in one factor accompany decreases in the other. The lack of any relationship is indicated by a correlation coefficient that is close to _____.

27. _____ observation is the observation of a naturally occurring behavior without intervention in the situation. It employs _____, a method borrowed from the field of anthropology in which researchers act as _____ observers. _____ studies involve extensive, in-depth interviews with a particular individual or small group of individuals. In _____ research, people chosen to represent some larger population are asked questions about their attitudes, behavior, or thinking on a given topic.

Experiments: Determining Cause and Effect

28. An experimenter typically devises two different experiences or _____ for participants. The group receiving the treatment is called the treatment or _____ group; the one with no-treatment or an alternative treatment is the _____ group. The _____ variable is the variable that the researchers manipulate; whereas the _____ variable is the one that is measured and expected to _____ as a result of the experimental manipulation. In experiments, there is _____ assignment of participants who make up the _____.

29. A _____ study is a research investigation carried out in a naturally occurring setting. A _____ study is conducted in a controlled setting explicitly designed to hold events _____.

Theoretical and Applied Research: Complementary Approaches

30. _____ research is designed specifically to test some developmental explanation and expand scientific knowledge; whereas _____ research is meant to provide practical solutions to immediate problems.

Measuring Developmental Change

31. In _____ research, the behavior of study participants is measured as they age. This type of research provides information about _____ over time, but there is the problem of participant _____ and participants becoming _____.

32. In _____ research, people of different ages are compared at the same point in time. There may be problems in this research because everyone belongs to a _____, a group of people born around the same time and in the same place, and there is the risk of selective _____ in which participants in some age groups are more likely to quit participating in a study than are others.

33. In _____ studies, researchers examine a number of different age groups at several points in time combining the advantages of _____ and _____ research. It permits developmental researchers to tease out the consequences of age _____ versus age _____.

Ethics and Research

34. The major organizations of developmentalists have comprehensive ethical guidelines for researchers which include freedom from _____, informed _____, the use of _____, and maintenance of _____.

35. Not all advice is equally _____. To determine whether recommendations and suggestions are reasonable, consider the _____, evaluate the _____ of the person providing the advice, understand the difference between anecdotal evidence and _____ evidence, keep _____ context in mind, and don't assume that because many people _____ something, it is necessarily true.

CRITICAL THINKING QUESTIONS

To further your mastery of the topics, write out the answers to the following essay questions in the space provided.

1. What are some possible advantages of taking a lifespan approach to the study of human development? What are some possible disadvantages?

2. How might each of the four elements of the bioecological approach influence a major developmental step, such as the decision to marry or not to marry?

3. What are some events that might have a shared significance for members of your age cohort as normative history-graded influences? How might they produce different effects from events shared by members of different age cohorts?

4. Describe one aspect of human development in each area (physical, cognitive, personality, and social) that is affected by both nature and nurture.

5. What problems might affect a study of age-related changes in sexual attitudes and practices conducted at one time among a cross section of adults aged 20 to 70?

6. How can reinforcement (or punishment) be used to explain how students might be motivated to earn good grades?

7. How do the concepts of social learning and modeling relate to the mass media?

8. Formulate a theory about one aspect of human development and a hypothesis that relates to it.

9. Can you think of a correlation between two phenomena related to gender? What are some possible explanations for the correlation? How would you establish causality?

10. What sort of research strategy would be appropriate for investigating each of the statements (about comforting babies, spanking, and divorce) at the beginning of the Informed Consumer box? Would a laboratory or a field setting be most appropriate for each research strategy you identified?

PRACTICE TEST – POST TEST

Circle the correct answer for each multiple choice question and check your answers with the Answer Key at the end of the chapter.

1. Roberta is trying to decide whether or not she should breast-feed. She is most interested in whether breast-feeding helps a newborn fight off infections. Her question is of interest to developmentalists who specialize in
   a. social development.
   b. physical development.
   c. cognitive development.
   d. personality development.

2. A researcher studies how individuals born during the depression compare to individuals born during the prosperous 1970s. The groups of individuals are called
   a. cohorts.   c. macrosystems.
   b. mesosystems.   d. reference groups.

3. The church and school that Takesha attends are part of her
   a. microsystem.   c. exosystem.
   b. mesosystem.   d. macrosystem.

4. North American culture is characterized as _____; Asian cultures are characterized as _____.
   a. individualistic; collectivistic   c. collectivistic; individualistic
   b. individualistic; paternalistic   d. paternalistic; collectivistic

5. The fact that most people can learn new languages throughout their lives, yet we have an affinity for doing so during infancy and toddlerhood underscores the importance of
   a. critical periods.   c. continuous change.
   b. sensitive periods.   d. discontinuous change.

6. The group of children born in the United States approximately nine months after September 11, 2001, would be considered a(n)
   a. epidemic.   c. race.
   b. ethnic group.   d. cohort.

7. Laura forms a hypothesis as she starts to work on her latest research project; in doing so she will
   a. inform her participants of any risks involved.
   b. identify whether an association exists between two or more factors.
   c. make a prediction stated in a way that it can be tested.
   d. seek the guidance of other researchers who have completed similar work.

8. You would like to eat another piece of apple pie but you are on a diet. If you eat that second piece of pie, you will feel guilty. What part of your personality will cause this guilt?
   a. id   c. libido
   b. superego   d. ego

9. Freud is to _____ development as Erikson is to _____ development.
   a. cognitive; social   c. psychosexual; psychosocial
   b. psychosocial; psychosexual   d. social; cognitive

10. A friend of yours eats too much and talks too much. Freud's theory would indicate
    a. anal retention issues.
    b. fixation in the oral stage.
    c. fixation in the phallic stage.
    d. defense mechanisms being used to the extreme.

11. When Dave hears the horn blow on the catering truck at 10:30 a.m., he goes outside and buys a donut even though he isn't hungry. His association between the horn of the catering truck and his hunger is the result of
    a. shaping.   c. operant conditioning.
    b. counterconditioning.   d. classical conditioning.

12. What is the third step suggested in Bandura's social-cognitive learning theory?
    a. reproducing the behavior   c. recalling the behavior
    b. paying attention   d. motivation to learn

13. You and a friend worked with the homeless last summer and you both changed the way you thought about homelessness. What Piagetian process was at work?
   a.   assimilation
   b.   equilibration
   c.   psychosocialism
   d.   accommodation

14. Which type of research identifies whether a relationship between two factors exists?
   a.   survey
   b.   correlation
   c.   case study
   d.   experiment

15. A researcher is interested in determining the effect of phonics training on reading skills. Two groups of children in reading classes are studied. One group receives phonics training and the other group receives the current "whole word" method of teaching reading. At the end of four months the two groups are tested for reading skill level. What is the treatment in this experiment?
   a.   the two groups of children
   b.   the reading skill test scores
   c.   the "whole word" method
   d.   the phonics training

16. All of the following are disadvantages of longitudinal research EXCEPT
   a.   participants become "test-wise."
   b.   there is no measure of change over time.
   c.   a tremendous investment of time is required.
   d.   significant possibility of participant attrition exists.

17. A researcher studies three groups of people for one day; 15-year-olds, 30-year-olds, and 45-year-olds. The study compares the different age groups in terms of their sources of stress. What research strategy is the researcher using?
   a.   age cohort
   b.   longitudinal
   c.   cross-sectional
   d.   cross-sequential

18. Keith learns about etiquette by observing how his father interacts with his mother. This type of learning can be described as
   a.   habituation.
   b.   social-cognitive learning.
   c.   operant conditioning.
   d.   classical conditioning.

19. A 2 ½-year-old seems to be in a power struggle with her parents. What psychosexual stage is she experiencing?
   a.   oral stage
   b.   anal stage
   c.   phallic stage
   d.   latency stage

20. Joan wants to conduct a study whereby she examines the motor development of children over time. She plans to start with groups of 3-, 6-, and 9-year-olds and measure their development every two years for the next ten years. What research design must she employ?
   a.   cohort
   b.   longitudinal
   c.   cross-sectional
   d.   sequential

ANSWER KEYS

Practice Test - Pretest (with text page numbers)

Pretest

1.	c 6	6.	b 12	11.	a 26	16.	d 18
2.	c 6	7.	a 18	12.	b 26	17.	a 33
3.	d 6	8.	c 19	13.	a 22	18.	a 25
4.	b 9	9.	b 20	14.	b 34	19.	b 40
5.	c 10	10.	c 24	15.	a 33	20	b 35

Key Names

1.	n	5.	j	9.	b	13.	m
2.	l	6.	i	10.	h	14.	a
3.	c	7.	d	11.	g		
4.	e	8.	k	12.	f		

Key Vocabulary Terms

7. history-graded influences
8. age-graded influences
9. sociocultural-graded influences
10. nonnormative life events

Match the Definition

11.	g	13.	f	15.	e	17.	a
12.	c	14.	h	16.	d	18.	b

19. <u>Continuous change</u> is gradual; whereas <u>discontinuous change</u> occurs in distinct steps or stages.

20. <u>Critical periods</u> are specific times during development when a particular event has its greatest consequences; <u>sensitive periods</u> are points in development when organisms are particularly susceptible to certain kinds of stimuli in their environments.

21. <u>Classical conditioning</u> is learning in which an organism responds in a particular way to a neutral stimulus that normally does not bring about that type of response; <u>operant conditioning</u> is learning in which a voluntary response is strengthened or weakened, depending on its association with positive or negative consequences.

22. The <u>treatment group</u> receives the treatment; the <u>control group</u> receives either no treatment or alternative treatment.

23. The <u>independent variable</u> is manipulated by the researchers; the <u>dependent variable</u> is measured and expected to change as a result of the experimental manipulation.

24. <u>Theoretical research</u> is designed specifically to test some developmental explanation and expand scientific knowledge; <u>applied research</u> is meant to provide practical solutions to immediate problems.

31. Superego, Assimilation, Maturation, Psychodynamic, Longitudinal, Ego (Sample)

32. Laboratory, Id, Field study, Evolutionary, Scientific, Psychoanalytic, Accommodation, Naturalistic (Lifespan)

Programmed Review

1. change, scientific, human
2. physical, cognitive, Personality, Social
3. prenatal, infancy, toddlerhood, preschool, middle, adolescence, young, middle, late
4. social construction, individual differences
5. bioecological, microsystem, mesosystem, exosystem, macrosystem, chronosystem, interconnectedness
6. individualism, collectivism
7. Race, ethnic group, ethnicity
8. cohort, cohort effects, history-graded, age-graded, sociocultural-graded, Nonnormative
9. continuous, discontinuous, critical, sensitive
10. Nature, maturation, Nurture
11. theories
12. psychodynamic, psychoanalytic, unconscious, three, id, drives, pleasure, ego, reality, superego, conscience, five or six
13. psychosexual, oral, anal, phallic, genital, Fixation
14. psychosocial, eight, crisis
15. behavior, environment, Watson
16. classical, operant, Skinner, reinforcement, punishment, extinguished, modification
17. social-cognitive, model, four, attention, recall, reproduce, motivated
18. understand, internally, schemes, assimilation, accommodation
19. Information-processing, qualitative, quantitative
20. sociocultural, interactions, reciprocal
21. Cognitive neuroscience
22. decisions, control, free will, positive, self-actualization
23. genetic, Darwin, ethology, genetics
24. scientific, hypothesis
25. Correlational, causes, Experimental
26. coefficient, positive, negative, zero
27. Naturalistic, ethnography, participant, Case, survey
28. treatments, experimental, control, independent, dependent, change, random, sample
29. field, laboratory, constant
30. Theoretical, applied
31. longitudinal, change, attrition, test-wise
32. cross-sectional, cohort, dropout
33. sequential, longitudinal, cross-sectional, change, difference
34. harm, consent, deception, privacy
35. valid, source, credentials, scientific, cultural, believe

Practice Test – Post Test (with text page numbers)

1.	b	6	6.	d	12	11.	d	21	16.	b	38
2.	a	12	7.	c	31	12.	a	22	17.	c	38
3.	c	9	8.	b	18	13.	d	23	18.	b	22
4.	a	10	9.	c	18	14.	b	31	19.	b	19
5.	b	14	10.	b	19	15.	d	34	20.	d	39

Chapter 2

The Start of Life: Genetics and Prenatal Development

CHAPTER OUTLINE

◆ Earliest Development
- ♦ Genes and Chromosomes: The Code of Life
- ♦ The Basics of Genetics: The Mixing and Matching of Traits
- ♦ Inherited and Genetic Disorders: When Development Goes Awry
- ♦ Genetic Counseling: Predicting the Future from the Genes of the Present

◆ The Interaction of Heredity and Environment
- ♦ The Role of the Environment in Determining the Expression of Genes: From Genotypes to Phenotypes
- ♦ Studying Development: How Much Is Nature? How much Is Nurture?
- ♦ Physical Traits: Family Resemblances
- ♦ Intelligence: More Research, More Controversy
- ♦ Genetic and Environmental Influences on Personality: Born to Be Outgoing?
- ♦ Psychological Disorders: The Role of Genetics and Environment
- ♦ Can Genes Influence Environment?

◆ Prenatal Growth and Change
- ♦ Fertilization: The Moment of Conception
- ♦ The Stages of the Prenatal Period: The Onset of Development
- ♦ Problems in Pregnancy
- ♦ The Prenatal Environment: Threats to Development

LEARNING OBJECTIVES

After you have read and studied this chapter, you should be able to answer the following questions.

1. What is our basic genetic endowment, and how can human development go awry?
2. How do the environment and genetics work together to determine human characteristics?
3. Which human characteristics are significantly influenced by heredity?
4. What happens during the prenatal stages of development?
5. What are the threats to the fetal environment and what can be done about them?

PRACTICE TEST - PRETEST

Circle the correct answer for each of the following multiple choice questions and check your answers with the Answer Key at the end of this chapter.

1. Michelle is expecting twins that are the result of two eggs being fertilized by two sperm. Her babies are
   a. dizygotic.
   b. identical.
   c. monozygotic.
   d. multizygotic.

2. Becky's mother has blue eyes and her father has brown eyes. Becky has brown eyes. Becky's phenotype is
   a. blue eyes.
   b. brown eyes.
   c. two "brown eye" genes.
   d. one "brown eye" gene and one "blue eye" gene.

3. Which of the following is a genetically normal male?
   a. XY
   b. XX
   c. YX
   d. YY

4. A person with Down syndrome has
   a. only one chromosome 5.
   b. an extra X chromosome.
   c. an extra chromosome 21.
   d. two X and one Y chromosome.

5. At about the seventh week of pregnancy, a test was done on a patient that involved withdrawing and analyzing amniotic fluid. This test is called
   a. fetoscopy.
   b. ultrasound.
   c. amniocentesis.
   d. chorionic villus sampling.

6. Infertility is defined as the inability to conceive after
   a. 3 to 6 months of sexual intercourse.
   b. 10 months of sexual intercourse.
   c. 12 to 18 months of trying to get pregnant with unprotected intercourse.
   d. 24 months of trying to get pregnant with the help of fertility drugs.

7. _____ usually causes death before its victims reach school age and occurs mainly in Jews of eastern European ancestry and in French-Canadians.
   a. Sickle-cell anemia
   b. Tay-Sachs disease
   c. Klinefelter's syndrome
   d. Fragile X syndrome

8. What difference in temperament did Kagan find in his study that compared four-month-old infants in China, Ireland, and the United States?
   a. Chinese babies had significantly lower motor activity, irritability, and vocalization.
   b. American babies had abnormally high motor activity, irritability, and vocalization.
   c. American babies had significantly lower motor activity, irritability, and vocalization.
   d. Irish babies had significantly lower motor activity, irritability, and vocalization.

9. What is the first stage of prenatal development?
   a. zygotic
   b. embryonic
   c. germinal
   d. blastocyst

10. A patient took DES during pregnancy. Her daughter has a possible risk of
    a. sterility.
    b. toxemia.
    c. breast cancer.
    d. vaginal or cervical cancer.

17

11. The process by which a sperm and an ovum join to form a single new cell is called
   a. ovulation.
   c. fertilization.
   b. conception.
   d. insemination.

12. When couples use fertility drugs to help them conceive, what is the chance that they will have dizygotic twins?
   a. 1 in 10
   c. 1 in 100
   b. 1 in 50
   d. 1 in 1000

13. Polygenic inheritance is
   a. the phenotype of the individual.
   b. a trait that is expressed in the individual, but not inherited.
   c. a trait caused by an interaction of gene pairs.
   d. one gene of a gene pair causing a particular trait to be expressed.

14. The gender of the child is determined by
   a. the mother.
   b. the father.
   c. random distribution of chromosomes.
   d. the mother for a girl and the father for a boy.

15. Which of the following is an inherited disorder produced by a single allele?
   a. FAS
   c. PKU
   b. CVS
   d. FAE

16. Which of the following disorders does NOT result in some degree of mental retardation?
   a. Down syndrome
   c. Klinefelter's syndrome
   b. Tay-Sachs disease
   d. Fragile X syndrome

17. Basic units of genetic information are
   a. gametes.
   c. chromosomes.
   b. DNA.
   d. genes.

18. The determination of traits by a combination of both genetic and environmental factors is
   a. polygenic transmission.
   c. chorionic transmission.
   b. dizygotic transmission.
   d. multifactorial transmission.

19. _____ studied cross-pollination of pea plants to observe properties of dominant and recessive traits.
   a. Darwin
   c. Jensen
   b. Mendel
   d. Scarr

20. The conduit between the mother and fetus is the
   a. blastocyst.
   c. placenta.
   b. endoderm.
   d. amnion.

KEY NAMES

Match the following names with the appropriate description.

1. ___ Arthur Jensen   a. dominant and recessive traits

2. ___ Jerome Kagan   b. genotype-environment effects

3. ___ Gregor Mendel   c. inheritance of intelligence

4. ___ Sandra Scarr   d. temperament

KEY VOCABULARY TERMS

Explain the difference between the terms in each of the following groups.

1. Monozygotic twins; Dizygotic twins
2. Homozygous; Heterozygous
3. Dominant trait; Recessive trait
4. Fetal alcohol syndrome (FAS); Fetal alcohol effect (FAE)
5. Genes; DNA; Chromosomes
6. Down syndrome; Sickle-cell anemia

Look up the definitions of the following terms and given a specific example of each.

7. Polygenic inheritance
8. Behavioral genetics
9. Genetic counseling
10. Multifactorial transmission
11. Temperament
12. Tetrogen

Explain the relationship among the following.

13. Gametes, Fertilization, Zygote, Germinal stage, Embryonic stage, Fetal stage, Fetus

Differentiate among the following prenatal tests.

14. Amniocentesis; Chorionic villus sampling (CVS); Ultrasound sonography

Differentiate among the following methods of fertilization.

15. Artificial insemination; In vitro fertilization (IVF); Surrogate mother

Fill in the blanks in each of the following puzzles with the term that belongs with each definition. The first letter of each term will spell, from top to bottom, the term that matches the last definition. (NOTE: Some terms may be from previous chapters.)

16. _

A disorder produced by injury to a gene on the 23rd chromosome pair, producing mild to moderate mental retardation is called Fragile _ syndrome.

_ _ _ _ _ _ _ _ _ _

Research in which behaviors of one or more participants in a study are measured as they age.

_ _ _ _ _ _ _ _ _

The inability to conceive after 12 to 18 months of trying to become pregnant.

_ _ _ _ _ _ _ _ _ _

A type of observation in which naturally occurring behavior is observed without intervention.

_ _ _ _ _ _ _ _ _ _

A syndrome resulting from the presence of an extra X chromosome that produces males with underdeveloped genitals, extreme height, and enlarged breasts.

_ _ _ _ _ _

A milder version of FAS is Fetal Alcohol _____.

- - - - - - - -   The one trait that is expressed when two competing traits are present.

Genes that are recessive and located only on the X chromosome.   _ - _ _ _ _ _ _

17.   - - - - - - - -   A factor that produces a birth defect.

- - - - - - - -   A genotype-environment effect in which a child's genes elicit a particular type of environment.

- - - - - - - - -   The predetermined unfolding of genetic information.

- - - - - - - -   An observable trait.

- - -   According to Freud, the part of the personality that is rational and reasonable.

- - - - - - - -   A trait that is present but not expressed.

- - - - - - - - - - -   The process of identifying genetic defects by examining a small sample of fetal cells withdrawn by a needle inserted into the amniotic fluid.

- - - - - - - - - - - -   The determination of traits by a combination of both genetic and environmental factors in which a genotype provides a range within which a phenotype may be expressed.

- - - - - - - - -   The perspective suggesting that different levels of the environment simultaneously influence individuals.

- - - - - - - - - - -   An atypical event that occurs in a person's life at a time when it does not happen to most people.

- - -   - - - - -   An untreatable disorder that produces blindness and muscle degeneration prior to death.

Patterns of arousal and emotionality that represent consistent and enduring characteristics in an individual.   - - - -
- - - - - -

PROGRAMMED REVIEW

Fill in the blanks in the following programmed review and check your answers with the Answer Key at the end of the chapter.

Earliest Development

1.   The first cell of human life is created when a male reproductive cell, a _____ pushes through the membrane of the _____, the female reproductive cell. These _____ each contain huge amounts of genetic information. About an hour or so after sperm enters the ovum, the two gametes suddenly fuse, becoming one cell, a _____.

Genes and Chromosomes: The Code of Life

2. _____ are the basic units of genetic information and are composed of specific sequences of _____ molecules. They are arranged in specific locations and in specific order along 46 _____, rod-shaped portions of DNA that are organized in 23 pairs. Through a cell replication process called _____, all the cells of the body contain the same 46 chromosomes as the zygote.

3. When gametes are formed in the adult human body, in a process called _____, each gamete receives one of the body's two pairs of 23 chromosomes. There are some _____ different combinations possible. Other processes also add to the variability of the genetic brew. The ultimate outcome: tens of _____ of possible genetic combinations.

4. Less than _____ percent of all pregnancies produce twins. When a cluster of cells in the ovum splits off within the first two weeks after fertilization, two genetically identical zygotes or _____ twins are formed. More common is two separate ova fertilized by two separate sperm forming _____ twins. The chances of multiple births rise considerably with the use of _____ drugs.

5. The 23rd chromosome pair determines the sex of the child: the female being _____ and the male being _____. The _____ sperm determines the sex of the child.

The Basics of Genetics: The Mixing and Matching of Traits

6. When two competing traits were both present, only one could be expressed and that was the _____ trait. The trait that was present but not expressed was the _____ trait.

7. A _____ is the underlying combination of genetic material present (but outwardly invisible) and a _____ is the observable trait.

8. Some genes form pairs called _____, genes governing traits that may take alternate forms. If the child receives similar genes, he or she is said to be _____ for the trait. If the child receives different forms of the gene, he or she is said to be _____ for the trait.

9. PKU, _____, is an inherited disorder in which a child is unable to make use of phenylalanine. It is produced by a _____ allele, or pair of genes. Most traits are the result of _____ inheritance, a combination of multiple gene pairs.

10. Genes also vary in terms of their _____ range, the potential degree of variability in the actual expression of a trait due to environmental conditions. A number of _____ genes, called X-linked genes, are located only on the X chromosome. A blood disorder called _____ is produced by X-linked genes.

11. In early 2001, molecular biologists succeeded in _____ the specific sequence of genes on each chromosome. They found that the number of human genes is _____ and that _____ percent of the gene sequence is shared by all humans. The field of _____ genetics studies the effects of heredity on behavior.

Inherited and Genetic Disorders: When Development Goes Awry

12. Genes may spontaneously change their form, a process called spontaneous _____. PKU occurs once in _____ thousand births. Down syndrome is a disorder produced by an extra chromosome on the _____ pair and is the most frequent cause of mental _____. _____ syndrome occurs from damage to a gene on the X chromosome resulting in mild to moderate mental _____. Sickle-cell _____ is a blood disorder that gets its name from the shape of the red blood cells in those who have it. Occurring mainly in Jews of Eastern European ancestry, _____ disease usually causes death before its victims reach school age. One male out of every 400 is born with _____ syndrome, the presence of an extra X chromosome. There are disorders produced by an extra _____ chromosome (XYY), a missing _____ chromosome called Turner's syndrome (X0), and three _____ chromosomes (XXX).

Genetic Counseling: Predicting the Future from the Genes of the Present

13. Genetic counseling focuses on helping people deal with issues relating to _____ disorders. Possible genetic defects can be identified by assembling a _____, a chart containing enlarged photos of each of the chromosomes.

14. In _____ sonography, high frequency sound waves bombard the mother's womb. These waves produce an indistinct image of the unborn baby. A more invasive test, _____ samplings can be employed if blood tests and ultrasound have identified potential problems. In _____ a small sample of fetal cells is drawn by a tiny needle inserted into the amniotic fluid surrounding the unborn fetus.

15. The newest role of genetic counselors involves testing to identify whether an individual is susceptible to _____ disorders because of genetic abnormalities. _____ disease is a fatal disorder marked by tremors and intellectual deterioration that does not appear until people reach their _____.

Advancing Gene Therapy: Are We Heading Toward a Clone Age?

16. In _____ therapy, researchers inject genes targeted to correct a disease into a patient's blood stream. In _____ gene therapy, genetic modifications can correct problems not only for unborn individuals, but for future generations as well.

The Interaction of Heredity and Environment

The Role of the Environment in Determining the Expression of Genes: From Genotypes to Phenotypes

17. Patterns of arousal and emotionality that represent consistent and enduring characteristics in an individual are _____. Many traits represent _____ transmission, determined by a combination of both genetic and environmental factors. In this type of transmission, a _____ provides a particular range within which a _____ may achieve expression.

Studying Development: How Much Is Nature? How Much Is Nurture?

18. By observing animals with similar _____ backgrounds in different _____, scientists can determine the effects of specific kinds of environmental stimulation. Examining groups of animals that have been bred to have significantly different _____ backgrounds exposed to identical _____ can determine the role that genetic background plays.

19. _____ twins share an identical genetic code so variations in their behavior must be due to _____ factors. If these twins are more similar on a particular trait than dizygotic twins, we can assume that _____ plays an important role in the determination of the expression of that trait.

Physical Traits: Family Resemblances

20. The more genetically similar two people are, the more likely they are to share _____ characteristics.

Intelligence: More Research, More Controversy

21. Genetics plays a significant role in _____. The impact of genetics on intelligence increases with _____. Jensen argues that as much as _____ percent of intelligence is a result of the influence of heredity. Others have suggested figures ranging from _____ percent.

Genetic and Environmental Influences of Personality: Born to Be Outgoing?

22.   The term _____ refers to the degree of emotional stability an individual characteristically displays. _____ is the degree to which a person seeks to be with others, to behave in an outgoing manner, and generally to be sociable.

<u>Developmental Diversity - Cultural Differences in Physical Arousal: Might a Culture's Philosophical Outlook Be Determined by Genetics?</u>

23.   Kagan speculates that the underlying _____ of a given society is determined genetically and may predispose people in that society toward a particular philosophy. He suggests that the Chinese, who enter the world temperamentally _____, may find Buddhist philosophical notions of _____ more in tune with their natural inclinations. Westerners, who are emotionally more volatile and tense, and who report higher levels of _____, are more likely to be attracted to philosophies that articulate the necessity of controlling the unpleasant _____ that they are more apt to encounter in their everyday experience.

<u>Psychological Disorders: The Role of Genetics and Environment</u>

24.   Schizophrenia runs in _____. A monozygotic twin has close to a _____ percent risk of developing schizophrenia when the other twin develops the disorder. Major depression, alcoholism, autism, and attention-deficit hyperactivity disorder have significant _____ components. The role of genetics is often to produce _____ toward a future course of development.

<u>Can Genes Influence the Environment?</u>

25.   Scarr believes that the genetic endowment provided to children by their parents not only determines their genetic characteristics, but actively influences their _____. Children tend to _____ focus on those aspects of their environment that are most connected with genetically determined abilities. In some cases, the gene-environment influence is more _____ passive and less direct. Finally, the genetically-driven temperament of a child may _____ certain environmental influences.

Prenatal Growth and Change

<u>Fertilization: The Moment of Conception</u>

26.   _____, or conception, is the joining of a sperm and an ovum to create a single celled _____. Females are born with around 400,000 ova located in the two _____. The ova do not mature until the female reaches _____. From that point until she reaches menopause, the female will _____ about every 28 days, during which an egg is released and pushed through a _____ tube toward the _____. An adult male typically produces several hundred _____ sperm a day.

<u>The Stages of the Prenatal Period: The Onset of Development</u>

27.   The _____ stage is the first and shortest stage of prenatal development and takes place during the first two weeks following conception. The fertilized egg is now called a _____ and travels toward the _____ to become implanted in its wall. The cells of the organism become increasingly _____. Some cells form a protective layer around the mass of cells, whereas others begin to establish the rudiments of a _____ that serves as a conduit between the mother and fetus, providing nourishment and oxygen via the _____ cord.

28.   The _____ stage is the period from 2 to 8 weeks following fertilization. At the beginning of this stage, the developing child has _____ distinct layers. The outer layer of the embryo, the _____, will form skin, hair, teeth, sense organs, and the brain and spinal cord. The _____, the inner layer, produces the digestive system, liver, pancreas, and respiratory system. Between is the _____ from which muscles, bones, blood, and circulatory system are forged.

29. The _____ stage starts at about 8 weeks after conception and continues until birth. The child is now called a _____.

Problems in Pregnancy

30. Some 15 percent of couples suffer from _____, the inability to conceive after 12 to 18 months of trying. Some difficulties can be corrected through the use of drugs, surgery, or artificial _____, a procedure in which a physician places a man's sperm cells directly into a woman's vagina. In _____ fertilization, a woman's ova are removed from her ovaries and a man's sperm are used to fertilize the ova in a laboratory. The fertilized egg is then implanted in a woman's uterus. _____ intrafallopian transfer and _____ intrafallopian transfer are procedures in which an egg and sperm or fertilized egg are implanted in a woman's fallopian tubes. In IVF, GIFT, and ZIFT implantation is done in the woman who provided the donor eggs or a _____ mother.

31. A miscarriage, known as a _____ abortion, occurs when pregnancy ends before the developing child is able to _____ outside the mother's womb. Some _____ percent of all pregnancies end in miscarriage, usually in the first several _____ of pregnancy. In _____, a mother voluntarily chooses to terminate pregnancy.

The Prenatal Environment: Threats to Development

32. A _____ is an environmental agent that produces a birth defect. The _____ and _____ of exposure is crucial. The brain is most susceptible from _____ days after conception; the heart is most vulnerable from _____ days following conception.

33. A mother who eats a varied diet high in nutrients is apt to have fewer _____ during pregnancy, an easier _____, and a generally _____ baby.

34. Women who give birth when over the age of _____ are at greater risk for a variety of pregnancy and birth complications than younger ones. Older mothers are considerably more likely to give birth to children with _____ syndrome, a form of mental retardation. Women who become pregnant during _____ are more likely to have premature deliveries, and the mortality rate of infants born to these mothers is _____ that for mothers in their 20s.

35. Young mothers often face _____ social and economic factors which can affect infant health. Many teenage mothers do not have enough money or social support, a situation that prevents them from getting good _____ care and _____ support after the baby is born.

36. The onset of _____ or German measles, in the mother prior to the 11th week of pregnancy is likely to cause serious consequences in the baby. Chicken pox may produce _____ defects, and mumps may increase the risk of _____. Some sexually transmitted diseases such as _____ can be transmitted directly to the fetus, who will be born suffering from the disease. STDs such as _____ are communicated to the child as it passes through the birth canal to be born. Less than _____ percent of infants born to mothers with AIDS are born with the virus if the mother is treated with antiviral drugs such as ___ during pregnancy.

37. Aspirin taken for a headache can lead to _____ in the fetus. The drug _____ inhibited the growth of limbs. The daughters of mothers who took _____ stood a much higher than normal chance of developing a rare form of vaginal or cervical cancer. Sons of these mothers had a higher rate of _____ difficulties. Marijuana used during pregnancy can restrict the _____ that reaches the fetus. Cocaine produces an intense restriction of the _____ leading to the fetus.

38. Approximately 1 out of 750 infants is born with fetal _____ syndrome, a disorder that may include below-average intelligence and sometimes mental retardation, delayed growth, and facial deformities. Fetal alcohol _____ is a condition in which children display some, although not all of the problems of FAS. Smoking reduces the _____ content and increases the carbon monoxide of the mother's blood. The ultimate result is an increased possibility of _____ and a higher likelihood of _____ during infancy.

39. The father's use of alcohol and illegal drugs may lead to _____ damage that may affect the fetus at conception.

CRITICAL THINKING QUESTIONS

To further your mastery of the topics in this chapter, write out your answers to the following essay questions in the space provided.

1. How can the study of identical twins who were separated at birth help researchers determine the effects of genetic and environmental factors on human development? How might you design such a study?

2. How might adopted children develop traits similar to those of their adoptive parents? What sorts of traits do you think might be shared or be different in adoptive families?

3. What are some ethical and philosophical questions that surround the issue of genetic counseling? Might it sometimes be unwise to know ahead of time about possible genetically linked disorders that could afflict your child or yourself?

4. Do you think dizygotic (fraternal) twins are likely to be more similar to one another than two siblings born of the same parents at different times? Why? What genetic or environmental factors help determine your answer?

5. Describe how a child actively and passively influences her or his school environment.

6. Some people have used the proven genetic basis of intelligence to argue against strenuous educational efforts on behalf of individuals with below-average IQs. Does this viewpoint make sense based on what you have learned about heredity and environment? Why or why not?

7. Which of the prenatal stages of development is the most critical? Explain your answer.

8. Given the long-term importance of prenatal development do you feel that there should be legal consequences for mothers who have the means but neglect prenatal care and/or have been educated about the documented risks of drug use during pregnancy but choose to use drugs anyway?

9. Studies show that crack babies who are now entering school have significant difficulty dealing with multiple stimuli and forming close attachments. How might both genetic and environmental influences have combined to produce these results?

10. In addition to avoiding smoking, do you think there are other steps fathers might take to help their unborn children develop normally in the womb? What are they and how might they affect the environment of the unborn child? What are some steps both parents can take to give the fetus a healthy prenatal environment?

PRACTICE TEST – POST TEST

Circle the correct answer for each of the following multiple choice questions and check your answers with the Answer Key at the end of this chapter.

1. Your hair color is your
   a. gene.
   b. genotype.
   c. phenotype.
   d. heredity.

2. If Jamie has blue eyes, her mother has blue eyes and her father has brown eyes, Jamie is
   a. cross-modal.
   b. homozygous.
   c. heterozygous.
   d. multidimensional.

3. Bryan is an African-American with the following symptoms: yellowish eyes, poor appetite, stunted growth, and a swollen stomach. He may have
   a. hemophilia.
   b. Tay-Sachs disease.
   c. sickle-cell anemia.
   d. Klinefelter's syndrome.

4. A man is extremely ill, and has small external male sex organs, and breast enlargement. What genetic disorder does he have?
   a. Down syndrome
   b. Tay-Sachs disease
   c. Sickle-cell anemia
   d. Klinefelter's syndrome

5. Which of the following statements is true regarding a father's effect on the prenatal environment?
   a. Father's drug use and physical or emotional abuse of the mother can adversely affect the unborn child.
   b. Fathe's drug use can adversely affect unborn the child.
   c. Father's physical abuse of the mother can adversely affect the unborn child.
   d. Fathers have no effect on the prenatal environment

6. A couple having trouble getting pregnant went to an infertility specialist. The doctor shared with them that they were not alone in their difficulty conceiving, and that _____ percent of couples meet the criteria of infertility.
   a. 5   c. 15
   b. 10   d. 20

7. A patient of yours has schizophrenia. Her monozygotic twin has what chance of developing schizophrenia?
   a. 50 percent   c. 80 percent
   b. 60 percent   d. 95 percent

8. You notice that a child demands responses from her parents and babysitter. How would you describe this child's interaction with the environment?
   a. active   c. prosocial
   b. passive   d. evocative

9. A pregnant woman works around toxic fumes and her baby is born with birth defects. It is possible that the toxic chemical acted as a
   a. virus.   c. teratogen.
   b. bacteria.   d. pathogen.

10. You have a patient who admits to drinking several alcoholic beverages a day during her pregnancy. You will need to monitor her child for
    a. Down syndrome.   c. Klinefelter's syndrome.
    b. FAS.   d. diethylstilbestrol (DES).

11. When a cell duplicates itself exactly, the process is called
    a. mitosis.   c. fertilization.
    b. meiosis.   d. homozygotic.

12. Although Ashanti has a headache she decides not to take an aspirin during her pregnancy. Her decision is
    a. unwise, there are no risks associated with taking legal drugs during pregnancy.
    b. unwise, aspirin has no affect on a fetus during prenatal development.
    c. wise, the use of aspirin may cause fetal bleeding or growth impairments.
    d. wise, pregnant mothers should avoid all drugs during pregnancy.

13. A prenatal diagnostic procedure which involves high-frequency sound waves that form a picture of a fetus is called
    a. fetoscopy.   c. ultrasound sonography.
    b. amniocentesis.   d. chorionic villus sampling.

14. Who studied the role of genes in intelligence?
    a. Darwin   c. Mendel
    b. Kagan   d. Jensen

15. What percent of the gene sequence is shared by all humans?
    a. 25.3   c. 66.5
    b. 43.8   d. 99.9

16. A developing child is able to swallow and urinate. Its arms develop hands, hands develop fingers, and fingers develop nails. What stage of prenatal development is the child experiencing?
   a. germinal
   b. zygotic
   c. embryonic
   d. fetal

17. DNA tests are available for all of the following disorders EXCEPT
   a. cystic fibrosis.
   b. diabetes.
   c. hemophilia.
   d. retinoblastoma.

18. At the end of the _____ stage the developing human has rudimentary eyes, nose, and lips, although what appear to be gills and a tail-like structure may make it look nonhuman.
   a. conception
   b. germinal
   c. embryonic
   d. fetal

19. A physician places a man's sperm directly into a woman's vagina in
   a. CVS.
   b. IVF.
   c. artificial insemination.
   d. surrogate motherhood.

20. Which of the following is transmitted to the child as it passes through the birth canal?
   a. rubella
   b. syphilis
   c. AIDS
   d. gonorrhea

ANSWER KEYS

Practice Test – Pretest (with text page numbers)

1.	a 49	6.	c 77	11.	c 73	16.	b 56
2.	b 52	7.	b 56	12.	a 50	17.	d 49
3.	a 50	8.	a 69	13.	c 52	18.	d 62
4.	c 56	9.	c 74	14.	b 50	19.	b 51
5.	c 57	10.	d 81	15.	c 57	20.	c 74

Key Names

1. c   2. d   3. a   4. b

Key Vocabulary Terms

1.   Monozygotic twins are genetically identical; dizygotic twins are the result of two ova, each fertilized by a different sperm.

2.   Homozygous is inheritance of similar genes for a trait from both parents; heterozygous is inheritance of different forms of a gene for a given trait.

3.   A dominant trait is one that is expressed when two competing traits are present; a recessive trait is one that is within the organism, but is not expressed.

4.   FAS and FAE are both caused by the mother's use of alcohol; in FAE children display only some of the problems found in FAS.

5.   Genes are basic units of genetic information that are composed of DNA. Chromosomes are rod-shaped portions of DNA.

6.   Down syndrome is caused by chromosome damage on the 21st chromosome pair; sickle-cell anemia is an inherited disorder.

13. Gametes are sex cells that combine through fertilization to form a zygote, marking the beginning of the germinal stage of prenatal development which lasts 2 weeks. The embryonic stage of prenatal development follows and lasts 6 weeks; in turn being followed by the fetal stage of prenatal development in which the child is called a fetus.

14. Amniocentesis in a procedure in which cells are drawn from the amniotic fluid; in CVS samples are taken from material around the embryo; in ultrasound sonography sound waves are used to scan the mother's womb.

15. In artificial insemination, the sperm is placed directly into the vagina. In in vitro fertilization, the ova is fertilized by a sperm in a laboratory, and the ova either implanted in the mother or in a surrogate mother who will carry the child for the mother.

16. X, Longitudinal, Infertility, Naturalistic, Klinefelter's, Effect, Dominant (X-linked)

17. Teratogen, Evocative, Maturation, Phenotype, Ego, Recessive, Amniocentesis, Multifactorial, Ecological, Nonnormative, Tay-Sachs (Temperament)

Programmed Review

1. sperm, ovum, gametes, zygote
2. Genes, DNA, chromosomes, mitosis
3. meiosis, 8 million, trillions
4. 3, monozygotic, dizygotic, fertility
5. XX, XY, father's
6. dominant, recessive
7. genotype, phenotype
8. alleles, homozygous, heterozygous
9. phenylketonuria, single, polygenic
10. reaction, recessive, hemophilia
11. mapping, 25,000, 99.9, behavioral
12. mutation, 10 to 20, 21st, retardation, Fragile X, retardation, anemia, Tay-Sachs, Klinefelter's, Y, second, X
13. inherited, karyotype
14. ultrasound, chorionic villus, amniocentesis
15. future, Huntington's, 40s
16. gene, germ-line
17. temperament, multifactorial, genotype, phenotype
18. genetic, environments, genetic, environments
19. Monozygotic, environmental, genetics
20. physical
21. intelligence, age, 80, 50 to 70
22. neuroticism, extroversion
23. temperament, calmer, serenity, guilt, feelings
24. families, 50, inherited, tendency
25. environment, actively, passive, evoke
26. Fertilization, zygote, ovaries, puberty, ovulate, Fallopian, uterus, million
27. germinal, blastocyst, uterus, specialized, placenta, umbilical
28. embryonic, three, ectoderm, endoderm, mesoderm
29. fetal, fetus
30. infertility, insemination, in vitro, gamete, zygote, surrogate
31. spontaneous, survive, 15 to 20, months, abortion
32. teratogen, timing, quantity, 15 to 25, 20 to 40
33. complications, labor, healthier
34. 30, Down, adolescence, double
35. adverse, prenatal, parenting
36. rubella, birth, miscarriage, syphilis, gonorrhea, 5, AZT

37. bleeding, thalidomide, DES, reproductive, oxygen, arteries
38. alcohol, effect, oxygen, miscarriage, death
39. chromosome

Practice Test – Post Test (with text page numbers)

1.	c 52	6.	c 77	11.	a 49	16.	d 75
2.	b 52	7.	a 70	12.	c 81	17.	b 59
3.	c 56	8.	d 72	13.	c 57	18.	c 75
4.	d 56	9.	c 79	14.	d 66	19.	c 77
5.	a 84	10.	b 82	15.	d 54	20.	d 81

Chapter 3

Birth and the Newborn Infant

CHAPTER OUTLINE

◆ Birth
- ♦ Labor: The Process of Birth Begins
- ♦ Birth: From Fetus to Neonate
- ♦ Approaches to Childbirth: Where Medicine and Attitudes Meet

◆ Birth Complications
- ♦ Preterm Infants: Too Soon, Too Small
- ♦ Postmature Babies: Too Late, Too Large
- ♦ Cesarean Delivery: Intervening in the Process of Birth
- ♦ Infant Mortality and Stillbirth: The Tragedy of Premature Death
- ♦ Postpartum Depression: Moving from the Heights of Joy to the Depths of Despair

◆ The Competent Newborn
- ♦ Physical Competence: Meeting the Demands of a New Environment
- ♦ Sensory Capabilities: Experiencing the World
- ♦ Early Learning Capabilities
- ♦ Social Competence: Responding to Others

LEARNING OBJECTIVES

After you have read and studied this chapter, you should be able to answer the following questions.

1. What is the normal process of labor?
2. What complications can occur at birth and what are their causes, effects, and treatments?
3. What capabilities does the newborn have?

PRACTICE TEST - PRETEST

Circle the correct answer for each of the following multiple choice questions and check your answers with the Answer Key at the end of this chapter.

1. A patient calls and states that she is having regular contractions. What hormone has caused the uterus to contract?
    a. estrogen
    b. oxytocin
    c. androgen
    d. progesterone

2. A friend has asked you to describe an episiotomy. You explain to her that it is
   a. the second step of a Cesarean section.
   b. part of the Lamaze method of child birth.
   c. an incision to increase the size of the vaginal opening.
   d. the stage of birth in which the placenta and the umbilical cord are expelled.

3. Meg's cervix is fully open and her contractions are at their greatest intensity. Meg is
   a. beginning the first stage of labor.   c. in the second stage of labor.
   b. in the transition period.   d. expelling the placenta.

4. The Apgar scale measures all of the following qualities, EXCEPT
   a. pulse.   c. respiration.
   b. activity (muscle tone).   d. temperature regulation.

5. A couple wanting to use relaxation training to help with birthing would choose what method?
   a. Lamaze   c. Cesarean
   b. anesthesia   d. family birthing

6. Jennifer is considering a career as a physician who specializes in delivering babies. She will study to be a(n)
   a. midwife.   c. pediatrician.
   b. obstetrician.   d. gynecologist.

7. A child is considered preterm if he or she
   a. weighed less than 2,500 grams.
   b. was born prior to 38 weeks after conception.
   c. weighed 90 percent or less than the average weight of infants.
   d. is postmature.

8. When children are born several weeks premature, what is the main factor used to determine degree of risk?
   a. birth weight   c. ability to regulate temperature
   b. mother's age   d. ability to take in sufficient oxygen

9. Premature babies may experience respiratory distress syndrome. What would the likely treatment be for the respiratory problems?
   a. isolation   c. placement in an incubator
   b. use of a birth center   d. immersion in water

10. How many stages of labor are there?
    a. 1   c. 3
    b. 2   d. 4

11. Infant mortality, a serious concern in the United States, is defined as
    a. stillbirth.   c. death during the perinatal period.
    b. death within the first year of life.   d. death within the first month of life.

12. Babies are born with involuntary responses that occur in response to specific stimuli. These responses are called
    a. reflexes.   c. reactions.
    b. schemes.   d. overextensions.

13. Which is the shortest phase of labor?
    a. first   c. third
    b. second   d. fourth

14. About one-third of women who receive anesthesia do so in the form of
    a. epidural anesthesia.
    b. prescription narcotics.
    c. total anesthesia.
    d. episiotomies.

15. Of the following countries which has the highest rate of infant mortality?
    a. Spain
    b. New Zealand
    c. Czech Republic
    d. United States

16. Takeesha was born 2-1/2 weeks after her mother's due date. She would be classified as
    a. preterm.
    b. postmature.
    c. low birthweight.
    d. large-for-gestational age.

17. All of the following are environmental risk factors for low birthweight EXCEPT
    a. low altitude.
    b. smoking.
    c. poor nutrition.
    d. alcohol use.

18. A stillbirth indicates
    a. the labor has taken over 24 hours.
    b. the child was not alive when born.
    c. the child dies within the first year after birth.
    d. the child is physically and emotionally unresponsive at birth.

19. Whenever Jose cries, his mother picks him up, and Jose has increased his crying. Jose has been
    a. operantly conditioned.
    b. classically conditioned.
    c. habituated.
    d. influenced by modeling.

20. In a Cesarean delivery
    a. the baby is surgically removed.
    b. born with the use of a midwife and doula.
    c. no anesthesia or pain reducing drugs are used.
    d. the baby is born in a family birthing center.

KEY NAMES

Match the following names with the correct descriptive term and check your answer with the Answer Key at the end of this chapter.

1. ___ Virginia Apgar   a. birthing technique

2. ___ Ferdinand Lamaze   b. classical conditioning

3. ___ Ivan Pavlov   c. newborn assessment

KEY VOCABULARY TERMS

Explain the difference among the following terms.

1. Low-birthweight infants; Small-for-gestational-age infants; Very-low-birthweight infants
2. First stage of labor; Second stage of labor; Third stage of labor

Describe the relationship between the following.

3. Fetal monitors and Cesarean delivery
4. Age of viability and Apgar scale

Define each of the following terms and check the answers in your text.

5. Bonding
6. Anoxia
7. Classical conditioning

8. Neonate
9. States of arousal
10. Habituation

Fill in the blanks for the term for each definition. The first letters of each term will spell, from top to bottom, the term that matches the last definition. (NOTE: Some terms may be from previous chapters.)

11. _ _ _ _ _ _ _   Infants born prior to 38 weeks after conception.

_ _ _ _ _ _ _   A form of conditioning in which a voluntary response is strengthened or weakened depending on its association with positive or negative consequences.

_ _ _ _ _ _ _ _ _   The delivery of a child who is not alive.

_ _ _ _ _ _ _ _ _   The group in an experiment that receives the experimental condition.

_ _ _ _ _ _ _ _   Death within the first year of life is infant _____.

_ _ _ _ _ _   Different degrees of sleep and wakefulness through which newborns cycle are states of _____.

_ _ _ _ _ _ _ _ _ _   Patterns of arousal and emotionality that represent enduring characteristics of the individual.

_ _ _ _ _ _ _ _ _   The prenatal test that uses sound waves to scan the mother's abdomen.

_ _ _ _ _ _ _ _   Unlearned, organized involuntary responses that occur automatically in the presence of certain stimuli.

_ _ _ _ _ _ _ _ _   An incision made to increase the size of the opening of the vagina to allow the baby to pass.

Infants still unborn two weeks after the mother's due date. _ _ _ _ _ _ _ _ _ _

PROGRAMMED REVIEW

Fill in the blanks in the following programmed review and check your answers with the Answer Key at the end of this chapter.

Birth

1. The term used for newborns is _____.

Labor: The Process of Birth Begins

2. About 266 days after conception, a protein called _____ triggers the release of the hormone _____ from the mother's pituitary gland. When the concentration becomes high enough, the uterus begins periodic _____. After the fourth month, the uterus occasionally contracts in order to ready itself for the eventual _____. These contractions are called _____ contractions or false labor. When birth is imminent, intense contractions force the head of the fetus against the _____, the neck of the uterus that separates it from the vagina.

3. In the first stage of labor, the uterine contractions initially occur around every _____ minutes and last about _____ seconds. Toward the end of labor the contractions may occur every _____ minutes and last for almost _____ minutes. During the final part of the first stage of labor, the contractions increase to their greatest intensity, a period known as _____. The mother's cervix fully opens, usually to around _____ to allow the baby's head to pass through. Typically, labor takes _____ hours for firstborn children.

4. During the second stage of labor, the baby's _____ emerges further from the mother. Because the area between the vagina and rectum must stretch a good deal, an incision called an _____ is sometimes made to increase the size of the opening of the vagina.

5. The third stage of labor occurs when the _____ cord and the _____ are expelled from the mother. The nature of a woman's reactions to labor reflect, in part, _____ factors.

Birth: From Fetus to Neonate

6. Health care workers employ the _____ scale, a standard measurement system that looks for a variety of indications of good health. The scale directs attention to five basic qualities: _____ or color, _____ or heart rate, grimace or _____ irritability, activity or _____ tone, and _____. The vast majority of children score _____ or above.

7. A restriction of oxygen, or _____, lasting a few minutes can produce brain damage as brain cells die.

8. The thick greasy substance that covers the newborn called _____ smoothes the passage through the birth canal. Newborn's bodies are also covered with a fine, dark fuzz known as _____.

9. Some psychologists and physicians have argued that _____, the close physical and emotional contact between parent and child during the period immediately following birth, is a crucial ingredient for a lasting relationship. This argument is based on research conducted on nonhuman species, showing there was a critical period after birth when organisms _____. There is no _____ evidence for this process in humans.

Approaches to Childbirth: Where Medicine and Attitudes Meet

10. The _____ method makes use of breathing techniques and relaxation training. A _____ is trained along with the future mother. Participation in natural childbirth techniques is relatively rare among members of _____ income groups.

11. The decision to use _____ centers is becoming increasingly common. In a majority of cases labor and delivery are uneventful, permitting them to occur in _____ setting that these centers provide. Because of the popularity around these centers many hospitals have opened birthing _____ of their own.

12. Traditionally women have turned to _____, physicians who specialize in delivering babies. More recently other mothers have chosen to use a _____, a childbirth attendant who stays with the mother during labor and delivery. A _____ is trained to provide emotional, psychological, and educational support during birth.

13. During childbirth, _____ is actually a signal that the body is working appropriately. The nature of every woman's delivery depends on how much _____ and support she has before and during delivery, her _____ view of pregnancy and delivery, and the specific nature of the _____ itself.

14. About a third of women who receive anesthesia do so in the form of _____ anesthesia, which produces numbness from the waist down. A new form, known as _____ epidural or _____ spinal-epidural, uses smaller needles and a system for administering continuous doses of anesthetic.

15. Anesthetics may temporarily depress the flow of _____ to the fetus and slow _____. Newborns whose mothers have been anesthetized are less physiologically _____ and show poorer _____ control during the first days of life after birth.

16. The average hospital stay following normal births has decreased to _____ days in the 1990s. The American Academy of Pediatrics states that women should stay in the hospital no less than _____ hours after giving birth.

Birth Complications

17. Overall, the United States ranks _____ among industrialized countries in infant mortality with _____ deaths for every 1,000 live births.

Preterm infants: Too Soon, Too Small

18. Preterm infants, or _____ infants, are born prior to _____ weeks after conception. The average newborn weighs around 3400 grams (about _____ pounds), low-birthweight infants weigh less than 2500 grams (around _____ pounds).

19. Small-for- _____ -age infants are infants who because of delayed fetal growth, weigh 90 percent or less of the average weight of infants of the same gestational age. They are sometimes also _____.

20. Newborns who are born prematurely may experience _____ distress syndrome, with potentially fatal consequences. To deal with this syndrome, they are often placed in _____, enclosures in which temperature and oxygen are controlled. The immature development of preterm neonates makes them unusually sensitive to _____ in their environment.

21. Very-low-birthweight infants weigh less than 1250 grams (around _____ pounds) or, regardless of weight, have been in the womb less than _____ weeks. Medical advances have led to a much higher chance of survival pushing the age of _____, the point at which an infant can survive prematurely, to about _____ weeks. _____ care, in which infants are held skin-to-skin against their parents' chests appears to be effective in promoting development of preterm infants.

22. Half of preterm and low-birthweight births are _____. In some cases, difficulties relating to the mother's _____ system cause such births. In other cases, preterm and low-birthweight babies are a result of the _____ of the mother's reproductive system. Factors that affect the general _____ of the mother are related to prematurity and low birthweight as well.

Postmature Babies: Too Late, Too Large

23. Postmature infants are still unborn _____ weeks after the mother's due date. Blood supply from the _____ may become insufficient to nourish the fetus adequately and _____ becomes riskier for both the child and the mother.

Cesarean Delivery: Intervening in the Process of Birth

24. In a _____ delivery, the baby is surgically removed from the uterus. Fetal _____ is the most frequent cause, but they are also used in some cases of _____ position, in which the baby is positioned feet first in the birth canal, or _____ position, in which the baby lies crosswise in the uterus, or when the baby's _____ is so large that it has trouble moving through the birth canal. The routine use of _____ monitors, devices that measure the baby's heartbeat during labor, has contributed to the soaring rate of such deliveries.

25. A Cesarean is major _____ and the risk of maternal _____ is higher than in normal births. Cesarean deliveries may deter the normal release of certain _____ related hormones into the newborn's bloodstream and these infants are more prone to initial _____ problems upon birth.

Infant Mortality and Stillbirth: The Tragedy of Premature Death

26. The delivery of a child who is not alive is _____. Infant mortality is defined as death within the _____ of life. In the 1990s the overall rate in the United States was _____ per 1,000 lives births.

27. In particular, _____ -American babies are more than twice as likely to die before the age of 1 than white babies. The overall U.S. rate of infant mortality is _____ than the rate in many other countries and almost _____ that of Japan. The United States has a higher rate of _____ birthweight and _____ deliveries. It also has a higher proportion of people living in _____ who are less likely to have adequate _____ care. The lack of national health care insurance or a national health policy means that _____ care is often haphazardly provided to the poor. About one out of every _____ pregnant women has insufficient prenatal care.

Postpartum Depression: Moving from the Heights of Joy to the Depths of Despair.

28. Postpartum depression, a period of deep depression following the _____ of a child, affects _____ percent of all new mothers. It may be triggered by the pronounced swings in _____ production that occur after birth.

The Competent Newborn

29. The size of the brain of the average newborn is just _____ what it will be at adulthood, but infants enter this world with an astounding array of _____ in all domains of development.

Physical Competence: Meeting the Demands of a New Environment

30. Newborns show several _____, unlearned, organized involuntary responses that occur automatically in the presence of certain stimuli. The _____ reflex and the _____ reflex permit the neonate to begin right away to ingest food. The _____ reflex involves turning in the direction of a source of stimulation near the mouth and is also related to eating.

31. The neonate's digestive system initially produces _____, a greenish-black material that is a remnant of the neonate's days as a fetus. Almost half of all newborns develop a distinctly yellowish tinge to their bodies and eyes, a symptom of neonatal _____.

Sensory Capabilities: Experiencing the World

32. Neonates pay closest attention to portions of scenes in their field of vision that are highest in _____ and they can discriminate different levels of _____. Evidence suggests that newborns have a sense of _____ constancy. They distinguish different _____.

33. Newborns react to certain kinds of sounds, showing _____ reactions to loud, sudden noises. They are sensitive to _____ and the senses of _____ and _____ are well developed.

Early Learning Capabilities

34. In _____ conditioning, an organism learns to respond in a particular way to a neutral stimulus that normally does not bring about that type of response. The key feature is stimulus _____. One of the earliest examples of the power of classical conditioning is the case of Little _____.

35. _____ conditioning is a form of learning in which a _____ response is strengthened or weakened depending on its association with positive or negative consequences. Infants learn to act _____ on their environments.

36. The most primitive form of learning is _____, the decrease in response to a stimulus that occurs after repeated presentations of the same stimulus. When newborns are presented with a new stimulus, they produce a _____ response. It occurs in every _____ system and is linked to _____ and _____ maturation.

Social Competence: Responding to Others

37. Newborns have the capability to _____ others' behavior, providing an important foundation for _____ interaction later in life.

38. Newborns cycle through various states of _____, different degrees of sleep and wakefulness. They tend to pay particular attention to their _____ voices.

CRITICAL THINKING QUESTIONS

To further your mastery of the topics in this chapter, write out your answers to the following essay questions in the space provided.

1. Why might cultural differences exist in expectations and interpretations of labor? Do you think such cultural differences are due primarily to physical or psychological factors?

2. While 99 percent of births in the United States are attended by professional medical workers or birthing attendants, this is the case in only about half of births worldwide. What do you think are some causal factors and implications of this statistic?

3. What are some arguments for and against the use of pain-reducing drugs during birth? What advice would you give a mother-to-be about anesthetics, and why?

4. Are there differences in postdelivery care for families without adequate medical insurance in the United States? Are there long-term developmental concerns associated with a poor medical care? What could be done about this situation?

5. The number of Cesarean deliveries has increased dramatically in the United States in recent years. What cultural differences could have accounted for this change? Should there be policies for families and physicians to govern the use of Cesarean procedures? How should these procedures be designed?

6. How are the racial and cultural differences that exist in infant mortality a product of genetics, SES, and/or larger societal factors? What can be done to address these concerns? What factors might make it difficult for a society to address these differences?

7. Developmental researchers no longer view the neonate as a helpless, incompetent creature, but rather as a remarkably competent, developing human being. What do you think are some implications of this change in viewpoint for methods of childrearing and child care?

8. How do newborns' reflexes help them in their new environment? How might the fetus have developed such organized responses to stimuli?

9. Classical conditioning relies on stimulus substitution. Can you think of examples of the use of classical conditioning in adults in everyday life, in such areas as entertainment, advertising, or politics?

10. How does the newborn's imitative capability help him or her to develop social competence later in life? In what ways might this process be different or similar for a baby born without sight?

PRACTICE TEST – POST TEST

Circle the correct answer for each of the following multiple choice questions and check your answers with the Answer Key at the end of this chapter.

1. Braxton-Hicks contractions begin to occur
   a. after the first month.
   b. after the third month.
   c. after the fourth month.
   d. after the eighth month.

2. What happens during the second stage of childbirth?
   a. expulsion of the placenta
   b. the actual birth of the baby
   c. breakage of the amniotic sac
   d. expulsion of the umbilical cord

3. Which of the following is NOT a concern associated with the use of anesthesia or pain reducing drugs during labor?
   a. Anesthetics may heighten sensory capabilities.
   b. Anesthetics may temporarily depress the flow of oxygen and slow labor.
   c. Newborns show poorer motor control during the first days after birth.
   d. Newborns less physiologically responsive during the first few days of life.

4. Anoxia is the restriction of oxygen and is serious because it can cause
   a. brain damage.
   b. liver damage.
   c. visual damage.
   d. muscular damage.

5. Which of the following does NOT do medical exams, but may be an integral part of the birthing process?
   a. pediatrician
   b. doula
   c. midwife
   d. obstetrician

6. Which statement is TRUE regarding early learning capabilities?
   a. Newborns can only learn through classical conditioning.
   b. It takes a considerable amount of time before infants are capable of learning through operant conditioning.
   c. Newborns can only learn through habituation.
   d. Infants are capable of learning very early through classical conditioning.

7. Research on bonding indicates that
   a. all infants imprint on their mothers.
   b. bonding occurs only if the infant is breast fed.
   c. there is no scientific evidence for bonding.
   d. infants bond with both parents in the first week after birth.

8. What is the age of viability?
   a. 16 weeks
   b. 18 weeks
   c. 22 weeks
   d. 24 weeks

9. All of the following may cause preterm deliveries, EXCEPT
   a. twin births.
   b. the mother's occupation.
   c. short interpregnancy interval.
   d. immaturity of the mother's reproductive system.

10. When a baby is born feet first, the birth is called
    a. fetal distress.
    b. breech position.
    c. Cesarean section.
    d. transverse position.

11. A healthcare worker has just completed an Apgar and the newborn has received a score of 3. What does this score indicate?
    a. The newborn will most likely need immediate life saving interventions.
    b. The newborn demonstrates all reflexes.
    c. A Cesarean section will be needed to correct the difficulties.
    d. The newborn is healthy; most newborns receive a score of or higher.

12. By touching an infant's cheek you stimulate her to turn in that direction. This reflex is called the
    a. plantar reflex.
    b. rooting reflex.
    c. Babinski reflex.
    d. grasping reflex.

13. Infants are able to tell the difference among many facial expressions, such as sad, happy, or surprise. An infant's response to his or her mother's sad face would be to
    a. act confused.
    b. touch the mother's face.
    c. imitate the facial expression.
    d. begin to ignore the facial expression.

14. Which government provides the least amount of economic support following childbirth?
    a. Austria
    b. Germany
    c. Canada
    d. United States

15. Larry's new son weighed 2.1 pounds at birth. His son is classified as
    a. low-birthweight.
    b. small-for-gestational-age.
    c. very-low-birthweight.
    d. viable.

16. Which of the following statements is an accurate comparison of preterm infants and postmature infants?
    a. Preterm infants are more likely to have an insufficient blood supply from the placenta.
    b. Postmature infants are more likely to have RDS.
    c. Difficulties are more preventable in postmature infants.
    d. Preterm infants require induced labor.

17. When the baby lies crosswise in the uterus, it is in a _____ position.
    a. breech
    b. Cesarean
    c. transverse
    d. normal

18. A basic type of learning in infants, first identified by Pavlov, is
    a. modeling.
    b. classical conditioning.
    c. operant conditioning.
    d. habituation.

19. When an infant no longer responds to the sound of a clock's hourly chimes, the infant has become
    a. conditioned.
    b. accommodated.
    c. habituated.
    d. intimidated.

20. Different degrees of sleep and wakefulness are infant states of
    a. consciousness.
    b. attentiveness.
    c. wakefulness.
    d. arousal.

ANSWER KEYS

Practice Test – Pretest (with text page numbers)

1.	b 91	6.	b 98	11.	b 108	16.	b 104
2.	c 92	7.	b 102	12.	a 114	17.	a 105
3.	b 91	8.	a 102	13.	c 92	18.	b 108
4.	d 93	9.	c 103	14.	a 99	19.	a 116
5.	a 96	10.	c 91	15.	d 109	20.	a 105

Key Names

1. c   2. a   3. b

Key Vocabulary Terms

1. Low-birthweight infants weigh less than 5.5 pounds at birth; small-for-gestational-age infants weigh 90 percent or less than average weight for infants of the same gestational age; very-low-birthweight infants weigh less than 2.25 pounds or have been in the womb less than 30 weeks.

2. During the first stage of labor the uterine contractions initially occur. This stage of labor is the longest and may last several hours. The second stage of labor begins with the emergence of the baby and lasts about 90

41

minutes, ending when the baby has completely left the mother's body. The <u>third stage of labor</u>, which last only few minutes, is when the umbilical cord and placenta are expelled from the mother.

3.   The use of <u>fetal monitors</u> often results in <u>Cesarean sections</u> when not necessarily needed because minor problems are discovered.

4.   The <u>age of viability</u> is the age at which an infant can survive on its own. The <u>Apgar Score</u> measures the condition of the infant immediately after birth to determine if the infant is able to survive without extraordinary measures.

11. Preterm, Operant, Stillbirth, Treatment, Mortality, Arousal, Temperament, Ultrasound, Reflexes, Episiotomy (Postmature)

Programmed Review

1.   neonate
2.   corticotrophin, oxytocin, contractions, delivery, Braxton-Hicks, cervix
3.   8 to 10, 30, 2, 2, transition, 10cm, 16 to 24
4.   head, episiotomy
5.   umbilical, placenta, cultural
6.   Apgar, appearance, pulse, reflex, muscle, respiration, 7
7.   anoxia
8.   vernix, lanugo
9.   bonding, imprint, scientific
10. Lamaze, coach, lower
11. birthing, homelike, rooms
12. obstetrician, midwife, doula
13. pain, preparation, culture's, delivery
14. epidural, walking, dual
15. oxygen, labor, responsive, motor
16. two, 48
17. 26th, 7.3
18. premature, 38, 7-1/2, 5-1/2
19. gestational, preterm
20. respiratory, incubators, stimuli
21. 2-1/4, 30, viability, 22, Kangaroo
22. unexplained, reproductive, immaturity, health
23. two, placenta, labor
24. Cesarean, distress, breech, transverse, head, fetal
25. surgery, infection, stress, breathing
26. stillbirth, first year, 8.5
27. African, higher, double, low, preterm, poverty, medical, prenatal, six
28. birth, 10, hormone
29. one-quarter, capabilities
30. reflexes, sucking, swallowing, rooting
31. meconium, jaundice
32. information, brightness, size, colors
33. startle, touch, smell, taste
34. classical, substitution, Albert
35. Operant, voluntary, deliberately
36. habituation, orienting, sensory, physical, cognitive
37. imitate, social
38. arousal, mothers'

Practice Test – Post test (with text page numbers)

1. c 91	6. d 116	11. a 93	16. c 106
2. b 92	7. c 94	12. b 114	17. c 107
3. a 99	8. c 104	13. c 117	18. b 116
4. a 93	9. b 104	14. d 110	19. c 116
5. b 98	10. b 107	15. c 103	20. d 118

Chapter 4

Physical Development in Infancy

CHAPTER OUTLINE

◆ Growth and Stability
- ♦ Physical Growth: The Rapid Advances of Infancy
- ♦ The Nervous System and Brain: The Foundations of Development
- ♦ Integrating the Bodily Systems: The Life Cycles of Infancy

◆ Motor Development
- ♦ Reflexes: Our Inborn Physical Skills
- ♦ Motor Development in Infancy: Landmarks of Physical Achievement
- ♦ Nutrition in Infancy: Fueling Motor Development
- ♦ Breast or Bottle?
- ♦ Introducing Solid Foods: When and What?

◆ The Development of the Senses
- ♦ Visual Perception: Seeing the World
- ♦ Auditory Perception: The World of Sound
- ♦ Smell and Taste
- ♦ Sensitivity to Pain and Touch
- ♦ Multimodal Perception: Combining Individual Sensory Inputs

LEARNING OBJECTIVES

After you have read and studied this chapter, you should be able to answer the following questions.

1. How do the human body and nervous system develop?
2. Does the environment affect the pattern of development?
3. What developmental tasks must infants accomplish in this period?
4. How does nutrition affect physical development?
5. What sensory capabilities do infants possess?

PRACTICE TEST - PRETEST

Circle the correct answer for each of the following multiple choice questions and check your answers with the Answer Key at the end of this chapter.

1. What principle states that simple skills develop independently and are later integrated into more complex skills?
    a. proximocaudal
    b. hierarchical integration
    c. continuity
    d. cephalocaudal

2. Frank is six months old and can reach out and grab a toy with his hand, but he will not be able to pick up a small toy with his finger and thumb until he is nine months old. This illustrates what developmental principle?
    a. cephalocaudal principle
    b. proximodistal principle
    c. principle of hierarchical integration
    d. principle of the independence of systems

3. An infant received brain damage as the result of an accident, but through various experiences the brain was able to develop to overcome most of the problems. This ability of the brain is called
    a. plasticity.
    b. kwashiorkor.
    c. sensitivity.
    d. integrity.

4. The rate of SIDS in the United States has been declining partially due to the
    a. respiratory occlusion reflex.
    b. reflexes present at birth.
    c. back-to-sleep guideline.
    d. undertanding sensitive periods for the formation of sleep habits.

5. Newborns do not sleep the same amount as their parents. Approximately how long do newborns sleep each day?
    a. 10 hours
    b. 12 hours
    c. 14 hours
    d. 16 hours

6. What is the incidence of sudden infant death syndrome?
    a. 1 in 300
    b. 2 in 100
    c. 1 in 1000
    d. 2 in 1000

7. Newborns react to loud noises automatically. This reaction is called the
    a. Babinski reflex.
    b. Moro reflex.
    c. rooting reflex.
    d. startle reflex.

8. Zelazo and his colleagues conducted a study in which they provided two-week-old infants practice in walking for four sessions of three minutes each over a six-week period. The results showed that the children who had the walking practice actually began to walk unaided several months earlier than those who had had no such practice. What did the researchers conclude?
    a. Exercise of the stepping reflex was performed qualitatively better in practiced infants than in unpracticed infants.
    b. Exercise of the stepping reflex helps the brain's cortex to develop the ability to walk.
    c. Early gains in stepping reflex are associated with proficiency in motor skills in adulthood.
    d. Parents should make extraordinary efforts to stimulate their infant's reflexes.

9. When does crawling typically appear?
    a. 3-5 months
    b. 6-8 months
    c. 8-10 months
    d. 10-12 months

10. At what age can you expect a child to walk by herself?
    a. 8 months
    b. 10 months
    c. 12 months
    d. 15 months

11. On television you see a child from a poor country whose growth has stopped. This child is suffering from malnutrition and has a disease called
    a. anemia.
    b. marasmus.
    c. kwashiorkor.
    d. acetycholine deficiency.

12. What is the best form of nourishment for infants under the age of one?
    a. bottle formula
    b. breast milk
    c. cereals
    d. All of the answers are correct.

13. By the age of 5 months, the average infant's birth weight has _____ to around _____ pounds.
    a. doubled; 22
    b. tripled; 15
    c. doubled; 15
    d. tripled; 22

14. The gap between neurons through which they communicate with each other is the
    a. synapse.
    b. myelin.
    c. dendrite.
    d. axon.

15. What specific skill permits infants to pinpoint the direction from which a sound is emanating?
    a. sensation
    b. perception
    c. sound habituation
    d. sound localization

16. Which of the following reflexes is permanent?
    a. rooting
    b. sucking
    c. stepping
    d. swimming

17. In the United State the poverty rate for children under the age of three has
    a. decreased.
    b. remained the same.
    c. stabilized.
    d. increased.

18. Joan's baby has stopped growing due to a lack of stimulation and attention. Her baby is suffering from
    a. marasmus.
    b. kwashiorkor.
    c. nonorganic failure to thrive.
    d. SIDS.

19. Who developed the visual cliff?
    a. Gibson
    b. Pavlov
    c. Fantz
    d. Skinner

20. Which of the following is an example of a gross motor skill?
    a. rolling over
    b. placing a peg in a board
    c. coping circles
    d. pincer grasp

KEY NAMES

Match the following names with the most accurate description and check your answers with the Answer Key at the end of this chapter.

1. ___ Esther Thelen

a. "blooming, buzzing confusion"

2. ___ Robert Fantz

b. Dynamic systems theory

3. ___ Eleanor Gibson

c. SIDS

4. ___ William James   d. visual preferences

5. ___ Lewis Lipsitt   e. visual cliff

KEY VOCABULARY TERMS

Explain the difference between the following pairs of terms.

1. Cephalocaudal principle; Proximodistal principle
2. Principle of hierarchical intergration; Principle of the independence of systems
3. Marasmus; Kwashiorkor
4. Sensation; Perception

How are the following terms related?

5. Neuron, Myelin, Synapse

Fill in the blanks next to each definition with the appropriate term. The first letter of each term from top to bottom will spell out the term for the final definition. (NOTE: Some terms may be from previous chapters.)

6. _ _ _ _ _ _ _ _ _ _   The degree to which a developing structure or behavior is modifiable due to experience.

  _ _ _   Freud's term for the rational part of the personality.

  _ _ _ _ _ _ _ _   Unlearned, organized, involuntary responses that occur automatically in the presence of certain stimuli.

  _ _ _ _ _ _ _ _   The upper layer of the brain is the _____ cortex.

  _ _ _ _ _ _ _ _ _ _ An incision made to increase the vaginal opening to allow the baby to pass during birth.

  _ _ _ _ _ _ _ _ _ _ _ _ Growth from the center of the body outward.

  _ _ _ _ _ _   In nonorganic failure to _____, infants stop growing due to a lack of stimulation and attention.

  _ _ _ _ _ _   SIDS or sudden _____ death syndrome occurs in the first year of life.

  _ _ _ _ _ _ _   A form of conditioning in which a response is strengthened or weakened depending on its consequences.

  _ _ _ _ _   The average performance of a large sample of children of a given age.

  The sorting out, interpretation, analysis, and integration of stimuli involving the sense organs and brain is

  _ _ _ _ _ _ _ _ _ _ .

Look up the definitions of each of the following terms and write a specific example of each.

7. SIDS   12. Sensitive period
8. Rhythms   13. Rapid eye movement (REM)
9. Infant states   14. Brazelton Neonatal Behavioral Scale

10. Multimodal approach to perception
11. Affordances

15. Nonorganic failure to thrive
16. Dynamic system theory

PROGRAMMED REVIEW

Fill in the blanks in the following programmed review and check your answers with the Answer Key at the end of this chapter.

Growth and Stability

1. The average newborn weighs just over _____ pounds and its length is _____ inches.

Physical Growth: The Rapid Advances of Infancy

2. Over the first two years of a human's life, growth occurs at a _____ pace. By the age of 5 months, the average infant's birthweight has _____, and by the first birthday, weight has _____. By the end of its second year, the average child weighs _____ times its birthweight. Of course there is a good deal of variation among infants.

3. By the end of the first year, the typical baby is _____ inches tall, and by its second birthday, the child usually has attained a height of _____ feet.

4. Four major principles govern infant growth. According to the _____ principle, growth follows a pattern that begins with the head and upper body parts and then proceeds to the rest of the body. According to the _____ principle, development proceeds from the center of the body outward. The principle of _____ integration states that simple skills typically develop separately and independently. The principle of _____ of systems suggests that different body systems grow at different rates.

The Nervous System and Brain: The Foundations of Development

5. The nervous system comprises the _____ and the _____ that extend throughout the body. Like all cells, neurons have a cell body containing a _____. They communicate using _____ to receive messages and an _____ to carry messages. Neurons communicate by means of _____ that travel across small gaps, know as _____, between neurons.

6. Infants are born with between _____ billion neurons. Unused neurons are eliminated in a process called synaptic _____. The result of this process allows established neurons to build more elaborate _____ networks with other neurons.

7. After birth, neurons continue to _____ in size and become coated with _____, the fatty substance that helps insulate them and speeds the transmission of nerve impulses. The brain _____ its weight in the first two years and reaches more than _____ of adult weight and size by the age of two.

8. Neurons become arranged by _____. Some move into the _____ cortex, the upper layer of the brain, and others move to _____ levels.

9. The brain's _____, or degree to which a developing structure or behavior is modifiable due to experience, is relatively great for the brain. A _____ period is a specific but limited time during which the organism is particularly susceptible to environmental influences.

Integrating the Bodily Systems: The Life Cycles of Infancy

10. One of the most important ways that behavior becomes integrated is through the development of various body _____, repetitive cyclical patterns of behavior. An infant's _____ is the degree of awareness it displays to both internal and external stimulation.

11. Some of the different states that infants experience produce changes in _____ activity in the brain reflected in different patterns of brain _____ which can be measured by an _____.

12. On average, newborn infants sleep _____ hours a day. They experience a period of active sleep similar though not identical to _____ eye movement or REM sleep found in older children and adults. REM sleep provides a means for the brain to stimulate itself, a process called _____.

13. When seemingly healthy infants die in their sleep, it is probably due to _____ infant death syndrome (SIDS). The number of SIDS deaths has decreased since the American Academy of Pediatrics suggests the _____ guideline that babies sleep on their back. SIDS is the leading cause of death in children under the age of _____. Lipsitt believes that SIDS hinges on infant reflexes, specially the _____ occlusion reflex.

Motor Development

Reflexes: Our Inborn Physical Skills

14. Reflexes are _____, organized involuntary responses that occur automatically in the presence of certain stimuli. The _____ reflex makes a baby who is lying face down in a body of water paddle and kick. The _____ reflex seems designed to protect the eye from too much direct light. Most researchers attribute the gradual disappearance of reflexes to the increase in _____ control over behavior.

15. Reflexes are _____ determined and _____ throughout all infants. The _____ reflex is activated when support for the neck and head is suddenly removed. There are some _____ variations in the ways they are displayed however. Reflexes can serve as helpful _____ tools for pediatricians.

Motor Development in Infancy: Landmarks of Physical Achievement

16. By the age of _____ months, many infants become rather accomplished at moving themselves in particular directions. Crawling appears typically between _____ months. At around the age of _____ months, most infants are able to walk by supporting themselves on furniture. Babies are able to sit without support by the age of _____ months.

17. By the age of _____ months, infants show some ability to coordinate the movements of their limbs. By the age of _____ months, infants are able to pick small objects off the ground, and by the time they are _____ old, they can drink from a cup. Infants first begin picking up things with their whole hand, but as they get older they use a _____ grasp where the thumb and index finger meet to form a circle.

18. The _____ systems theory described how motor behaviors are assembled. This theory is noteworthy for its emphasis on a child's own _____.

19. The timing of the milestones is based on _____, the average performance of a large sample of children at a given age. One of the most widely used techniques to determine infants' normative standing is the _____ Neonatal Behavior Assessment Scale, a measure designed to determine infants' _____ and behavioral responses to their environment.

20. Variations in the timing of motor skills seem to depend in part on parental _____ of what is the appropriate schedule for the emergence of specific skills; that is by _____ factors. However, there are certain _____ determined constraints on how early a skill can emerge.

Nutrition in Infancy: Fueling Motor Development

21. The rapid physical growth that occurs during infancy is fueled by the _____ that infants receive. _____ is the condition of having an improper amount and balance of nutrients. Children who have been chronically malnourished during infancy later score lower on _____ tests and tend to do less well in _____. The problem of malnutrition is greatest in _____ countries.

49

22. Some _____ children live in poverty in the United States and the poverty rate for children under the age of _____ has increased. Although these children rarely become severely malnourished, they are susceptible to _____ .

23. Malnutrition during the first year can produce _____ , a disease in which infants stop growing because of a severe deficiency in _____ and _____ . Older children are susceptible to _____ , a disease in which a child's stomach, limbs, and face swell with water. Some children fail to grow for no biological reasons, a condition known as nonorganic failure to _____ .

24. _____ is defined as weight greater than 20 percent above the average for a given height. Research suggests that overfeeding during infancy may lead to the creation of unnecessary _____ cells, but _____ factors are an important determinant as well.

Breast or Bottle?

25. Child-care authorities agree that for the first 12 months of life, there is no better food for an infant than _____ milk. It contains all the nutrients necessary for _____ , and offers some degree of _____ to a variety of childhood diseases. And it is more easily _____ than cow's milk or formula.

26. Research suggests that women who breast-feed may have lower rates of _____ cancer and _____ cancer prior to menopause. The hormones produced during breast-feeding help shrink the _____ following birth, and inhibit _____ .

27. Only about _____ percent of all new mothers in the United States employ breast-feeding. The rates of breast-feeding are highest among women who are _____ , have better _____ , and are of higher _____ status. Breast-feeding among _____ mothers in the United States occurs at a rate almost double that for _____ mothers.

Introducing Solid Foods: When and What?

28. Solid foods are introduced into an infant's diet gradually around _____ months although they are not needed unitl _____ months. Most often _____ comes first. The timing of _____ , the cessation of breast-feeding, varies greatly.

The Development of the Senses

29. According to _____ , the world of the infant is a "blooming, buzzing confusion." The processes that underlie infants' understanding of the world around them are _____ , the stimulation of the sense organs, and _____ , the sorting out, interpretation, analysis, and integration of stimuli.

Visual Perception: Seeing the World

30. A newborn cannot discern visual material beyond _____ feet that an adult with normal vision is able to see from a distance of between 200 and 600 feet. By _____ months of age, the average infant's vision is already 20/20.

31. _____ vision, the ability to combine the images coming to each eye to see depth and motion, is achieved at around 14 weeks. _____ perception is a particularly useful ability for which Gibson and Walk developed the _____ cliff to test. Infants reliably prefer to look at stimuli that include _____ rather than simple stimuli. They are _____ preprogrammed to prefer particular kinds of stimuli.

Auditory Perception: The World of Sound

32. Even in the womb, the fetus responds to _____ outside of its mother. Sound _____ permits infants to discern the direction from which a sound is emanating.

33. Infants are able to discriminate certain characteristics that differentiate one _____ from another and can distinguish different _____ on the basis of voice. Infants can become acclimated to a sound thought a process called _____.

Smell and Taste

34. Some 12- to 18-day-old babies can distinguish their mothers on the basis of _____ alone. Some taste preferences are well developed at birth, such as disgust over _____ tastes. Infants seem to have a preference for _____ tastes.

Sensitivity to Pain and Touch

35. Pain produces signs of _____ in infants. It is possible that the delayed reaction to pain in infants is produced by the relatively slower _____ of information within the newborn's nervous system.

36. One of the most highly developed sensory systems in a newborn is _____, and it is also one of the _____ to develop. The basic _____ present at birth require touch sensitivity to operate.

37. Gentle _____ stimulates the production of certain chemicals in an infant's brain that instigate growth. In one study, _____ infants who were massaged were discharged earlier from the hospital, and their medical costs were significantly _____ than infants who were not massaged.

Multimodal Perception: Combining Individual Sensory Inputs

38. The multimodal approach to perception considers how information that is collected by various individual sensory systems is _____ and _____. Perceptual growth is aided by _____, the options that a given situation or stimulus provides.

CRITICAL THINKING QUESTIONS

To further your mastery of the topics in this chapter, write out your answers to the following essay questions in the space provided.

1. The cephalocaudal principle seems to imply that babies should learn how to talk before they learn how to walk, and yet most babies can walk long before they can form understandable utterances. How does another major growth principle explain this apparent contradiction?

2. Research indicates that there is a sensitive period during childhood for normal language acquisition. Individuals deprived of normal language stimulation as babies and children may never use language with the same skill as others who were not so deprived. For babies who are born deaf, what are the implications of this research finding, particularly with regard to signed languages?

3. What do you suppose that infants, without language capabilities or formal thought processes, dream about? Is this different from adult dreaming?

4. What are some cultural influences on infants' daily patterns of behavior that operate in the culture of which you are a part? How do they differ from the influences of other cultures (either within or outside of the United States) of which you are aware?

5. What advice might you give a friend who is concerned about the fact that her infant is still not walking at 14 months, when every other baby she knows started walking by the first birthday?

6. How would you design an experiment to determine whether early development of physical skills produces lasting effects? Why do you think a definitive answer to this question has not yet been found? How would you eliminate factors other than early development from your study?

7. Given that malnourishment negatively affects physical growth, how can it also adversely affect IQ scores and school performance?

8. Given the way the brain and nervous system develop, what sort of sensory environment would probably be most conducive to healthy neural development in the infant? Why?

9. Given that research indicates that infants can sense pain, do you feel there are moral or ethical considerations surrounding controversial practices such as circumcision?

10. The nervous system develops by "pruning down" unnecessary neurons that do not form links with other neurons. Do you think an infant's early preference for the sounds of its home language gives evidence that such a process operates in the area of language development? How?

PRACTICE TEST – POST TEST

Circle the correct answer for each of the following multiple choice questions and check your answers with the Answer Key at the end of this chapter.

1. An infant is brought into your medical office because his mother is concerned that he shows less development in his legs than he does in his trunk. Which of the following is a possible explanation?
   a. The boy is just demonstrating normal rhythmic development and does not need further evaluation.
   b. The boy should be evaluated because his development is not following the principle of hierarchical integration.
   c. The boy should be evaluated immediately because inconsistent developmental abilities indicate problems in brain development.
   d. If the differential development is within normal range, it is probably just normal cephalocaudal development.

2. The cells that carry information in the nervous system are called
   a. somas.
   b. neurons.
   c. synapse.
   d. myelin.

3. An infant had repeated ear infections and later developed problems telling certain words apart, for example, bat and pat. This led to the development of problems with spelling and understanding certain new words. His older sibling had no lasting effects from ear infections at age 6 years. This demonstrates the principle of
   a. sensitive periods.
   b. teratogenic development.
   c. proximodistal development.
   d. cephalocaudal development.

4. An awake state characterized by attentive scanning, and the infant's eyes open, bright and shining is called
   a. alert.
   b. cry.
   c. fuss.
   d. transitional.

5. What is the function of REM sleep in infants?
   a. achieving quiet sleep
   b. achieving active sleep
   c. warding off SIDS
   d. autostimulation

6. Rob and Julie are concerned about SIDS. Their doctors tell them that SIDS occurs most often in babies
   a. under one year old.
   b. 6 to 12 months old.
   c. 12 to 18 months old.
   d. 18 to 24 months old.

7. Babies will spread their toes when the soles of their feet are stroked. This reflex is called the
   a. startle reflex.
   b. Moro reflex.
   c. rooting reflex.
   d. Babinski reflex.

8. What is a possible function of the stepping reflex?
   a. protection
   b. avoidance of danger
   c. preparation for independent locomotion
   d. unknown

9. Dr. Brazelton developed an assessment called the Brazelton Neonatal Behavioral Assessment Scale primarily to assess
   a. neonatal reflexes.
   b. respiratory effort.
   c. responses to the environment.
   d. use of fine and gross motors skills.

10. When a child goes in for his well baby checkup, his height and weight will be compared to typical values. These values are obtained by averaging the values for a large number of normal babies and are called
    a. norms.
    b. factors.
    c. standards.
    d. neurological levels.

11. Obesity is defined as weight greater than
    a. 20 percent above the average.
    b. 30 percent above the average.
    c. 40 percent above the average.
    d. 50 percent above the average.

12. Rachel wants to start her baby on solid food. What should she start with first?
    a. eggs
    b. cereals
    c. vegetables
    d. strained fruits

13. Different body systems grow at different rates. This is the principle of
    a. proximodistal growth.
    b. cephalocaudal growth.
    c. hierarchical organization.
    d. independence of systems.

14. Synaptic pruning
    a. occurs as a result of brain damage.
    b. allows established neurons to build more elaborate communication networks.
    c. impedes the development of the nervous system.
    d. occurs early in adolescence.

15. Louisa's eyes are heavy-lidded, but opening and closing slowly and she is exhibiting a low level of motor activity. She is exhibiting which infant state?
    a. drowse
    b. quiet sleep
    c. daze
    d. active sleep

16. Which of the following is NOT a fine motor skill?
    a. drawing
    b. standing
    c. grasping a rattle
    d. building a tower out of cubes

17. All of the following children live in the United States in a mother-only family. Which child is most likely to live in poverty?
    a. two-year-old Jerome, who is black
    b. two-year-old Mark, who is white
    c. six-year-old Maria, who is Hispanic
    d. ten-year-old Kate, who is white

18. The stimulation of the sense organs is
    a. attenuation.
    b. habituation.
    c. perception.
    d. sensation.

19. According to research by Fantz, babies prefer to look at
    a. straight lines to curved lines.
    b. two-dimensional figures to three-dimensional figures.
    c. human faces to nonhuman faces.
    d. circles to squares.

20. Which of the following is an accurate statement about pain in infancy?
    a. Infants can't feel pain before the age of three months.
    b. Pain sensitivity decreases with age.
    c. There is a developmental progression in reaction to pain.
    d. Pain is most severe in the first week after birth.

ANSWER KEY

Practice Test – Pretest (with text page numbers)

1.	b 126	6.	c 134	11.	b 142	16.	b 136
2.	b 125	7.	d 136	12.	b 144	17.	d 141
3.	a 128	8.	b 136	13.	c 124	18.	c 142
4.	c 134	9.	c 137	14.	a 126	19.	a 147
5.	d 130	10.	c 138	15.	d 149	20.	a 137

Key Names

1. b   2. d   3. e   4. a   5. c

Key Vocabulary Terms

1. The cephalocaudal principle states growth follows a pattern that begins with the head and upper body and then proceeds down to the rest of the body; the proximodistal principle states that development proceeds from the center of the body outward.

2. The principle of hierarchical integration states that simple skills develop separately but are later integrated into more complex skills; the principle of independence of systems states that different body systems grow at different rates.

3. Marasmus is a disease characterized by the cessation of growth; kwashiorkor is a disease in which a child's stomach, limbs, and face swell with water. They are both caused by forms of malnutrition.

4. Neurons are coated with myelin and separated by a synapse, both serving to speed the transmission of the nerve impulse.

5. Sensation is the physical stimulation of the sense organs; and perception is the mental process of sorting out, interpreting, analyzing, and integrating sensory stimuli.

6. Plasticity, Ego, Reflexes, Cerebral, Episiotomy, Proximodistal, Thrive, Infant, Operant, Norms (Perception)

Programmed Review

1. 7, 20
2. rapid, doubled, tripled, four
3. 30, 3
4. cephalocaudal, proximodistal, hierarchical, independence
5. brain, nerves, nucleus, dendrites, axon, neurotransmitters, synapses
6. 100 to 200, pruning, communication
7. increase, myelin, triples, three-quarters
8. function, cerebral, subcortical
9. plasticity, sensitive
10. rhythms, state
11. electrical, waves, electroencephalogram
12. 16 to 17, rapid, autostimulation
13. sudden, back-to-sleep, one year, respiratory
14. unlearned, swimming, eye-blink, voluntary
15. genetically, universal, moro, cultural, diagnostic
16. six, 8 and 10, nine, six
17. three, 11, 2 years, pincer

18. dynamic, motivation
19. norms, Brazelton, neurological
20. expectations, cultural, genetically
21. nutrients, Malnutrition, IQ, school, underdeveloped
22. 12 million, three, undernutrition
23. marasmus, proteins, calories, kwashiorkor, thrive
24. Obesity, fat, genetic
25. breast, growth, immunity, digested
26. ovarian, breast, uterus, ovulation
27. 70, older, education, socioeconomic, Caucasian, African-American
28. 6, 9 to 12, cereal, weaning
29. William James, sensation, perception
30. 20, six
31. Binocular, Depth, visual, patterns, genetically
32. sounds, localization
33. language, people, habituation
34. smell, bitter, sweet
35. distress, transmission
36. touch, first, reflexes
37. massage, preterm, lower
38. integrated, coordinated, affordances

Practice Post Test (with text page numbers)

1.	d	125	6.	a	134	11.	a	143	16.	b 138
2.	b	126	7.	d	136	12.	b	146	17.	a 140
3.	a	129	8.	c	136	13.	d	125	18.	d 147
4.	a	130	9.	c	140	14.	b	127	19.	c 148
5.	d	132	10.	a	139	15.	a	130	20.	c 151

Chapter 5

Cognitive Development in Infancy

CHAPTER OUTLINE

◆ Piaget's Approach to Cognitive Development
- ♦ Key Elements of Piaget's Theory
- ♦ The Sensorimotor Period: Earliest Cognitive Growth
- ♦ Appraising Piaget: Support and Challenges

◆ Information-Processing Approaches to Cognitive Development
- ♦ Encoding, Storage, and Retrieval: The Foundations of Information Processing
- ♦ Memory During Infancy: They Must Remember This...
- ♦ Individual Differences in Intelligence: Is One Infant Smarter than Another?

◆ The Roots of Language
- ♦ The Fundamentals of Language: From Sounds to Symbols
- ♦ The Origins of Language Development: The Learning Theory Approach
- ♦ Speaking to Children: The Language of Infant-Directed Speech

LEARNING OBJECTIVES

After you have read and studied this chapter, you should be able to answer the following questions.

1. What are the fundamental features of Piaget's theories of cognitive development?
2. How do infants process information?
3. How is infant intelligence measured?
4. By what processes do children learn to use language?
5. How do children influence adults' language?

PRACTICE TEST QUESTIONS- PRETEST

Circle the correct answer for each of the following multiple choice questions and check your answer with the Answer Key at the end of this chapter.

1. Eight-month-old Angela picked up a crayon. She had never seen one before and did not know how to use it. She treated the crayon as if it were like her other toys, handling and mouthing it. Because she was functioning from her toy-manipulating schema she
   a. assimilated the crayon into her existing schemes.
   b. adapted to the crayon with a tertiary circular schema.
   c. accommodated the crayon into her existing schemes.
   d. adapted to the crayon with a secondary circular schema.

2. If Piaget designed an early educational program, he would be most likely to focus on
   a. the environment.
   b. direct motor behavior.
   c. facts communicated by others.
   d. learning through sensation and perception.

3. When Michael cannot directly see his mother he does not understand that she still exists. This illustrates a lack of which of Piaget's sensorimotor concepts?
   a. object permanence
   b. differed imitation
   c. infantile amnesia
   d. goal-directed behavior

4. Rebecca copies the behavior of her mother who is no longer present. Rebecca's actions are called
   a. mirror imaging.
   b. object permanence.
   c. deferred imitation.
   d. stimulus substitution.

5. Most people cannot remember their early childhood. This is called infantile amnesia and is defined as the lack of memory for experiences that occurred prior to
   a. birth.
   b. six months of age.
   c. 12 months of age.
   d. three years of age.

6. An overall developmental score that relates to performance on motor skills, language use, adaptive behavior, and personal-social domains is called the
   a. mental age.
   b. chronological age.
   c. intelligence quotient.
   d. developmental quotient.

7. Many children get frustrated because they know what they want to express but they cannot say it. This is due to the fact that
   a. production precedes comprehension.
   b. comprehension precedes production.
   c. comprehension does not always occur with articulation.
   d. comprehension and production are not part of the child's repertoire.

8. Juan has spoken his first words. We would expect that an infant developing normally would reach this milestone at approximately
   a. 6-8 months.
   b. 8-10 months.
   c. 10-14 months.
   d. 14-18 months.

9. When two-year-old Christine speaks, she leaves out words like " to." For example, if she wants something she will say "give me," instead of "give that to me." This language is called
   a. egocentric speech.
   b. telegraphic speech.
   c. holophrastic speech.
   d. infant-directed speech.

10. When a child is not able to see that a general term like "dog" can apply to more dogs than just to her German shepherd, the child is experiencing a normal developmental aspect of language called
    a. overextending.
    b. overregulating.
    c. underextending.
    d. underregulating.

11. Which theory of language acquisition is most fully supported by research?
    a. learning theory
    b. interactionist approach
    c. nativist perspective
    d. universal grammar

12. According to Piaget, an organized pattern of sensorimotor functioning is a(n)
    a. scheme.   c. holophrase.
    b. reaction.   d. expression.

13. Vicky has just begun to coordinate separate actions into single, integrated activities. What substage of sensorimotor development is Vicky in?
    a. one   c. three
    b. two   d. four

14. Who suggested that cognitive development proceeds in waves rather than stages?
    a. Jean Piaget
    b. Noam Chomsky
    c. Robert Siegler
    d. Nancy Bayley

15. What is the second step of memory according to the information-processing approach?
    a. consciousness   c. cognition
    b. retrieval   d. storage

16. The degree to which an activity requires attention is
    a. conceptualization.   c. intellectualization.
    b. accommodation.   d. automization.

17. Piaget focused on _____ changes, whereas the information-processing approach focused on _____ change.
    a. qualitative; quantitative   c. referential; expressive
    b. quantitative; qualitative   d. expressive; referential

18. Three formal characteristics of language that must be mastered are
    a. morphemes, phonology, and semantics.
    b. pragmatics, phonology, and semantics.
    c. nouns, verbs, and prepositions.
    d. adjectives, subject, and verbs.

19. Which of the following statements is TRUE regarding gender and infant language development?
    a. Girls are prone to hear twice as many diminutives as boys.
    b. Boys are prone to hear twice as many diminutives as girls.
    c. Girls hear firmer, clearer language than do boys.
    d. Language is largely unaffected by gender.

20. Noam Chomsky is associated with all of the following EXCEPT
    a. nativist approach.   c. universal grammar.
    b. infant-directed speech.   d. language acquisition device.

KEY NAMES

Match the following names with the most accurate description and check your answers with the Answer Key at the end of this chapter.

1. ____ Nancy Bayley   a. developmental quotient

2. ____ Noam Chomsky   b. gender differences in speech

3. ____ Arnold Gesell   c. LAD

4. ____ Jean Berko Gleason   d. scales of infant development

5. ___ Jean Piaget   e. stages of cognitive development

6. ___ Robert Siegler   f. "waves" of cognitive development

KEY VOCABULARY TERMS

Distinguish between each of the terms in the following groups.

1. Assimilation; Accommodation
2. Holophrases; Telegraphic speech
3. Underextension; Overextension
4. Explicit memory; Implicit memory

Explain how the following terms are related.

5. Prelinguistic language, Babbling

Fill in the blanks next to each definition with the correct term. The first letters of the terms will spell, from top to bottom, the term for the definition at the bottom of each puzzle. (NOTE: Some terms may be from previous chapters.)

6. _ _ _ _ _ _   An internal image of a past event or object is a ____ representation.

    _ _ _ _ _ _ _ _ _   A style that uses language primarily to express feelings and needs.

    _ _ _ _ _   The ability to identify a stimulus previously experienced only through one sense is cross _____ transference.

    _ _ _ _ _ _   Understanding that something still exists even if it is out of sight is _____ permanence.

    _ _ _ _ _ _ _ _ _ _   A style that uses language primarily to label objects.

    _   The chromosome on the 23rd pair that signifies a male.

The process by which information is recorded, stored, and retrieved is _ _ _ _ _ _.

7. _ _ _ _ _ _ _ _   The _____ theory approach uses basic laws of reinforcement and conditioning.

    _ _ _ _ _ _ _   The lack of memory for experiences that occurred prior to three years of age is infantile _____.

    _ _ _ _ _ _ _ _   The approach that states that genetically determined innate mechanisms direct development.

    _ _ _ _   Behavior in which schemes are combined and coordinated to generate a single act to solve a problem is _____ directed.

    _ _ _ _ _ _ _ _   The theory of _____ grammar states that all the world's languages share a similar underlying structure.

    _ _ _ _ _ _ _ _ _ _   The language _____ device is a hypothesized neural system of the brain that permits the understanding of language.

_ _ _ _ _   The basic units of heredity.

_ _ _ _ _ _   The prenatal child from two to eight weeks after conception.

A systematic, meaningful arrangement of symbols for communication is _ _ _ _ _ _ _ _.

Look up the definition of each of the following terms and provide a specific example of each.

8. Infantile amnesia
9. Developmental quotient
10. Visual-recognition memory
11. Bayley Scales of Infant Development
12. Information-processing approaches
13. Language
14. Circular reactions
15. Infant-directed speech
16. Semantics

PROGRAMMED REVIEW

Fill in the blanks in the following programmed review and check your answers with the Answer Key at the end of this chapter.

Piaget's Approach to Cognitive Development

1. Piaget 's views of the ways infants learn could be summed in a simple equation: _____ = _____. He suggested that knowledge is the product of direct _____ behavior and that infants learn by _____.

Key Elements of Piaget's Theory

2. According to Piaget all children pass through four universal _____ in a fixed order when they are at an appropriate level of physical _____ and exposed to relevant types of _____. It is critical to consider the changes in _____ of knowledge and understanding that occur as the child moves from one stage to another.

3. Piaget believed that infants have mental structures called _____, organized patterns of functioning, that adapt and change with _____ development. Two principles underlie the growth in children's schemes: _____, the process in which people understand an experience in terms of their current stage of cognitive development and way of thinking, and _____, changes in existing ways of thinking, understanding, or behaving in response to encounters with new stimuli or events.

4. Piaget believed that the earliest schemes are primarily limited to the _____ with which children are all _____.

The Sensorimotor Period: Earliest Cognitive Growth

5. Piaget suggests that the sensorimotor stage can be broken down into _____ substages. The first substage is simple _____ encompassing the first month of life.

6. The second substage is first habits and _____ circular reactions and occurs from 1 to 4 months of age. Infants begin to _____ what were separate actions into single, integrated activities. A _____ reaction permits the construction of cognitive schemes through the repetition of a chance motor event. Primary circular reactions are schemes reflecting an infant's _____ of interesting or enjoyable actions.

7. The third substage is _____ circular reactions occurring from 4 to 8 months. Infants shift their cognitive horizons beyond themselves and begin to act on the _____ world. These reactions are schemes regarding repeated actions meant to bring about a desirable _____. The major difference between primary circular reactions and secondary circular reactions is whether the infant's activity is focused on the infant or his or her own _____, or involves actions relating the outside _____. The degree of _____ increases substantially as infants come to notice that if they make noises, other people around them will _____ with noises of their own.

8. Substage 4, coordination of secondary circular reactions, lasts from around _____ months to _____ months. Infants employ _____ behavior, in which several schemes are combined and coordinated to generate a single act to solve a problem. The developmental achievement of _____ permanence emerges, but it takes several _____ for the concept to be fully comprehended.

9. Around the age of 12 months, infants develop what Piaget labeled _____ circular reactions, schemes regarding the deliberate variation of actions that bring desirable consequences. What is most striking about infants' behavior in this substage is their interest in the _____.

10. Beginnings of thought is the major achievement of substage 6 and is the capacity for mental _____ or _____ thought. Children's understanding of _____ becomes more sophisticated. Using the skill Piaget refers to as deferred _____, in which a person who is no longer present is imitated, allows children to be able to _____.

Appraising Piaget: Support and Challenges

11. Most developmental researchers agree that Piaget's description of cognitive development during infancy is quite _____, but critics believe that development proceeds in a much more _____ fashion . Seigler suggests that cognitive development proceeds not in stages but in _____. Other critics of Piaget dispute the notion that cognitive development is grounded in _____ activities and that such a view ignores the importance of the sophisticated _____ and _____ systems that are present from very early in infancy. Some work suggests that younger infants may not appear to understand object _____ because the techniques used to test their abilities are too insensitive. There is also some evidence that the _____ for the emergence of various cognitive skills among children in _____ cultures differs from that observed in children living in Europe and the United States.

Information-Processing Approaches to Cognitive Development

12. Information-processing approaches seek to identify the way that individuals take in, use, and store _____, and hold that the _____ changes in infants' abilities to organize and manipulate information represent the hallmark of cognitive development.

Encoding, Storage, and Retrieval: The Foundations of Information Processing

13. Information processing has three basic aspects: _____ is the process by which information is initially recorded in a form usable to memory; _____ refers to the maintenance of material saved in memory; and _____ is the process by which material in memory storage is located, brought into awareness, and used. Information-processing approaches suggest that these processes are analogous to different parts of a _____.

14. The degree to which an activity requires attention is _____. Processes that require relatively little attention are _____; processes that require relatively large amounts of attention are _____. Children also develop an understanding of _____, categorizations of objects, events, or people that share common properties.

Memory During Infancy: They Must Remember This

15. Infants have memory capabilities, defined as the process by which information is initially _____, _____, and _____.

16. Although the processes that underlie memory retention and recall seem similar throughout the life span, the _____ of information stored and recalled does differ. Older infants can remember information _____ and they can retrieve it more _____.

17. Older research supports the notion of infantile _____, the lack of memory for experiences that occurred prior to three years of age. More recent research shows surprising _____ in infants. Memories are susceptible to _____ from other newer information and recall of memories is sensitive to the _____ context in which the memories were initially formed. Infants' memories may be highly detailed and can be enduring if the infants experience repeated _____.

18. _____ is memory that is conscious and can be recalled intentionally. _____ is a memory that is recalled unconsciously.

Individual Differences in Intelligence: Is One Infant Smarter than Another?

19. Developmental psychologist, _____, formulated the earliest measure of infant development. He developed a _____ quotient that is an overall developmental score relating performance in four domains: _____ skills, _____ use, adaptive _____, and personal-_____.

20. The _____ Scales of Infant Development evaluate an infant's development from 2 to 30 months in two areas: _____ and _____ abilities. The association between most measures of behavior during infancy and adult intelligence is _____.

21. Contemporary approaches to infant intelligence suggest that the _____ with which infants process information may correlate most strongly with later intelligence. Measures of _____ memory, the memory and recognition of a stimulus that has been previously seen, also relate to _____.

22. _____ transference, the ability to identify a stimulus that previously has been experienced through only one sense by using another sense, is associated with intelligence.

23. Piaget focused on _____ changes; whereas information-processing approaches focus on _____ changes. Piaget sees cognitive growth in sudden _____; information-processing theories see more _____ growth.

24. To promote infants' cognitive development, parents should provide opportunities to _____ the world, be _____ on a verbal and nonverbal level, _____ to their infants, keep in mind they _____ have to be with an infant 24 hours a day, and do not _____ infants or _____ too much.

The Roots of Language

The Fundamentals of Language: From Sounds to Symbols

25. Language is the systematic, meaningful arrangement of _____ and provides the basis for _____. It has several formal characteristics including _____, the basic sounds of language (called _____); _____, the smallest language unit that has meaning; and _____, the rules that govern the meaning of words and sentences.

26. In considering the development of language, we need to distinguish between linguistic _____, the understanding of speech, and linguistic _____, the use of language to communicate. _____ precedes _____.

27. _____ communication occurs through sounds, facial expressions, gestures, imitation, and other nonlinguistic means. The most obvious manifestation is_____ (making speechlike but meaningless sounds), a _____ phenomenon, and infants spontaneously produce all of the sounds found in every _____. By the age of _____, babbling differs according to the language to which infants are exposed.

28. First words generally are spoken around the age of _____ months. Once an infant starts to produce words, the rate of increase in vocabulary is _____. The first words are often _____, one-word utterances whose meaning depends on the particular context in which they are used.

29. Children first create two-word phrases around _____ months after they say their first word. Most early sentences are merely _____ and observations about events occurring in the child's world.

30. Two-year-olds produce _____ speech in which words not critical to the message are left out. Early language also contains _____, using words too restrictively, and _____ using words too broadly. Some children use a _____ style, primarily labeling objects; and some use an _____ style, to express feelings.

The Origins of Language Development: The Learning Theory Approach

31. Evidence for the innate theory of gestures is that blind children gesture in the _____ way as sighted children, gesturing follows a set of _____, and similar areas of the _____ are activated by gestures and speech.

32. According to the _____ theory approach, language acquisition follows the basic laws of reinforcement and conditioning. Through the process of _____, language becomes more and more similar to adult speech. But this theory doesn't explain adequately how readily children acquire the _____ of language.

33. Chomsky supports the _____ approach that argues that there is a _____ determined _____ mechanism that directs the development of language. His analysis of different languages suggests that all the world's languages share a similar underlying structure which he calls _____ grammar and that the human brain is wired with a neural system called the _____ device or LAD.

34. The _____ perspective suggests that language development is produced through a combination of _____ determined predispositions and _____ circumstances that help teach language.

Speaking to Children: The Language of Infant-Directed Speech

35. Infant-directed speech, previously called _____, is characterized by short, simple sentences. Pitch becomes _____, the range of frequency _____, and the intonation is more _____.

36. Virtually from the time of birth, the language parents employ with their children differs depending on the child's _____. Gleason found that by the age of 32 months, girls hear _____ as many diminutives as boys hear. Consequently, _____ tend to hear firmer, clearer language, whereas _____ are exposed to warmer phrases, often referring to inner _____ states.

CRITICAL THINKING QUESTIONS

To improve your understanding of the topics covered in this chapter, write out your answers to the following essay questions in the spaces provided.

1. Name some examples of different ways that adults and children understand and interpret objects or events in their worlds.

2. Give some examples of the principles of assimilation and accommodation at work in child development. Do these principles function in adult human learning? Explain your answer.

3. In what ways do you think the concept of object permanence might foster the infant's social and emotional development?

4. Why is the emergence of a capacity for mental representation essential for the development of thought? How do the mental representations of a blind infant differ from those of a sighted infant? In what ways might they be the same?

5. In general, what are some implications for childrearing practices of Piaget's observations about the ways children gain an understanding of the world?

6. Use an example to explain how goal-directed behavior evolves throughout the sensorimotor period of cognitive development.

7. In what way is the use of such developmental scales as Gesell's, Bayley's, or visual recognition helpful? In what way is it dangerous? How would you maximize the helpfulness and minimize the danger?

8. Information-processing speed in infants correlates moderately well with one sort of adult intelligence. Might there be other indicators in infants that correlate with other adult skills or intelligences? Of what use would such indicators be? What would be their limitations?

9. Give some examples of how individuals who do not use verbal communication might develop language abilities.

10. What are some implications of differences in the ways adults speak to boys and girls? How might such speech differences contribute to later differences not only in speech, but in attitudes?

PRACTICE TEST – POST TEST

Circle the correct answer for each of the following multiple choice questions and check your answer with the Answer Key at the end of this chapter.

1. John makes minor changes in his schemes every time he has a new experience. This process is called
    a. assimilation.
    b. accommodation.
    c. developmental reflexes.
    d. adapted secondary circular schema.

2. Ryan accidentally hits his crib and it makes an interesting noise. Ryan decides to repeat the action again. This is known as a
    a. simple reflex.
    b. primary circular reaction.
    c. secondary circular reaction.
    d. tertiary circular reaction.

3. What is the major achievement of the final sensorimotor substage?
    a. acting on the outside world
    b. deliberate variation of actions
    c. capacity for mental representation
    d. coordination of separate actions into single, integrated activities

4. Kyle, a 20-month-old, mainly uses words to express his feelings about himself and others. This use of language describes an
    a. expressive style.
    b. referential style.
    c. learning approach.
    d. universal approach.

5. All of the following are domains measured by Gesell's developmental quotient EXCEPT
    a. visual-recognition.
    b. motor skills.
    c. adaptive behavior.
    d. personal-social.

6. When a child is able to recognize the smell of something he has previously seen, the child is displaying
    a. habituation.
    b. sensory integration.
    c. cross-modal transference.
    d. visual-recognition memory.

7. Becky is making speechlike sounds to herself in her crib. Although the sounds resemble vowels and consonants, they do not form recognizable words. Becky is expressing herself by
    a. babbling.
    b. telegraphic speech.
    c. linguistic lag.
    d. holophrastic speech.

8. When Amy puts her arms up and says "up," she means "Mother, please pick me up." This is an example of what form of speech?
    a. scaffolding
    b. a holophrase
    c. overextension
    d. telegraphic speech

9. Laura says "kitty" whenever she sees a four-legged animal. This is an example of an aspect of speech called
    a. overextending.
    b. overregulating.
    c. underextending.
    d. underregulating.

10. Which type of speech is also known as motherese?
    a. telegraphic speech
    b. holophrastic speech
    c. infant-directed speech
    d. underextended speech

11. When a child begins to conduct trial-and-error experiments, she is in what sensorimotor stage?
    a. reflexes
    b. secondary circular reactions
    c. tertiary circular reactions
    d. the coordination of object permanence

12. Amit's ability to tie her shoes with without conscious cognitive effort demonstrates her
    a. memory decoding.
    b. explicit memory.
    c. implicit memory.
    d. infantile amnesia.

13. The combination and coordination of several schemes to generate a single act to solve a problem is
    a. tertiary circular reactions.
    b. secondary circular reactions.
    c. object-directed behavior.
    d. goal-directed behavior.

14. Critics of Piaget's theory have stated all of the following EXCEPT
    a. development proceeds in a much more continuous fashion.
    b. the theory ignores the importance of sensory and perceptual systems.
    c. facial imitation does not begin until age two years.
    d. object permanence can be mastered earlier than the theory states.

15. Which of the following is NOT an element of information processing?
    a. encoding
    b. decoding
    c. retrieval
    d. storage

16. The Bayley Scales of Infant Development evaluate all of the following EXCEPT
    a. fine motor skills.
    b. problem solving.
    c. intelligence quotient.
    d. gross motor skills.

17. The notion that all of the world's languages share a similar underlying structure was described by Chomsky as
    a. common communication.
    b. global semantics.
    c. universal grammar.
    d. the LAD.

18. Prelinguistic communication includes all of the following EXCEPT
    a. gestures.
    b. facial expressions.
    c. sounds.
    d. words.

19. Sara is learning to talk and her vocabulary consists primarily of words used to label objects. Her language style is
    a. overextended.
    b. linguistic.
    c. referential.
    d. expressive.

20. As a child reaches the end of the first year, infant-directed speech
    a. increases dramatically.
    b. involves longer, more complex sentences.
    c. is directed at girls but no longer at boys.
    d. stops completely.

ANSWER KEYS

Practice Test – Pretest (with test page numbers)

1.	a 160	6.	d 173	11.	b 183	16.	d 168
2.	b 159	7.	b 177	12.	a 159	17.	a 175
3.	a 163	8.	c 179	13.	b 161	18.	a 177
4.	c 165	9.	b 181	14.	c 166	19.	a 186
5.	d 170	10.	c 181	15.	d 168	20.	b 183

Key Names

1. d   3. a   5. e
2. c   4. b   6. f

Key Vocabulary Terms

1.   Assimilation is understanding an experience in terms of current stage of cognitive development and way of thinking; accommodation is changing existing ways of thinking in response to encounters with new stimuli or events.

2.   Holophrases are single words used to express an entire thought; telegraphic speech follows and is comprised of sentences with only the critical words.

3.   Underextension is the overly restrictive use of words; overextension is the overly broad use of words.

4.   Explicit memory is memory that is recalled consciously; implicit memory is memory that is recalled unconsciously.

5.   Babbling is a form of prelinguistic language.

6.   Mental, Expressive, Modal, Object, Referential, Y (Memory)

7.   Learning, Amnesia, Nativist, Goal, Universal, Acquisition, Genes, Embryo (Language)

Programmed Review

1.   Action, Knowledge, motor, doing
2.   stages, maturation, experience, quality
3.   schemes, mental, assimilation, accommodation
4.   reflexes, born
5.   six, reflexes
6.   primary, coordinate, circular, repetition
7.   secondary, outside, consequence, body, world, vocalization, respond
8.   8, 12, goal-directed, object, months
9.   tertiary, unexpected
10. representation, symbolic, causality, imitation, pretend
11. accurate, continuous, waves, motor, sensory, perceptual, permanence, timetable, non-Western
12. information, quantitative
13. encoding, storage, retrieval, computer
14. automatization, automatic, controlled, concepts
15. recorded, stored, retrieved
16. quantity, longer, rapidly
17. amnesia, retention, interference, environmental, reminders
18. Explicit, Implicit
19. Arnold Gesell, developmental, motor, language, behavior, social
20. Bayley, mental, motor, minimal
21. speed, visual-recognition, IQ
22. Cross-modal
23. qualitative, quantitative, spurts, gradual
24. explore, responsive, read, don't, push, expect
25. symbols, communication, phonology, phonemes, morphemes, semantics
26. comprehension, production, Comprehension, production
27. Prelinguistic, babbling, universal, language, 6 months
28. 10 to 14, rapid, holophrases

29. 8 to 12, comments
30. telegraphic, underextension, overextension, referential, expressive
31. same, rules, brain
32. learning, shaping, rules
33. nativist, genetically, innate, universal, language acquisition
34. interactionist, genetically, environmental
35. motherese, higher, increases, varied
36. sex, twice, boys, girls, emotional

Practice Test - Post Test (with test page numbers)

1.	b 160	6.	c 174	11.	c 161	16.	c 172
2.	c 161	7.	a 178	12.	c 171	17.	c 182
3.	c 161	8.	b 180	13.	d 162	18.	d 173
4.	a 182	9.	a 181	14.	c 166	19.	c 182
5.	a 172	10.	c 183	15.	b 168	20.	b 183

Chapter 6

Social and Personality Development in Infancy

CHAPTER OUTLINE

◆ Forming the Roots of Sociability

- ♦ Emotions in Infancy: Do Infants Experience Emotional Highs and Lows?
- ♦ Social Referencing: Feeling What Others Feel
- ♦ The Development of Self: Do Infants Know Who They Are?
- ♦ Theory of Mind: Infants' Perspectives on the Mental Lives of Others–and Themselves

◆ Forging Relationships

- ♦ Attachment: Forming Social Bonds
- ♦ Interactions Producing Attachment: The Roles of the Mother and Father
- ♦ Infant Interactions: Developing a Working Relationship
- ♦ Infants' Sociability with Their Peers: Infant-Infant Interaction

◆ Differences Among Infants

- ♦ Personality Development: The Characteristics That Make Infants Unique
- ♦ Temperament: Stabilities in Infant Behavior
- ♦ Gender: Why Do Boys Wear Blue and Girls Wear Pink?
- ♦ Family Life in the 21st Century

LEARNING OBJECTIVES

After you have read and studied this chapter, you should be able to answer the following questions.

1. Do infants experience emotions?
2. What sort of mental life do infants have?
3. What is attachment in infancy and how does it affect a person's future social competence?
4. What roles do other people play in infants' social development?
5. What individual differences distinguish one infant from another?
6. How does nonparental childcare impact infants?

PRACTICE TEST QUESTIONS - PRETEST

Circle the correct answer for each of the following multiple choice questions and check your answers with the Answer Key at the end of this chapter.

1. When a three-month-old infant smiles as her aunt plays with her, the response is called a(n)
   a. social smile.
   b. reciprocal smile.
   c. undifferentiated smile.
   d. mutually interactive smile.

2. Becky, who is 18 months old, and her older brother are on a sled being pulled by their father. As the sled takes off very quickly, Becky looks at her older brother and notices that he is smiling and really enjoying the ride. On seeing this, Becky smiles too. Becky's reliance on her brother to see how he reacts is called
   a. synchrony.
   b. attachment.
   c. social referencing.
   d. mutual regulation.

3. At what age do infants and their social partners have roughly equal mutual influence on each other's behavior?
   a. 6 months
   b. 9 months
   c. 12 months
   d. 18 months

4. Laura shared her toy with Wes because his toy broke. Laura has reached the age when she is beginning to demonstrate
   a. trust.
   b. empathy.
   c. sympathy.
   d. self-awareness.

5. Harlow experimented with infant monkeys to study
   a. empathy.
   b. attachment.
   c. temperament.
   d. social referencing.

6. In the strange situation test, infants' behaviors are used to
   a. measure reinforcement.
   b. classify parenting styles.
   c. measure orienting behaviors.
   d. classify children's attachment.

7. What traits do mothers of securely attached children appear to exhibit?
   a. a strong sense of discipline and order
   b. strong relationships with their husbands
   c. sensitivity to their infants' needs and desires
   d. a good understanding of child development patterns

8. How do mothers and fathers play differently with their infants?
   a. Fathers' play is more physical.
   b. Fathers' play is more conventional.
   c. Mothers' play is more spontaneous.
   d. Mothers' play is more unconventional.

9. Social referencing is
   a. smiling in response to other individuals.
   b. knowledge of one's self.
   c. search for information to explain uncertain circumstances.
   d. knowledge and beliefs about how the mind works and affects behavior.

10. When a caregiver responds promptly to an infant's needs, for example, feeds him when he is hungry and holds him when he cries, Erikson believed that the child develops
    a. trust.
    b. intimacy.
    c. initiative.
    d. generativity.

11. Research by Thomas and Chess has classified what percent of infants as "slow-to-warm"?
    a. 15 percent   c. 35 percent
    b. 25 percent   d. 45 percent

12. What dimension of temperament refers to the degree to which environmental stimuli alter behavior?
    a. adaptability   c. differentiation
    b. distractibility   d. threshold of stimulation

13. Stranger anxiety is common after the age of
    a. 3 months.   c. 18 months.
    b. 6 months.   d. 24 months.

14. With respect to infant emotions, most developmental researchers believe that
    a. infants experience the same emotions as adults do.
    b. facial expressions in infants are not accompanied by emotions.
    c. infant nonverbal expressions reflect emotions.
    d. positive emotions are expressed more frequently than negative emotions.

15. Enrico is 8 months old and experiences stranger anxiety. He will exhibit more stranger anxiety if
    a. the stranger is male rather than female.
    b. the stranger is a child rather than an adult.
    c. he had a lot of experience with strangers.
    d. he has experience with siblings.

16. Babies begin to smile reliably by what age?
    a. 1 to 2 weeks   c. 7 months
    b. 6 to 9 weeks   d. 9 months

17. Whose theory explored imprints as a way to examine human attachment styles?
    a. Harlow   c. Bowlby
    b. Lorenz   d. Freud

18. What percent of one-year-olds are classified as having ambivalent attachment?
    a. 66   c. 12
    b. 20   d. 10

19. Testing in the Strange Situation reveals that infants from Germany tend to be
    a. disorganized.   c. avoidant.
    b. secure.   d. ambivalent.

20. Patterns of arousal and emotionality that are consistent and enduring characteristics of an individual are
    a. temperament.   c. traits.
    b. personality.   d. socialized.

KEY NAMES

Match the following names with the most accurate descriptive terms and check your answers with the Answer Key at the end of the chapter.

1. ___ Mary Ainsworth   a. contact comfort

2. ___ John Bowlby   b. MAX

3. ___ Buss and Plomin   c. "safety and security" in attachment

4. ___ Erik Erikson   d. theory of mind

5. ___ John Flavell   e. imprinting

6. ___ Sigmund Freud   f. infant temperament

7. ___ Harry Harlow   g. inherited traits

8. ___ Carroll Izard   h. oral needs

9. ___ Konrad Lorenz   i. psychosocial development

10.___ Thomas and Chess   j. Strange Situation

KEY VOCABULARY TERMS

Differentiate between the terms in the following groups.

1. Securely attached; Avoidant; Ambivalent; Disorganized-disoriented

2. Trust v. mistrust; Autonomy v. shame and doubt

3. Difficult; Slow-to-warm

4. Personality; Temperament

Briefly explain each of the following.

5. Mutual regulation model

6. Erikson's theory of psychosocial development

Fill in the blanks with the appropriate term for each of the definitions. The first letter of each term will spell, from top to bottom, the term for the last definition. (NOTE: Some terms may be from previous chapters.)

7. _ _ _ _ _   A smile that is in response to other individuals.

_ _ _ _ _ _   An emotional response that corresponds to the feelings of another.

_ _ _ _ _ _ _ _ _ _   A study that follows the same group of individuals over a period of time.

_ _ _   Goodness of ____ is the notion that development is dependent on the match between a child's temperament and the environment.

_ _ _ _ _ _ _ _   The positive emotional bond between a child and a particular adult.

_ _ _ _ _ _   The first American psychologist to advocate the behavioral approach.

_ _ _ _ _ _ _   Stranger and separation are both a form of this.

_ _ _ _ _ _ _ _ _   Socialization in which an infant's behavior invites further responses from parents, which, in turn, invites further responses from the infant.

_ _ _ _ _ _ _ _   Differential _____ theory states that emotional expression reflects emotional experience.

_ _ _ _   The average performance of a large sample of children of a given age.

_ _ _ _   Children who have a positive disposition and are adaptable.

_ _ _ _ _ _   The intentional search for information about others' feelings is _ _ _ _ _ referencing.

_ _ _ _ _ _ _   Ainsworth developed the _ _ _ _ _ _ situation test.

Knowledge of oneself is _ _ _ _ - _ _ _ _ _ _ _ _ _

Look up the definition for each of the following terms and give a specific example of each.

8. Gender
9. Theory of mind
10. Attachment
11. Reciprocal socialization
12. Goodness-of-fit

PROGRAMMED REVIEW

Fill in the blanks in the following programmed review and check your answers with the Answer Key at the end of this chapter.

Forming the Roots of Sociability

Emotions in Infancy: Do Infants Experience Emotional Highs and Lows?

1. Basic facial expressions are remarkably _ _ _ _ _ _ across the most diverse cultures. The nonverbal expression of emotion, called nonverbal _ _ _ _ _ _, is fairly consistent throughout the life span. These consistencies have led researchers to conclude that we are _ _ _ _ _ with the capacity to display basic emotions.

2. Research using the Maximally Discriminative Facial Movement Coding system, also know as _ _ _ _ _, finds that interest distress, and disgust are present at _ _ _ _ _. Although infants display similar _ _ _ _ _ of emotions, the _ _ _ _ _ of emotional expressivity varies.

3. In addition to _ _ _ _ _ a wider variety of emotions as they develop they also _ _ _ _ _ a wider array of emotions.

4. By the end of the first year, infants often develop _ _ _ _ _ _ anxiety (caution and wariness displayed when encountering an unfamiliar person), and _ _ _ _ _ _ anxiety (the distress displayed by infants when a customary care provider departs). Separation anxiety peaks at _ _ _ _ _ _ . The infant's growing _ _ _ _ _ _ skills contribute to separation anxiety.

5. The first smiles tend to be relatively _ _ _ _ _ _. As infants get older, they become more _ _ _ _ _ _ in their smiles. Smiling in response to other individuals is considered a _ _ _ _ _ _ smile.

6. Imitative abilities pave the way for future nonverbal _ _ _ _ _ _. Infants are able to discriminate happy and sad vocal expressions at the age of _ _ _ _ _ months. Scientist know more about the _ _ _ _ _ in which this ability progresses. By _ _ _ _ _ months, infants may already have begun to understand emotions that lie behind _ _ _ _ _ and _ _ _ _ _ expression of others.

Social Referencing: Feeling What Others Feel

7. Social referencing is the _____ search for information about others' feelings to help explain the meaning of uncertain circumstances and events. It first tends to occur around the age of _____ months. Infants make particular use of _____ expressions in their social referencing.

The Development of Self: Do Infants Know Who They Are?

8. The roots of _____, knowledge of oneself, begin to grow at around the age of 12 months. By the age of _____ months, infants have developed at least the rudiments of awareness of their own physical characteristics and capabilities, and they understand that their appearance is _____ over time.

Theory of Mind: Infants' Perspectives on the Mental Lives of Others—and Themselves

9. Flavell has investigated children's theory of mind, their _____ and beliefs about the mental world. Children learn to see others as _____ agents, beings similar to themselves who behave under their own power and who have the capacity to _____ to infants' requests.

10. By the age of 2, infants begin to demonstrate the rudiments of _____, an emotional response that corresponds to the feelings of another person. Further, during the second year infants begin to use _____, in outright attempts to fool others.

Forging Relationships

Attachment: Forming Social Bonds

11. The most important form of social development that takes place during infancy is _____, the positive _____ bond that develops between a child and a particular individual.

12. Lorenz observed the process of _____ in goslings, behavior that takes place during a critical period and involves attachment to the first moving object that is observed. His findings suggested that attachment was based on _____ determined factors. Freud suggested that attachment grew out of a mother's ability to satisfy a child's _____ needs.

13. Harlow suggested that infants have a need for contact _____. His works illustrates that _____ alone is not the basis for attachment.

14. Bowlby believed that attachment is based primarily on infants' needs for _____ and _____, their genetically determined motivation to avoid predators. Infants develop a special relationship with an individual who is typically the _____.

15. Ainsworth developed a technique to measure attachment called the _____ Situation. She found that children with _____ attachment use the mother as a home base and explore independently. _____ children do not seek proximity to the mother, and after the mother has left, they seem to avoid her when she returns. _____ children display a combination of positive and negative reactions to their mothers. Later researchers identified the category of _____ disoriented children who show inconsistent, often contradictory behaviors.

Interactions Producing Attachment: The Roles of the Mother and Father

16. Sensitivity to their infants' needs and desires is the hallmark of mothers of _____ attached infants. Such a mother tends to be aware of her child's _____, and she takes into account her child's _____ as they interact. She is also responsive during face-to-face _____, provides feeding on _____, and is warm and _____ to her infant. These mothers provide the appropriate _____ of response.

17. Mothers whose communication involves interactional _____ are more likely to produce secure attachment. Mothers' behavior toward infants is a reaction to the children's ability to provide effective _____.

18. Bowlby suggested that there was something unique about the _____-child relationship. But research has shown that some infants form their primary initial relationship with their _____. Although most infants form their first primary relationship with one person, around _____ have multiple relationships.

19. Mothers spend a greater proportion of their time feeding and directly _____ their children. Fathers spend more time, proportionally, _____ with infants. Fathers engage in more _____ rough-and-tumble activities with their children. Mothers play traditional games with more _____ elements.

20. Bowlby suggested that seeking attachment was a _____ universal. But cross-cultural and within-cultural differences in attachment reflect the nature of the _____ employed. Secure attachment may be seen earliest in cultures that promote _____.

21. Attachment is now viewed as susceptible to cultural _____ and expectations.

Infant Interactions: Developing a Working Relationship

22. According to the mutual _____ model, infants and parents learn to communicate emotional states to one another and to respond appropriately. By the age of _____ months, infants have more control over turn-taking. The development of attachment is a process of _____ socialization, in which infants' behaviors invite further responses from parents and other caregivers. Ultimately, these actions and reactions lead to an increase in _____.

Infants' Sociability with Their Peers: Infant - Infant Interaction

23. Infants engage in rudimentary forms of _____ interaction. From the earliest months, they start to show more interest in _____ than inanimate objects and they begin to show preferences for people with whom they are _____. An infant's level of sociability generally _____ with age, and they begin to _____ each other. Infants learn new behaviors, skills, and abilities due to exposure to other _____.

Differences Among Infants

Personality Development: The Characteristics that Make Infants Unique

24. The origins of _____, the sum total of the enduring characteristics that differentiate one individual from another, stem from infancy. From _____ onward, infants begin to show unique, stable traits.

25. Erikson's theory of _____ development includes the period of infancy when children are in the stage of _____. If infants are able to develop trust, they experience a sense of _____. During the end of infancy, children enter the _____ stage, which lasts from around 18 months to 3 years. During this period, children develop _____ and autonomy if parents encourage _____ and _____.

Temperament: Stabilities in Infant Behavior

26. Temperament encompasses patterns of arousal and _____ that are consistent and _____ characteristics of an individual. Infants show temperamental differences in general disposition from the time of _____, largely due initially to _____ factors. Temperament is fairly _____ well into adolescence.

27. One central dimension of temperament is _____ level, which reflects the degree of overall movement. The nature and quality of an infant's mood, or _____, is another dimension.

28. Thomas and Chess carried out a large-scale study of infants known as the _____ Longitudinal Study. _____ babies have a positive disposition, their body functions operate regularly, and they are adaptable. This category applies to about _____ percent of infants. _____ babies have more negative moods and are slow to adapt to new situations. About _____ percent of infants belong in this category. _____ babies are inactive,

showing relatively calm reactions to their environment. Approximately _____ percent of infants are in this category. The remaining _____ cannot be consistently categorized.

29. Children's long-term adjustment depends on the goodness of _____ of their particular temperament and the nature and demands of the _____ in which they find themselves.

30. Buss and Plomin argue that temperamental characteristics represent inherited traits and are fairly stable during childhood and across the _____. _____ reactivity, which has been termed inhibition to the unfamiliar, is exhibited as shyness.

Gender: Why Do Boys Wear Blue and Girls Wear Pink?

31. From birth on, fathers tend to interact more with _____ than _____, and mothers interact more with _____. Male and female infants are clearly exposed to different styles of _____ and interaction from their parents. The behavior exhibited by girls and boys is _____ in very different ways by adults.

32. _____ refers to a sense of being male or female; _____ typically refers to sexual anatomy and sexual behavior. All cultures prescribe _____ for males and females.

33. Male infants tend to be more _____ and fussier than female infants, and boys' sleep tends to be more _____ than that of girls.

34. The differences among male and female infants are generally _____. By the age of _____, infants are able to distinguish between males and females.

35. The amount of reinforcement _____ receive for playing with toys that society deems appropriate increases with age. By the time they reach the age of 2, boys behave more _____ and less _____ than girls. Much of this behavior can be traced to parental _____ to earlier behaviors. Exploratory behavior tends to be encouraged more in _____.

Family Life in the 21st Century

36. The number of single-parent families has _____ dramatically in the last two decades. Today, on average, there are _____ persons per household. By the 1990s, more than 25 percent of births were to _____ mothers. Every minute, an _____ in the United States gives birth. More than 5 million children under the age of 3 are cared for by other adults while their parents _____ and more than half of _____ of infants work outside the home. One in six children lives in _____ in the United States.

37. Parents should look for a ratio of one adult for every _____ infants, groups of infants no larger than _____, and compliance with all governmental _____. They should ask about the motivation and training of _____ and if the environment is _____ and _____.

38. More than _____ of infants are cared for by people other than their mothers at some point during their first year of life. Most research finds little or no difference in the strength or nature of parental _____ bonds of infants in day care, but research does suggest that infants were less likely to be _____ when they had been placed in low-quality child care and if their mothers are relatively _____ and_____.

39. Boys who experienced _____ levels of child care and girls who had _____ amounts of care were less apt to be securely attached.

40. Children who participate in Head Start later are better able to _____ problems, pay greater _____ to others, and use _____ more effectively

CRITICAL THINKING QUESTIONS

To further your mastery of the topics, write out your answers to the following essay questions in the spaces provided.

1. If the facial expressions that convey basic emotions are similar across cultures, how do such expressions arise? Can you think of facial expressions that are culture-specific? How do they arise?

2. In what situations do adults rely on social referencing to work out appropriate responses? How might social referencing be used to manipulate an individual's responses?

3. In what sort of society might the attachment style labeled "avoidant" be encouraged by cultural attitudes toward childrearing? In such a society, would characterizing the infant's consistent avoidance of its mother as anger be an accurate interpretation?

4. In what ways might overly responsive and underresponsive caregivers equally contribute to insecure attachment in their infants?

5. Although there is no clear evidence that suggests clear benefits of parental or nonparental childcare most, individuals in the United States have a preference for one or the other. Why factors might influence this type of preferences?

6. Can you discern a relationship between reciprocal socialization and operant conditioning? Explain.

7. Why do you think that learning from peers is so effective for young children? Does this finding have implications for educational practices? Explain.

8. Does the concept of social referencing help explain the development of gender-based behavioral differences in young children? How?

9. What are some social implications of the changes in family life described in this chapter? What sorts of family policies might be instituted to address these changes?

10. Are the animal studies used in the chapter sufficient to shed light upon human patterns of attachment? Why or why not?

PRACTICE TEST – POST TEST

Circle the correct answer for each of the following multiple choice questions and check your answers with the Answer Key at the end of this chapter.

1. When Rachel approached the hot stove, her mother showed fear and yelled "don't touch that." Rachel was able to interpret her mother's vocal and facial expressions and did not touch the stove. This illustrates Rachel's ability for
   a. social referencing.
   b. nonverbal encoding.
   c. nonverbal decoding.
   d. reciprocal socialization.

2. When is a child over the age of nine months most likely to pay attention to another person's facial expression in determining how to react to the situation?
   a. when a situation is ambiguous
   b. when a situation is unambiguous
   c. in situations involving the opposite sex
   d. when self-awareness is fully developed

3. An infant's ability to show an emotional response that corresponds to the feelings of another person is
   a. deception.
   b. temperament.
   c. empathy.
   d. gender differentiation.

4. The positive emotional bond that develops between a child and a particular individual is called
   a. empathy.
   b. attachment.
   c. temperament.
   d. social referencing.

5. Which of the following statements is true regarding culture and attachment?
   a. Western cultures show the best attachment in the Strange Situation.
   b. Eastern cultures show the best attachment in the Strange Situation.
   c. Both Eastern and Western cultures show adequate attachment within the Strange Situation.
   d. The Strange Situation may be insufficient to describe cultural differences in attachment.

6. A mother drops her daughter off at childcare. The child is not upset and begins to explore the center while interacting with other people. Mary Ainsworth would classify the child's attachment with her mother as
   a. secure.
   c. avoidant.
   b. disoriented.
   d. ambivalent.

7. What proportion of infants form their first primary relationships with more than one individual?
   a. two-thirds
   c. one-quarter
   b. one-half
   d. one-third

8. Infants and parents learn to communicate emotional states to one another and to respond appropriately to that communication. This is called
   a. attachment.
   c. mutual regulation.
   b. social referencing.
   d. mutual generalization.

9. The lasting characteristics that differentiate one person from another make up a person's
   a. identity.
   c. personality.
   b. character.
   d. differentiated self.

10. If an infant develops normally during the first stage of psychosocial development, she experiences a sense of
    a. joy.
    c. identity.
    b. hope.
    d. autonomy.

11. Which of the following is NOT a dimension of temperament?
    a. adaptability
    c. differentiation
    b. activity level
    d. threshold of responsiveness

12. Harlow's experiment with the infant monkey's choice of cuddling showed that
    a. monkeys preferred the warm, soft "mother" over the wire "monkey".
    b. monkeys preferred the wire "monkey" over the warm, soft "mother".
    c. monkeys showed secure attachment no matter which stimulus was present.
    d. monkeys showed ambivalent attachment no matter which stimulus was present.

13. Which of the following statements about infant emotional expression is accurate?
    a. Basic facial expressions differ widely among cultures.
    b. Nonverbal encoding changes frequently over the life span.
    c. Infants display a narrowly focused range of emotions.
    d. The degree of emotional expressivity varies among infants.

14. Who proposed the theory of minds?
    a. Izard
    c. Bowlby
    b. Harlow
    d. Flavell

15. Separation anxiety peaks around
    a. 7 months.
    c. 12 months.
    b. 9 months.
    d. 14 months.

16. A child's knowledge and beliefs about the mental world is
    a. a theory of mind.
    c. self-awareness.
    b. empathy.
    d. a differential emotion theory.

17. Kathy is not distressed when her mother leaves, and stays away from her when she returns. Kathy would be classified as
    a. secure.
    c. ambivalent.
    b. avoidant.
    d. disorganized.

18. Which attachment style is characterized by low seeking proximity with caregiver, low maintaining contact with caregiver, high avoiding proximity with caregiver, and low resisting contact with caregiver?
    a. secure
    b. avoidant
    c. ambivalent
    d. disorganized

19. The process in which infants' behaviors invite further response from parents which in turn brings about further responses from infants is
    a. mutual responsiveness.
    b. assimilation.
    c. accommodation.
    d. reciprocal socialization.

20. What percent of children between four months and three years of age spend time in nonparental childcare?
    a. 50
    b. 66
    c. 75
    d. 80

ANSWER KEY

Practice Test Questions – Pretest (with text page numbers)

1.	a 195	6.	d 201	11.	a 210	16.	b 195
2.	c 196	7.	c 203	12.	b 210	17.	b 201
3.	b 207	8.	a 204	13.	b 194	18.	c 202
4.	b 199	9.	c 196	14.	c 196	19.	c 205
5.	b 201	10.	a 209	15.	a 194	20.	a 210

Key Names

1. j		4. i		7. a		10. f	
2. c		5. d		8. b			
3. g		6. h		9. e			

Key Vocabulary Terms

1. <u>Securely attached</u> children use the mother as a kind of home base, are at ease when she is present, become upset when she leaves, and go to her as soon as she returns. <u>Avoidant</u> children do not seek proximity to the mother, and if mother leaves, seem to avoid her when she returns as if they are angered by her behavior. <u>Ambivalent</u> children show great distress when the mother leaves, but upon her return they may simultaneously seek close contact but also hit and kick her. <u>Disorganized-disoriented</u> children show inconsistent, often contradictory behavior, such as approaching the mother when she returns but not looking at her.

2. In Erikson's stage of <u>trust v. mistrust</u>, infants develop a sense of trust or mistrust, largely depending on how well their needs are met by their caretakers; in <u>autonomy v. shame and doubt</u>, toddlers develop either independence and autonomy if they are allowed the freedom to explore, or shame and self-doubt if they are restricted and overprotected.

3. <u>Difficult babies</u> have negative moods, are slow to adapt to new situations, and when confronted with a new situation, tend to withdraw; <u>slow-to-warm babies</u> are inactive, showing relatively calm reactions to their environment, have generally negative moods, withdraw from new situations, and adapt slowly.

4. <u>Personality</u> is the sum total of the enduring characteristics that differentiate one individual from another; <u>temperament</u> is patterns of arousal and emotionality that are consistent and enduring characteristics of an individual.

5. Social, Empathy, Longitudinal, Fit, Attachment, Watson, Anxiety, Reciprocal, Emotions, Norm, Easy, Social, Strange (Self-awareness)

Programmed Review

1. similar, encoding, born
2. MAX, birth, kinds, degree
3. expressing, experience
4. stranger, separation, 14 months, cognitive
5. indiscriminate, selective, social
6. decoding, 5, sequence, 4, facial, vocal
7. intentional, 8 or 9, facial
8. self-awareness, 18 to 24, stable
9. knowledge, compliant, respond
10. empathy, deception
11. attachment, emotional
12. imprinting, biologically, oral
13. comfort, food
14. safety, security, mother
15. Strange, secure, Avoidant, Ambivalent, disorganized
16. securely, moods, feelings, interactions, demand, affectionate, level
17. synchrony, cues
18. mother, fathers, one-third
19. nurturing, playing, physical, verbal
20. biological, measure, independence
21. norms
22. regulation, 6, reciprocal, attachment
23. social, peers, familiar, rises, imitate, children
24. personality, birth
25. psychosocial, trust versus mistrust, hope, autonomy versus shame and doubt, independence, exploration, freedom
26. emotionality, enduring, birth, genetic, stable
27. activity, irritability
28. New York, Easy, 40, Difficult, 10, Slow-to-warm, 15, 35
29. fit, environment
30. lifespan, high
31. sons, daughters, daughters, activity, interpreted
32. Gender, sex, gender roles
33. active, disturbed
34. minor, one year
35. boys, independently, compliantly, reactions, boys
36. increased, 2.6, unmarried, adolescent, work, mothers, poverty
37. three, eight, regulations, caregivers, happy, cheerful
38. 80, attachment, secure, insensitive, unresponsive
39. high, minimal
40. solve, attention, language

Practice Test – Post test   (with text page numbers)

1. c 196	6. a 202	11. c 210	16. a 198
2. a 196	7. d 200	12. a 201	17. b 202
3. c 199	8. c 206	13. d 196	18. b 202
4. b 200	9. c 209	14. d 198	19. d 207
5. d 206	10. b 210	15. d 195	20. b 216

Chapter 7

Physical and Cognitive Development in the Preschool Years

CHAPTER OUTLINE

◆ Physical Growth
- ♦ The Growing Body
- ♦ Silent Danger: Lead Poisoning in Young Children
- ♦ The Growing Brain
- ♦ Motor Development

◆ Intellectual Development
- ♦ Piaget's Stage of Preoperational Thinking
- ♦ Information Processing Approaches to Cognitive Development
- ♦ Vygotsky's View of Cognitive Development: Taking Culture into Account

◆ The Growth of Language and Learning
- ♦ Language Development
- ♦ Television: Learning from the Media
- ♦ Early Childhood Education: Taking the "Pre" Out of the Preschool Period

LEARNING OBJECTIVES

After you have read and studied this chapter, you should be able to answer the following questions.

1. What is the state of children's bodies and overall health during the preschool years?
2. How do preschool children's brains and physical skills develop?
3. How does Piaget interpret cognitive development during the preschool years?
4. How do other views of cognitive development differ from Piaget's?
5. How does children's language develop in the preschool years?
6. What effects does television have on preschoolers?
7. What kinds of preschool educational programs are available?

PRACTICE TEST - PRETEST

Circle the correct answer for each question and check your answers with the Answer Key at the end of the chapter.

1. The age at which toilet training takes place has
   a. been rising over the last few decades.
   b. been lowering over the last few decades.
   c. stayed steady over the last few decades.
   d. become unpredictable over the last few decades.

2. What is the most frequent health problem during the preschool years?
   a. flu
   b. rubella
   c. mumps
   d. common cold

3. Left hemisphere of the brain is to _____, as the right hemisphere of the brain is to _____.
   a. music; language competence
   b. verbal competence; music
   c. recognition of patterns and drawings; spatial relationships
   d. spatial relationships; recognition of patterns and drawings

4. Drawing a picture is an example of a(n)
   a. fine motor skill.
   b. gross motor skill.
   c. adaptive motor skill.
   d. functional motor skill.

5. Most children show a clear-cut preference for their left or right hand (handedness) by
   a. the end of the preschool years.
   b. toddlerhood.
   c. early infancy.
   d. late infancy.

6. According to Piaget, the preoperational period of cognitive development occurs during
   a. infancy.
   b. the preschool years.
   c. the grade school years.
   d. adolescence.

7. Which of the following is NOT a feature of preoperational thought?
   a. conservation
   b. intuitive thought
   c. centration
   d. symbolic function

8. Mental processes that are logical and organized are called
   a. symbols.
   b. concepts.
   c. schemas.
   d. operations.

9. A child is playing hide-and-seek and puts a toy in front of her face. She thinks no one can see her because she cannot see past the toy. This illustrates what aspect of preoperational thought?
   a. centration
   b. artificialism
   c. egocentricity
   d. irreversibility

10. When a child understands that quantity is unrelated to the arrangement and physical appearance of objects, he has an understanding of
    a. functionality.
    b. conservation.
    c. intuitive thought.
    d. mastered seriation.

11. Brahman understands how nouns, verbs, adjectives, and prepositions go together to form complete sentences. He has learned about
    a. syntax.
    b. cognition.
    c. semantics.
    d. pragmatics.

12. Preschool education is viewed differently in China, Japan, and the United States. Research has found that in Japan parents view preschool as a way of
    a. teaching discipline.
    b. giving children basic academics.
    c. making children more independent and self-reliant.
    d. giving children the opportunity to be members of a group.

13. Kali is a preschooler. Statistically speaking, she is at greatest danger from
    a. illness.
    b. lead poisoning.
    c. nutritional problems.
    d. accidents.

14. Which of the following is NOT a guideline for keeping preschoolers healthy?
    a. Avoid contact with those who are ill.
    b. Follow an appropriate schedule for immunizations.
    c. Adhere to a strict sleep schedule.
    d. Encourage exercise.

15. Who proposed that children as young as three can easily tell the difference between rows of two and three animals regardless of spacing?
    a. Gelman
    b. Piaget
    c. Vygotsky
    d. Elkind

16. Four-year-old Michelle is most likely to be able to
    a. jump a distance of 24 to 33 inches.
    b. make a running jump of 28 to 36 inches.
    c. easily hop a distance of 16 feet.
    d. descend a stairway alternating feet.

17. The aspect of language that relates to communicating effectively and appropriately with others is
    a. private speech.
    b. social speech.
    c. grammar.
    d. pragmatics.

18. Marcus believes he knows how to change a tire on his father's car even though he has never been shown how to do so, and he is confident in this knowledge. This is an example of
    a. centration.
    b. conservation.
    c. logical relations.
    d. intuitive thought.

19. Memory for particular events in one's own life is
    a. categorical.
    b. autobiographical.
    c. conceptual.
    d. intellectual.

20. Providing clues to children and helping them to frame a task is
    a. zoning.
    b. scaffolding.
    c. conserving.
    d. parenting.

KEY NAMES

Match the following names with the most accurate description and check your answers with the Answer Key at the end of this chapter.

1. ___ T. Berry Brazelton
2. ___ David Elkind

a. poverty and language
b. flexible toilet training

3. ___ Rachel Gelman   c. counting abilities

4. ___ Hart and Risley   d. preoperational thinking

5. ___ Jean Piaget   e. stress in children

6. ___ Lev Vygotsky   f. zone of proximal development

KEY VOCABULARY TERMS

Explain the difference among the following terms.

1. Child-care centers; Family child care; Preschools; School day care

Explain the relationship between the following terms

2. Scaffolding; Zone of proximal development.
3. Private speech; Social speech
4. Grammar; Pragmatics

In the space provided, fill in the term for each of the following definitions. When read from top to bottom, the first letter of each term will spell out the term for the definition at the bottom. (NOTE: Some of the terms come from earlier chapters.)

5. _ _ _ _ _ _ _ _ _ _   The positive emotional bond that develops between a child and a particular individual.

   _ _ _ _ _ _ _ _   The theory of ____ grammar states that the world's languages share a similar underlying structure.

   _ _ _ _ _ _ _ _ _ _ _ _ _ _   The process by which one state is changed into another.

   _ _ _ _ _ _ _   Body weight more than 20 percent higher than the average weight for a person of a given age and height.

   _ _ _ _ _ _ _ _ _   An approach focusing on reinforcement and conditioning.

   _ _   According to Freud, the raw, unorganized, inborn part of the personality, present at birth.

   _ _ _ _ _ _ _ _ _   Organized, formal, and logical mental processes.

   _ _ _ _ _ _   The system of rules that determines how our thoughts can be expressed.

   _ _ _ _ _ _ _ _ _ _   A style that uses language primarily to label objects.

   _ _ _ _ _ _ _ _ _ _   A developmentally ____ education is based on typical development and the unique characteristics of the child.

   _ _ _ _ _ _ _   Speech by children that is spoken and directed to themselves is _____ speech.

   _ _ _ _ _ _ _ _ _   The preference of using one hand over the other.

_ _ _ _ _ _ _ _   Thought that reflects preschoolers' use of primitive reasoning and their avid acquisition of knowledge.

_ _ _ _ _ _ _ _ _ _   Concentrating on one limited aspect of a stimulus.

_ _ _ _ _ _ _   Stranger and Separation are both forms of ____ .

_ _ _ _ _ _ _ _ _ _ _ _ _   The process in which cognitive functions are located more in one hemisphere of the brain than the other.

Memory of particular events from one's own life is _ _ _ _ _ _ _ _ _ _ _ _ _ _ _ .

Look up the definition for each of the following terms and give a specific example of each.

6. Syntax
7. Developmentally appropriate educational practice
8. Preoperational stage
9. Social speech
10. Scripts
11. Fast mapping
12. Egocentric thought
13. Conservation
14. Transformations
15. Intuitive thought

PROGRAMMED REVIEW

Physical Development

The Growing Body

1. Two years after birth, the average child in the United States weighs around _____ pounds and is _____ inches tall, half the height of the average adult. Children grow _____ during the preschool period.

2. Average differences in height and weight between boys and girls _____ during the preschool years. During the preschool years, boys begin to be _____ and _____, on average, than girls. Differences in height and weight reflect _____ factors in the United States as well as other countries.

3. During the preschool years, boys and girls begin to burn off some of the _____ they have carried from their infancy, and their arms and legs _____. By the time children reach 6 years of age, their _____ are quite similar to those of adults. The _____ tube in the ear moves to a more angular position, sometimes leading to an increase in the frequency of _____ during the preschool years.

4. Preschoolers need _____ food to maintain their growth. Some children's food consumption can become so high as to lead to _____, which is defined as a body weight more than _____ percent higher than average.

5. Foods that have a relatively high _____ content are particularly important. Iron deficiency _____, which causes chronic _____, is one of the prevalent nutritional problems in developed countries.

6. For the average child in the United States, the common _____ and other minor respiratory illnesses are the most frequent kind of health problem during the preschool years. Such minor illness may offer some unexpected _____. An increasing number of children are being treated with drugs for _____ disorders.

7. The greatest risk that preschoolers face comes from _____. The danger of injuries during the preschool years is in part a result of the children's high levels of _____ activity. Children lack the _____ to know that their activities may hold some danger.

8. Boys tend to take more _____ and have a higher rate of _____. Asian-American children in the United States have one of the _____ accident rates for children. Children raised under conditions of poverty in urban areas are _____ times more likely to die of injuries.

Silent Danger: Lead Poisoning in Young Children

9. Some _____ million children are at risk for lead poisoning due to exposure to potentially toxic levels of lead, according to the Centers for Disease Control. Lead is still found on _____ walls and window frames. People who live in areas of substantial air _____ due to automobile and truck traffic may also be exposed to high levels of lead. The U.S. Department of Health and Human Services has called lead poisoning the most hazardous health threat to children under the age of _____.

10. Exposure to lead has been linked to lower _____, problems in _____ and _____ processing, _____, and distractibility. High lead levels have also been linked to higher levels of _____ behavior. At yet higher levels of exposure, lead poisoning results in illness and _____. _____ children are particularly susceptible to lead poisoning.

The Growing Brain

11. The brain grows at a _____ rate than any other part of the body. By age 5, children's brains weigh _____ percent of average adult brain weight. The brain grows so rapidly because of an increase in the number of _____ among cells that allow for more complex communication between _____, and permit the rapid growth of _____ skills. In addition, the amount of _____, a protective insulation that surrounds parts of neurons, increases. The _____, a bundle of nerve fibers that connect the two hemispheres becomes considerably thicker.

12. The two halves of the brain also begin to become increasingly _____ and specialized. _____, the process in which certain functions are located more in one hemisphere than the other, becomes more pronounced during the preschool years.

13. For most people, the left hemisphere concentrates on tasks that necessitate _____ competence. The right hemisphere develops strengths in areas such as comprehension of _____ relationships, _____ or patterns and drawings, _____ and _____ expression. The left hemisphere considers information _____, the right hemisphere processes information in a more _____ manner. The two hemispheres are _____ and there are many individual differences in the nature of _____.

14. There are _____ and _____ differences in lateralization. Males tend to show _____ lateralization of language in the left hemisphere. Data suggest that there are minor _____ differences between males' and females' brains. A section of the _____ is proportionally larger in women than in men.

15. It appears there are periods during childhood where the brain shows unusual growth _____, and these periods are linked to advances in cognitive _____.

Motor Development

16. By the time they are age 3, children have mastered a variety of skills, which by 4 and 5 have become more _____ as they gain increasing _____ over their muscles. Motor skills develop at such a rapid pace because preschool children spend a great deal of time _____ them. The activity level is higher at age _____ than at any other point in the entire life span.

17. Girls and boys differ in certain aspects of gross motor coordination in part due to differences in _____ strength. Muscle strength is somewhat _____ in boys than in girls. A boy's overall _____ level tends to be greater, but girls generally surpass boys in tasks that involve the _____ of limbs. Children progress in their ability to use

_____ motor skills, which involve more delicate, smaller body movements. These skills require a good deal of _____.

18. Beginning in early infancy, many children begin to show signs of a preference for the use of one hand over another—the development of _____. Most children display a clear-cut tendency to use one hand over the other by the end of the _____ years. Some _____ percent are right-handed. More boys than girls are _____-handed.

19. Brazelton suggests a _____ approach to toilet training advocating that it be put off until the child shows signs of _____. The age at which toilet training takes place has been _____. In 1999, only _____ percent of 18-month-olds were trained and _____ percent of 36 month olds. Children younger than 12 months have no _____ or _____ control.

20. The signs for readiness for toilet training include staying dry at least _____ hours at a time, or waking up dry after _____, regular and predictable _____ movements, an indication through _____ expressions or words that urination or bowel movement is about to occur, the ability to follow simple _____, the ability to undress _____, discomfort with _____ diapers, _____ to use the toilet, and desire to wear _____.

21. Preschoolers should eat a well-balanced diet containing the proper _____. Caregivers should encourage preschoolers to _____. Children should get as much _____ as they wish. Children should avoid contact with those who are _____ and follow an appropriate schedule of _____. Minor illnesses sometimes provide _____ to more serious illness later on.

Intellectual Development

Piaget's Stage of Preoperational Thinking

22. Piaget saw the _____ years as a time of both stability and great change. During the preoperational stage, children's use of _____ thinking grows, mental _____ emerges, and the use of _____ increases. Children become better at representing events _____, yet they are still not capable of _____ (organized, formal, logical mental processes).

23. _____ function, the ability to use a mental symbol, word, or object to stand for or represent something that is not physically present, is a key aspect of preoperational thought and is at the heart of the increasingly sophisticated use of _____.

24. Piaget suggests that language and _____ are inextricably intertwined. The use of language allows children to think beyond the _____ to the _____. Piaget suggests that language development is based on the development of more sophisticated modes of _____.

25. A key element and limitation of the thinking of children in the preoperational period is _____, the process of concentrating on one limited aspect of a stimulus and ignoring other aspects. Preschoolers are unable to consider all available information about a _____. Instead, they focus on _____ obvious elements.

26. Conservation is the knowledge that _____ is unrelated to the arrangement and physical appearance of objects. Children in the preoperational period make errors in conservation because their tendency towards _____ prevents them from focusing on the relevant features of the situation and they cannot follow the sequence of _____ that accompanies changes in the appearance of a situation.

27. One hallmark of the preoperational period is _____ thought that does not take into account the viewpoints of others. Egocentric thought takes two forms: the lack of _____ that others see things from a different physical perspective, and the failure to realize that others may hold thoughts, feelings, and viewpoints that _____ from one's own. Lack of awareness that their _____ acts as a trigger to others' reactions and responses means that a considerable amount of verbal behavior on the part of preschoolers has no _____ motivation behind it.

28. Intuitive thought refers to preschoolers' use of _____ reasoning and their avid acquisition of _____ about the world, and it leads them to believe that they know _____ to all kinds of questions.

29. By the end of the preoperational stage, preschoolers begin to understand the notion of _____, the concept that actions, events, and outcomes are related to one another in fixed patterns. Children begin to show an awareness of the concept of _____, the understanding that certain things stay the same, regardless of changes in shape, size, and appearance that is necessary for children to develop an understanding of _____.

30. Recent research indicates that Piaget _____ children's capabilities. Gelman concludes that children have an _____ ability to count. Such a conclusion is at odds with Piagetian notions which suggest that children's _____ abilities do not appear until after the preoperational period. Some developmentalists believe that cognitive skills develop in a more _____ manner than Piaget's stage theory implies. Critics of Piaget suggest that developmental changes are more _____ in nature. Performance on _____ tasks can be improved by providing preoperational children with certain kinds of training and experiences. Piaget tended to concentrate on preschoolers' _____ in thinking; whereas more recent theorists have focused more on children's _____.

Information Processing Approaches to Cognitive Development

31. Most people have unambiguous and seemingly accurate memories dating as far back as the age of _____. Information-processing approaches focus on changes in the kinds of _____ programs, and it views the changes that occur in children's cognitive abilities as analogous to how a _____ becomes more sophisticated when modified.

32. Gelman suggests that preschoolers follow a number of _____ in their counting. They know they should assign just _____ number to each item, and that each item should be counted only _____. Even when they get the _____ of numbers wrong they are still consistent in their usage.

33. _____ memory, memory of particular events from one's own life, achieves little accuracy until after 3 years of age. Unless an event is particularly vivid or _____, it is not likely to be remembered at all. Preschoolers' autobiographical memories not only _____, but the ones that are remembered may not be wholly _____. Preschoolers' memories of familiar events are often organized in terms of _____.

34. According to information-processing approaches, _____ development consists of gradual improvements in the ways people perceive, understand, and remember information. As preschoolers grow older, they have _____ attention spans, can _____ and plan what they are attending to more effectively, and become increasingly aware of their cognitive _____.

35. Proponents of information-processing theory have focused on processes such as _____ and attention and suggest that information processing provides a clear, logical, and full account of _____ development. Information processing pays relatively little attention to _____ and _____ factors.

36. Young children may recall things quite mistakenly, but with great _____. Children's memories are susceptible to the _____ of adults asking them questions. Preschoolers are also more prone to make inaccurate _____ about the reasons behind others' behavior, and less able to draw appropriate _____ based on their knowledge. The error rate for children is further heightened when the same question is asked _____. False memories may be more _____ than actual memories. The _____ the time between the actual event and questioning, the less firm are children's recollections.

Vygotsky's View of Cognitive Development: Taking Culture into Account

37. Vygotsky viewed cognitive development as a result of social interactions in which children learn through _____ participation. He focused on the child's _____ and _____ world as their source of cognitive development. Children grow intellectually and begin to function because of the assistance that _____ and _____ partners provide.

38. Vygotsky proposed that children's cognitive abilities increase through exposure to information that resides within the child's zone of _____ development, the level at which a child can almost, but not fully, perform a task independently, but can do so with the assistance of someone more competent. The assistance provided by others has been termed _____, the support for learning and problem solving that encourages independence and growth.

39. The aid that more accomplished individuals provide to learners comes in the form of _____ tools, actual physical items as well as an intellectual and conceptual framework for solving problems. This framework includes the _____ that is used within a culture, its _____ and _____ schemes, its _____ and _____ systems, and even its _____ systems.

40. The idea that children's comprehension of the world is an outcome of their interactions with other members of society is _____ supported by research findings. However, broad concepts such as the zone of proximal development are not _____, and they do not lend themselves to _____ tests. Vygotsky was largely silent on how basic cognitive processes such as _____ and memory develop and how natural cognitive abilities unfold.

The Growth of Language and Learning

Language Development

41. Between the late twos and mid threes, sentence length _____ at a steady pace, and the ways that children combine words and phrases to form sentences known as _____ doubles each month. There are enormous leaps in the _____ of words children use. By age 6, the average child has a vocabulary of around _____ words. They manage this feat through _____, in which new words are associated with their meaning after only a brief encounter. Preschoolers acquire the principles of _____, the system of rules that determine how our thoughts can be expressed.

42. Some developmentalists suggest that _____ speech by children that is spoken and directed to themselves is used as a guide to behavior and thought. This speech facilitates children's _____ and helps them _____ their behavior. Private speech may foster the development of _____, the aspect of language related to communicating effectively with others. The preschool years also mark the growth of _____ speech, speech directed toward another person and meant to be understood by that person.

43. The language that preschoolers hear at _____ has profound consequences for future cognitive success. The rate at which language is addressed to children varies significantly according to the _____ level of the family. Professional parents spend almost _____ as much time interacting with their children as do parents who received _____ assistance.

44. Research indicates that the type of language to which children are exposed is associated with their performance on tests of _____. Such findings argue for the importance of _____ exposure to language. By the age of 5, children raised in poverty tend to have lower _____ scores and perform less well on other measure of _____ development. The _____ children live in poverty, the more severe are the consequences.

Television: Learning from the Media

45. The average preschooler watches more than _____ hours of TV a week. In comparison, they spend three-quarters of an hour _____ on the average day. Children do not fully _____ the plots of the stories they are viewing. They are unable to _____ significant story details and the _____ they make about the motivations of characters are limited and often erroneous. They have difficulty separating _____ from _____ in television programming. Preschoolers are able to decode the _____ expressions they see on television, but much of what they view on TV _____ from what they find in the every day world.

46. *Sesame Street* was devised with the express purpose of providing an _____ experience for preschoolers. A two-year longitudinal study indicated that children who watched *Sesame Street* had significantly _____ vocabularies. Formal evaluations find that preschoolers living in _____ income households who watch the

show are better prepared for school, and they perform significantly higher on several measures of _____ and _____ ability at ages 6 and 7. Viewers of *Sesame Street* spend more time _____ than nonviewers.

Early Childhood Education: Taking the "Pre" Out of the Preschool Period

47. Almost _____ of children in the United States are enrolled in some form of care outside the home. One major factor is the rise in the number of families in which both parents _____ outside the home. Developmental psychologists have found increasing evidence that children can _____ substantially from involvement in some form of educational activity before they enroll in formal schooling.

48. _____ centers typically provide care for children all day, while their parents work. Today they provide some form of _____ stimulation, but their primary purpose tends to be more _____ and _____ than cognitive. Some child care is provided in _____ child-care centers, small operations run in private homes. Preschools or _____ schools are more explicitly designed to provide intellectual and social experiences for children. _____ child care is provided by some local school systems in the United States. Almost half the states fund _____ programs for 4-year-olds.

49. Studies find that early and long-term participation in child care is particularly helpful for children from _____ home environments or who are otherwise at risk. Children in high-quality programs tend to be more self-confident, _____, and knowledgeable about the _____ world in which they live. But children in child care have also been found to be less _____, less _____, less _____ of adults, and sometimes more _____ and _____.

50. One key factor is program _____. High-quality facilities have _____ care providers. Single groups should not have many more than _____ children and there should be no more than _____ 3-year-olds per caregiver, or _____ 4- or 5-year-olds per caregiver. The curriculum should be carefully _____ out and _____ among the teachers.

51. In the United States, the best known program designed to promote future academic success is _____. Graduates tend to show immediate _____ gains, but these increases do not last. Participants are more ready for future _____ and have better future school _____. They are less likely to be in _____ education classes or to be _____ in grade.

52. The United States has no coordinated national _____ on preschool education. Decisions about education have been traditionally left to the _____ and local school _____. The United States has no tradition of teaching _____, and the status of preschools has been traditionally _____. Parents in China tend to see preschools primarily as a way of giving children a good start _____, Japanese parents view them primarily as a way of giving children the opportunity to be members of a _____. In the United States, parents regard the primary purpose of preschools as making children more _____ and _____.

53. Elkind claims that society tends to push children so rapidly that they begin to feel _____ and pressure at a young age. He argues that academic success is largely dependent on factors out of parents' _____ such as _____ abilities and a child's rate of _____. Children require developmentally _____ educational practice. He suggests that a better strategy is to provide an environment in which learning is _____ but not pushed.

CRITICAL THINKING QUESTIONS

To further your mastery of the topics in this chapter, write out your answers to the following essay questions from the text in the spaces provided.

1. How might biology and environment combine to affect the physical growth of a child adopted as an infant from a developing country and taken to a more industrialized country to live?

2. Do you think the United States should formulate a national policy to combat childhood obesity? If yes, how could this be done? If no, what obstacles might prevent such a policy?

3. How would you develop specific a plan to reduce the amount of television that your 4-year-old niece watches? What problems might you encounter?

4. In your view, how do thought and language interact in preschoolers' development? Is it possible to think without language? How do prelingually deaf children think?

5. If children's cognitive development is dependent on interactions with others, what obligation does the broader society have regarding such social settings as preschools, schools, and neighborhoods?

6. Is private speech egocentric or useful? Do adults ever use private speech? What function does it serve?

7. Why is it difficult to set up an experiment on the effects of children's TV viewing? Why are results from TV viewing experiments so inconclusive?

8. Some negative outcomes of childcare outside the home are a lack of politeness and compliance. Do you think such outcomes are inherent in outside child care, or are they related to cultural views of the purpose of preschool programs?

9. Do you think the United States should formulate a national educational policy, like many other countries, or continue to leave most educational issues to the states? Why?

10. Do you accept the view that children in U.S. society are "pushed" academically to the extent that they feel too much stress and pressure at a young age? Why?

PRACTICE TEST – POST TEST

Circle the correct answer for each Multiple Choice question and check your answers with the Answer Key at the end of the chapter.

1. The eustachian tube in the ear moves during the preschool years from a position that is almost parallel to the ground at birth to a more angular position. This change can lead to
   a. hearing loss.
   b. enhanced hearing.
   c. a decrease in ear infections.
   d. an increase in frequency of earaches.

2. As a child grows, the hemispheres of the brain become specialized for specific functions. This process is called
   a. ossification.
   b. myelination.
   c. lateralization.
   d. regionalization.

3. Which of the following correctly describes the differences in lateralization of the brains of men and women?
   a. Men show greater lateralization of language in the right hemisphere, whereas females show greater lateralization of language in the left hemisphere.
   b. Men show greater lateralization of language in the left hemisphere, whereas females show greater lateralization of language in the right hemisphere.
   c. Men show greater lateralization of language in the left hemisphere, whereas language is more evenly divided between the two hemispheres for females.
   d. Women show greater lateralization of language in the left hemisphere, whereas language is more evenly divided between the two hemispheres for males.

4. Carlos weighs 35 percent more than peers of his same age and height. He would be classified as
   a. obese.
   b. an average male.
   c. developmentally delayed.
   d. developmentally advanced.

5. Exposure to lead has been linked to problems in the following area EXCEPT
   a. verbal processing.
   b. auditory processing.
   c. spatial reasoning.
   d. hyperactivity and distractibility.

6. What percent of children are left-handed?
   a. 5 percent
   b. 10 percent
   c. 15 percent
   d. 25 percent

7. Jamie is unable to use logical and organized mental processes, but she is able to use symbolic thinking for internal pictures of the world. According to the cognitive development theory of Piaget, what stage of development is she in?
   a. sensorimotor stage
   b. preoperational stage
   c. formal operational stage
   d. concrete operational stage

8. Five-year-old Amy is shown two rows of marbles, one with eight marbles that are spaced closely together, and the other with five marbles spread out to form a longer row. Amy says that the spread out row of five marbles has more marbles than the shorter row of eight. This reflects what aspect of preoperational thought?
   a. centration
   b. artificialism
   c. egocentricity
   d. operations

94

9. A four-year-old child is asked to draw a pencil falling. The child draws the pencil vertical and then horizontal, with no stages in between. This child shows that he does not understand
    a. centration.
    c. egocentricity.
    b. artificialism.
    d. transformation.

10. Who proposed the *zone of proximal development*?
    a. Piaget
    c. Vygotsky
    b. Erikson
    d. Chomsky

11. How many hours of TV does an average preschooler watch in a week?
    a. 5-10 hours
    c. 15-20 hours
    b. 10-15 hours
    d. 21 or more hours

12. Which developmental psychologist believes that society tends to push young children so hard that they experience excessive stress?
    a. Piaget
    c. Vygotsky
    b. Elkind
    d. Chomsky

13. What federal program was designed to promote future academic success of preschoolers?
    a. Head Start
    c. School child care
    b. Montessori schools
    d. *Sesame Street*

14. Which of the following children is most likely to be injured?
    a. an Asian American girl
    c. a boy living in an urban area
    b. a girl living in the country
    d. a boy living on a farm

15. By age 5, children's brains weigh _____ percent of average adult brain weight.
    a. 50
    c. 80
    b. 70
    d. 90

16. Which of the following is NOT a viable option for early childhood education
    a. preschool
    c. peer child care
    b. school child care
    d. family child care

17. Which type of conservation develops last?
    a. area
    c. length
    b. volume
    d. weight

18. The information-processing approach focuses on
    a. the kinds of mental programs children invoke.
    b. the strength and focus of intuitive thought.
    c. the zone of proximal development.
    d. conservation and centration.

19. Research into children's eyewitness testimony indicates that preschool children
    a. are not easily influenced by adults' suggestions.
    b. purposely lie to adults.
    c. are not able to remember accurately.
    d. usually believe their false memories are accurate.

20. Aisha is a one-year-old. According to the American Academy of Pediatrics she should watch no more than _____ hour(s) of television per day.
    a. 0
    c. 1-2
    b. 1
    d. 3-4

ANSWER KEYS

Practice Test – Pretest (with text page numbers)

1.	a 231	6.	b 235	11.	a 243	16.	a 231
2.	d 225	7.	a 239	12.	d 256	17.	d 250
3.	b 228	8.	d 235	13.	d 225	18.	d 239
4.	a 232	9.	c 238	14.	c 233	19.	b 241
5.	a 231	10.	b 237	15.	a 240	20.	b 245

Key Names

1. b	2. e	3. c	4. a	5. d	6. f

Key Vocabulary Terms

1. <u>Child-care centers</u> provide care for children all day, while their parents work; <u>family child-care</u> centers are small operations run in private homes, quality of care can be uneven because not all are licensed, <u>preschools</u> are designed to provide intellectual and social experiences for children; <u>school day care</u> is provided by some local school system in the United States.

2. <u>Scaffolding</u> is the support for learning and problem solving that encourages independence and growth and is provided when a child is in the <u>zone of proximal development</u> where he or she can almost, but not fully, perform a task independently and requires the assistance of someone more competent to do so.

3. <u>Private speech</u> is speech by children that is spoken and directed at themselves; <u>social speech</u> is directed toward another person and meant to be understood by that person.

4. <u>Grammar</u> is the system of rules that determine how our thoughts can be expressed; <u>pragmatics</u> is the aspect of language that relates to communicating effectively and appropriately with others.

5. Attachment, Universal, Transformation, Obesity, Behavioral, Id, Operations, Grammar, Referential, Appropriate, Private, Handedness, Intuitive, Centration, Anxiety, Lateralization (Autobiographical)

Programmed Review

1. 25 to 30, 36, steadily
2. increase, taller, heavier, economic
3. fat, lengthen, proportions, eustachian, earaches
4. less, obesity, 20
5. iron, anemia, fatigue
6. cold, benefits, emotional
7. accidents, physical, judgment
8. risks, injuries, lowest, two
9. 14, painted, pollution, 6
10. intelligence, verbal, auditory, hyperactivity, antisocial, death, poor
11. faster, 90, interconnections, neurons, cognitive, myelin, corpus callosum
12. differentiated, Lateralization
13. verbal, spatial, recognition, music, emotional, sequentially, global, interdependent, lateralization
14. individual, cultural, greater, structural, corpus callosum
15. spurts, abilities
16. refined, control, practicing, 3
17. strength, greater, activity, coordination, fine, practice
18. handedness, preschool, 90, left
19. flexible, readiness, rising, 25, 60, bladder, bowel
20. two, naps, bowel, facial, directions, alone, soiled, asking, underwear

21. nutrients, exercise, sleep, ill, immunizations, immunity
22. preschool, symbolic, reasoning, concepts, internally, operations
23. Symbolic, language
24. thinking, present, future, thinking
25. centration, stimulus, superficial
26. quantity, centration, transformation
27. egocentric, awareness, differ, behavior, social
28. primitive, knowledge, answers
29. functionality, identity, conservation
30. underestimated, innate, numerical, continuous, quantitative, conservation, deficiencies, competence
31. three, mental, computer
32. principles, one, once, names
33. Autobiographical, meaningful, fade, accurate, scripts
34. cognitive, longer, monitor, limitations
35. memory, cognitive, social, cultural
36. conviction, suggestion, inferences, conclusions, repeatedly, persistent, longer
37. guided, social, cultural, adult, peer
38. proximal, scaffolding
39. cultural, language, alphabetical, numbering, mathematical, scientific, religious
40. well, precise, experimental, attention
41. increases, syntax, number, 14,000, fast mapping, grammar
42. private, thinking, control, pragmatics, social
43. home, economic, twice, welfare
44. intelligence, early IQ, cognitive, longer
45. 21, reading, understand, recall, inferences, fantasy, reality, facial, differs
46. educational, larger, lower, verbal, mathematical, reading
47. three-quarters, work, benefit
48. Child-care, intellectual, social, emotional, family, nursery, School, prekindergarten
49. impoverished, independent, social, polite, compliant, respectful, competitive, aggressive
50. quality, well-trained, 14 to 20, 5 to 10, 7 to 10, planned, coordinated
51. Head Start, IQ, schooling adjustment, special, retained
52. policy, states, districts, preschoolers, low, academically, group, independent, self-reliant
53. stress, control, inherited, maturation, appropriate, encouraged

Practice Test – Post Test   (with text page numbers)

1. d 224	6. b 231	11. d 252	16. c 254
2. c 228	7. b 235	12. b 257	17. b 238
3. c 229	8. a 236	13. a 256	18. a 242
4. a 225	9. d 237	14. c 226	19. d 243
5. c 227	10. c 245	15. d 228	20. a 252

Chapter 8

Social and Personality Development in the Preschool Years

CHAPTER OUTLINE

◆ Forming a Sense of Self
  ◆ Psychosocial Development: Resolving the Conflicts
  ◆ Self-Concept in the Preschool Years: Thinking About the Self
  ◆ Gender Identity: Developing Femaleness and Maleness

◆ Friends and Family: Preschoolers' Social Lives
  ◆ The Development of Friendships
  ◆ Playing by the Rules: The Work of Play
  ◆ Preschoolers' Theory of Mind: Understanding What Others Are Thinking
  ◆ Preschoolers' Family Lives
  ◆ Effective Parenting: Teaching Desired Behaviors
  ◆ Child Abuse and Psychological Maltreatment: The Grim Side of Family Life
  ◆ Resilience: Overcoming the Odds

◆ Moral Development and Aggression
  ◆ Developing Morality: Following Society's Rights and Wrongs
  ◆ Empathy and Moral Behavior
  ◆ Aggression and Violence in Preschoolers

LEARNING OBJECTIVES

After you have read and studied this chapter, you should be able to answer the following questions.

1. How do preschool-age children develop a concept of themselves?
2. How do children develop their sense of racial identity and gender?
3. In what sorts of social relationships do preschool-age children engage?
4. What sorts of disciplinary styles do parents employ, and what effects do they have?
5. What factors contribute to child abuse and neglect?
6. How do children develop a moral sense?
7. How does aggression develop in preschool-age children?

PRACTICE TEST - PRETEST

Circle the correct answer in each of the following Multiple Choice questions and check your answers with the Answer Key at the end of this chapter.

1. When an 18-month-old child is encouraged to explore her environment and allowed to play with her toys as she desires, she is likely to develop
   a. trust.   c. initiative.
   b. industry.   d. autonomy.

2. Allison has an appreciation and can understand what Kyle feels when he falls from his bike. Allison is displaying
   a. abstract modeling.
   c. resilience.
   b. empathy.
   d. moral behavior.

3. What theory states that gender development results from the child moving through a series of stages related to biological urges?
   a. cognitive
   c. social learning
   b. biological
   d. psychoanalytic

4. Two preschoolers are sitting side by side and playing with different toys. What type of play are they engaged in?
   a. parallel play
   c. cooperative play
   b. functional play
   d. sociodramatic play

5. Parents that are controlling and inflexible are
   a. permissive.
   c. authoritative.
   b. disoriented.
   d. authoritarian.

6. Child abuse occurs most frequently in
   a. blended families.
   b. minority families.
   c. one-parent families.
   d. families living in stressful environments.

7. Emmy Werner (1995) studied children who overcame difficult environments to lead socially competent lives. She called these children
   a. focused children.
   c. authoritative children.
   b. resilient children.
   d. self-regulated children.

8. After a boy spills his milk at the dinner table, his father tells him he is clumsy and will grow up to be a loser. This is an example of
   a. dissonance.
   c. social learning.
   b. vulnerability.
   d. psychological maltreatment.

9. A boy believes that he will be punished immediately when he breaks a rule. He is demonstrating a belief in
   a. intentionality.
   c. "good boy" mentality.
   b. immanent justice.
   d. law-and-order mentality.

10. If children are playing 'hide and seek' and they all rigidity adhere to one standard for the rules, they are demonstrating the stage of morality called
    a. emotional group regulation.
    c. heteronomous morality stage.
    b. authoritarian cooperation stage.
    d. autonomous cooperation stage.

11. Which theory states that aggression is based on prior learning?
    a. biological
    c. psychoanalytic
    b. social learning
    d. cognitive developmental

12. What approach suggests that the key to understanding moral development is to examine preschoolers' interpretations of others' behavior?
    a. cognitive approach
    c. sociobiological approach
    b. social-learning approach
    d. psychodynamic approach

13. Larry Chang is five years old and has come to realize that he is a person in his own right. This is indicative of the stage of
   a. autonomy v. shame and doubt.
   b. heteronomous morality.
   c. initiative v. guilt.
   d. collectivistic orientation.

14. Juan is a Hispanic preschooler living in the United States. Juan has a tendency to prefer the music, literature, and media of the majority culture. Juan is displaying
   a. race dissonance.
   b. acculturation .
   c. assimilation.
   d. bi-cultural identity.

15. Research suggests that there are biological differences between males and females in which part of the brain?
   a. hypothalamus
   b. corpus callosum
   c. cerebral cortex
   d. brain stem

16. Advocates of which of the following approaches would be most likely to be concerned about the influence of television programming on children?
   a. biological
   b. psychoanalytic
   c. cognitive
   d. social learning

17. Simple repetitive muscular actions such as skipping and jumping are what type of play?
   a. constructive
   b. functional
   c. cooperative
   d. parallel

18. Cherise is very dependent on her parents, but her brother is unusually hostile. This indicates that their parents most likely were
   a. authoritarian.
   b. authoritative.
   c. permissive.
   d. uninvolved.

19. _____ aggression is motivated by the desire to obtain a concrete goal.
   a. All
   b. Emotional
   c. Instrumental
   d. Relational

20. Scientists who consider the biological roots of social behavior are
   a. ethologists.
   b. sociobiologists.
   c. biologists.
   d. sociologists.

KEY NAMES

Match the following names with the descriptions and check your answers with the Answer Key at the end of this chapter. (NOTE: Two names match one of the descriptions.)

1. ____ Albert Bandura   a. androgyny

2. ____ Diana Baumrind   b. children's play

3. ____ Sandra Bem   c. cognitive developmental theory

4. ____ Erik Erikson   d. ethologist

5. ____ Sigmund Freud   e. heteronomous morality

6. ____ Lawrence Kohlberg   f. parenting styles

7. ____ Konrad Lorenz   g. phallic stage

8. ___ Eleanor Maccoby   h. pretend play

9. ___ Mildred Parten   i. psychosocial development

10. ___ Jean Piaget   j. resilient children

11. ___ Lev Vygotsky   k. social learning

12. ___ Emmy Werner

KEY VOCABULARY TERMS

Describe the relationship among the terms in the following groups.

1. Gender identity; Gender constancy

2. Functional play; Constructive play; Parallel play; Cooperative play

3. Authoritative parents; Authoritarian parents

4. Permissive parents; Uninvolved parents

5. Instrumental aggression; Relational aggressions

In the following puzzles, fill in the blanks with the term that matches the definition. The first letters of the terms from top to bottom will spell out the term for the last definition. (NOTE: Some of the terms may be from previous chapters.)

6. _ _ _ _ _ _ _ _ _ _   A state in which gender roles encompass characteristics thought typical of both sexes.

    _ _ _ _ _ _ _ _   Parents who show almost no interest in their children and indifferent rejecting behavior.

    _ _ _ _ _ _ _ _ _   Patterns of arousal and emotionality that represent consistent and enduring characteristics.

    _ _ _ _ _ _ _ _ _ _   The stage of moral development in which rules are seen as invariant and unchangeable.

    _ _ _ _ _ _ _   Play in which children simply watch others at play but do not actually participate themselves.

    _ _ _ _   ____ dissonance is the phenomenon in which minority children indicate preferences for majority values or people.

    _ _ _ _ _ _ _ _ _ _ _ _ _   A philosophy that emphasizes personal identity and the uniqueness of the individual.

    _ _ _ _ _ _ _ _   A factor that produces a birth defect.

    _ _ _ _ _ _ _   The process in which modeling paves the way for the development of more general rules and principles.

101

_ _ _ _ _ _ _ _ _   The ability to overcome circumstances that place a child at high risk for psychological or physical damage.

_ _ _ _ _ _ _ _ _ _ _ _ _   The process in which children attempt to be similar to their same-sex parent, incorporating the parent's attitudes and values.

_ _ _ _ _ _ _ _ _   Intentional injury or harm to another person.

_ _ _ _ _ _ _   Another term for a newborn.

Parents who are controlling, punitive, rigid, and cold are _ _ _ _ _ _ _ _ _ _ _ _ _.

7.   _ _ _ _ - _ _ _ _ _ _ _   A person's identity, or set of beliefs about what he or she is like as an individual.

_ _ _ _ _ _ _ _ _ _ _ _ _ _   A philosophy that promotes the notion of interdependence.

_ _ _ _ _ _ _   _____-graded events are biological and environmental influences associated with a particular period of time.

_ _ _ _ _ _ _   The understanding of what another individual feels.

_ _ _ _ _   Development based on the changes in people's sense of justice and of what is right and wrong.

_ _ _ _ _ _ _ _ _ _   Play in which two or more children actually interact with one another by sharing or borrowing toys or materials, although they do not do the same thing.

A gender _ _ _ _ _ _ is a cognitive framework that organizes information relevant to gender.

Look up the definition for each of the following terms and write an example of each.

8. Empathy
9. Abstract modeling
10. Cycle-of-violence hypothesis
11. Psychological maltreatment
12. Immanent justice
13. Prosocial behavior
14. Resilience
15. Emotional self-regulation

PROGRAMMED REVIEW

Forming a Sense of Self

Psychosocial Development: Resolving the Conflicts

1. According to Erikson, _____ development encompasses changes both in the understanding individuals have of themselves as members of _____ and in their comprehension of the meaning of others' _____.

2. In the early part of the preschool period, children are ending the _____ stage, which lasts from around 18 months to 3 years. In this period, children either become more _____ and autonomous if their parents encourage _____ and freedom, or experience shame and self-doubt if they are _____ and overprotected.

3. The preschool years largely encompass the _____ stage, which lasts from around age 3 to age 6. In essence, preschool-age children come to realize that they are _____ in their own right, and they begin to make _____ and to shape the kind of persons that they will become.

Self-Concept in the Preschool Years: Thinking About the Self

4. Self-concept is a person's _____, or set of beliefs about what they are like as individuals. The statements that describe children's self-concepts are not necessarily _____. Preschool children typically _____ their skills and knowledge across all domains of expertise.

5. Preschool-age children also begin to develop a view of self that reflects the way their particular _____ considers the self. Asian societies tend to have a _____ orientation promoting the notion of _____. People in such cultures tend to regard themselves as parts of a larger _____ network. Children in Western cultures are more likely to develop an independent view of the self, reflecting an _____ orientation that emphasizes personal _____ and the _____ of the individual. They are more apt to see themselves as self-contained and _____, in _____ with others for scarce resources.

6. In the preschool years, children's answer to the question of who they are begins to take into account their _____ and _____ identity. Racial _____ comes relatively early, but it is only later that children begin to attribute _____ to different racial characteristics.

7. By the time they are _____ years of age, preschool children notice differences among people based on _____ color, and begin to identity themselves as members of a particular _____. Later they begin to understand the significance that society places on ethnic and racial _____.

8. Some preschool-age children start to experience _____ over the meaning of their racial and ethnic identity. Some preschoolers experience race _____, the phenomenon in which minority children indicate preferences for majority values or people.

9. _____ identity emerges somewhat later. Preschool-age children who were _____ were most apt to be aware of their racial identity.

Gender Identity: Developing Femaleness and Maleness

10. Differences in the ways males and females are treated begin at _____. _____ is the sense of being male or female and is well established by the time children reach the preschool years. Sex typically refers to sexual _____ and sexual _____, while gender refers to the _____ of maleness or femaleness related to membership in a given society. By the age of two, children consistently _____ themselves and those around them as male or female.

11. During the preschool years, boys spend more time than girls in _____ play, while girls spend more time than boys in _____ games and _____. Girls begin preferring _____ playmates a little earlier than boys. Gender outweighs _____ variables when it comes to play.

12. Expectations about gender-appropriate _____ are even more rigid and gender stereotyped than those of adults and may be less _____ during the preschool years than at any point in the lifespan. Preschool children expect that _____ are more apt to have traits involving competence, independence, forcefulness, and competitiveness. In contrast, _____ are viewed as more likely to have traits such as warmth, expressiveness, nurturance, and submissiveness.

13. _____ are one sex-related biological characteristic that have been found to affect gender-based behaviors. Girls exposed to unusually high levels of _____ are more likely to display behaviors associated with male stereotypes than their sisters who were not exposed. Boys prenatally exposed to unusually high levels of female hormones are apt to display more behaviors that are stereotypically _____ than is typical.

14. Part of the _____, the bundles of nerves that connect the hemispheres of the brain, is proportionally larger in _____ than in _____. It is important to note that environmental experiences can produce _____ change.

15. Freud's psychoanalytic theory suggests that we move through a series of stages related to _____ urges. The preschool years encompass the _____ stage in which the focus of a child's pleasure relates to _____ sexuality. The _____ conflict occurs at around the age of five. Boys begin to develop sexual interest in their _____, viewing their _____ as rivals. They view their fathers as all powerful, and develop a fear of retaliation which takes the form of _____ anxiety. To overcome this fear, boys begin to identify with their _____. _____ is the process in which children attempt to be similar to the same-sex parents, _____ the parents' attitudes and values.

16. Girls begin to feel sexual attraction towards their _____ and experience _____ envy. Girls ultimately identify with their _____. The result of identifying with the same-sex parents is that children adopt their parent's _____ attitudes and values.

17. Most developmentalists base their criticisms of Freud on the lack of _____ support for his theories.

18. According to social-learning approaches, children learn gender-related behavior and expectations from their _____ of others. Television also presents men and women in _____ gender roles. In some cases learning social roles occurs more _____. Such direct training sends a clear messages about the _____ expected of a preschool-age child.

19. In the view of some theorists, the desire to form a clear sense of identity leads children to establish a _____ identity, a perception of themselves as male or female. To do this, they develop a gender _____, a cognitive framework that organizes information relevant to gender. According to _____ developmental theory, proposed by _____, this rigidity is in part an outcome of changes in preschoolers' understanding of gender.

20. Young preschool children believe that sex differences are based on differences in _____ or _____. By the time they reach the age of 4 or 5, children develop an understanding of gender _____, the belief that people are permanently males or females.

21. According to Sandra Bem, children should be encouraged to be _____, a state in which gender roles encompass characteristics thought typical of both sexes.

Friends and Family: Preschoolers' Social Lives

The Development of Friendships

22. At around the age of _____, children develop real friendships. Preschoolers' relations with peers are based more on the desire for _____, _____, and _____. With age, they come to view friendship as a _____ state, a stable _____ that has meaning beyond the immediate moment and that bears implications for _____ activity.

23. The focus of friendship in three-year-olds is the enjoyment of carrying out _____ activities. Older preschool children pay more attention to _____ concepts such as trust, support, and shared interests.

Playing by the Rules: The Work of Play

24. _____ play is simple, repetitive activities typical of three-year-olds, involving doing something for the sake of being _____. In _____ play, children manipulate objects to produce or build something. Constructive play permits children to test their developing _____ and _____ skills and to practice their _____ muscle movements. They gain experience in solving problems about the ways and the _____ in which things fit together, they also learn to _____ with others.

25. According to pioneering work by Parten, preschoolers engage in _____ play, in which they play with similar toys in a similar manner but do not interact with each other. Preschoolers also engage in _____ play, simply watching others at play but not actually participating themselves. In _____ play, two or more children actually

interact with one another by sharing or borrowing toys or materials although they do not do the same thing. In _____, children genuinely play with one another, taking turns, playing games, or devising contests.

26. Children who have had substantial _____ experience are more apt to engage in _____ forms of behavior. Pretend play becomes increasingly _____ as preschool-age children change from using only realistic objects to using less concrete ones.

27. Vygotsky argued that pretend play, particularly if it involves _____ play, is an important means for expanding preschool-age children's _____ skills.

28. Korean-American children engage in a higher proportion of _____ play than their Anglo-American counterparts, while Anglo-American preschool children are involved in more _____ play.

Preschoolers' Theory of Mind: Understanding What Others Are Thinking

29. Theory of mind refers to knowledge and _____ about the mental world. During the preschool years, children increasingly can see the world from other's _____. By the age of 3 or 4, they can distinguish between _____ phenomena and _____ actuality. Preschool children can also understand that people have _____ and reasons for their behavior.

30. Although preschoolers understand the concept of pretend by the age of _____, their understanding of belief is still not complete, which is illustrated by the _____ task. _____ is a psychological disorder that produces significant language and emotional difficulties.

31. _____ maturation is an important factors in children's theory of mind as well as developing _____ skills. Opportunities for _____ interaction and _____ play are critical in promoting the development of a theory of mind, and _____ factors also play a role.

Preschoolers' Family Lives

32. In the 1960s less than _____ of all children under the age of 18 lived with one parent. In 2000, a single parent headed _____ percent of white families, _____ percent of Hispanic families, and _____ of African-American families.

Effective Parenting: Teaching Children Desired Behavior

33. _____ parents are controlling, punitive, rigid, and cold. Their word is law and they value strict, unquestioning _____ from their children. _____ parents provide lax and inconsistent feedback. _____ parents are firm, setting clear and consistent limits, and they try to _____ with their children, and encourage their children to be _____. _____ parents show virtually no interest in their children.

34. Children of authoritarian parents tend to be _____, showing relatively little sociability. Girls who are raised by authoritarian parents are especially _____ on their parents, whereas boys are unusually _____. Children with permissive parents tend to be _____ and moody and low in social skills and _____. Children of _____ parents fare best. If this parenting style is related to _____ parenting, children show better adjustment and are protected from the consequences of later adversity. Children whose parents show _____ parenting styles are the worst off. Findings regarding child-rearing styles are particularly applicable to _____ society.

35. The Chinese concept of _____ suggests that parents should be strict, firm, and in tight control of their children's behavior. Children's acceptance of such an approach to discipline is seen as a sign of parental _____. Parents in China are typically highly _____ with their children.

105

Child Abuse and Psychological Maltreatment: The Grim Side of Family Life

36. At least _____ children are killed by their parents or caretakers every day, and _____ are physically injured every year. More than _____ million children are abused or neglected in the United States each year.

37. Child abuse is most frequent in families living in _____ environments. _____ are more likely to commit abuse against stepchildren than genetic fathers are against their own offspring. Child abuse is related to the presence of _____ between spouses.

38. Abused children are more likely to be fussy, resistant to _____ and not readily _____. The children most likely to be abused by their parents are _____ -year-olds as well as _____ -year-olds.

39. One reason for child abuse is the vague demarcation between permissible and impermissible forms of physical _____. The use of physical punishment of _____ sort is not recommended by child-care experts.

40. _____ teaches children that violence is an acceptable solution to problems. _____ plays a key role in the prevalence of child abuse.

41. One additional source of abuse is insensitivity to _____ norms on the part of parents. According to the _____ hypothesis, the abuse and neglect that children suffer predispose them as adults to _____ and _____ of their own children. Victims of abuse have learned from their childhood experience that violence is an acceptable form of _____.

42. _____ maltreatment occurs when parents or other caregivers harm children's behavioral, cognitive, emotional, or physical functioning. It takes the form of _____ in which parents ignore their children or act emotionally unresponsive to them.

43. Psychological maltreatment has been associated with low _____, lying, misbehavior, and _____ in school. In extreme cases, it can produce _____ behavior, aggression, and murder. In other instances, children who have been psychologically maltreated become depressed and even commit _____.

Resilience: Overcoming the Odds

44. Resilience is the ability to _____ circumstances placing a child at high risk for psychological or physical damage. Resilient children have _____ that evoke positive responses from a variety of caregivers. They tend to be _____, easy-going, and good-natured. They are easily _____ as infants, and they are able to elicit _____ from the most nurturant people in any environment in which they find themselves. The most resilient school-age children are those who are socially _____, outgoing, and have good _____ skills. They tend to be _____ and they are _____. The characteristics of resilient children suggest ways to improve the prospects of children who are at the risk from a variety of _____ threats.

45. For most children in Western cultures, _____ parenting is best. _____ is never an appropriate discipline technique. Use _____ for punishment. Parental discipline should be tailored to the _____ of the child and the situation. Use _____ to avoid noncompliance.

Moral Development and Aggression

Developing Morality: Following Society's Rights and Wrongs

46. Moral development refers to changes in people's sense of _____ and of what is right and wrong, and in their _____ related to moral issues.

47. _____ was one of the first to study moral development. He claimed that _____ morality is the earliest stage of moral development in which rules are seen as invariant and unchangeable. During this stage, which lasts from about age _____ through age _____, children play games _____, assuming that there is one, and only one, way to play. In the incipient _____ stage, which lasts from about age 7 to age 10, children's games become

106

more clearly _____. Children actually learn the formal _____ of games. It is not until the _____ cooperation stage, which begins at about age 10, that children become more fully aware that formal game rules can be _____.

48. Children in the heteronomous morality stage do not take _____ into account. They believe in _____ justice, the notion that rules that are broken earn immediate punishment.

49. Piaget _____ the age at which children's moral skills are honed. It is now clear that preschool children understand the notion of intentionally by about age ___.

50. Social-learning approaches focus more on how the _____ in which preschoolers operate produces _____ behavior, helping behavior that benefits others. Children learn moral behavior more indirectly by observing the behavior of others, called _____. By observing moral conduct, they are reminded of society's _____ about the importance of moral behavior, and modeling paves the way for the development of more general rules and principles in a process called _____ modeling.

51. According to some developmentalists, _____, the understanding of what another individual feels, lies at the heart of some kinds of moral behavior.

52. The notion that negative emotions promote moral development is one that _____ first suggested in his theory of psychoanalytic personality development. A child's _____, the part of the personality that represents societal do's and don'ts, is developed through the resolution of the _____ conflict.

Aggression and Violence in Preschoolers

53. Aggression is _____ injury or harm to another person. The amount of aggression _____ as they move through the preschool years. _____ self-regulation is the capability to adjust emotions to a desired state and level of _____.

54. _____ self-regulation is the capability to adjust emotions to a desired state and level of intensity. _____ aggression is motivated by the desire to obtain a concrete goal. _____ aggression is intended to hurt another person's feelings.

55. Freud's psychoanalytic theory suggests that we all have a _____ drive, which leads us to act aggressively towards others as we turn our inward _____ outward. According to ethologist Konrad Lorenz, animals, including humans, share a fighting _____ that stems from primitive urges to preserve _____, maintain a steady supply of _____, and weed out weaker animals.

56. Evolutionary theorists and _____, scientists who consider the biological roots of social behavior, argue that aggression leads to _____ success, increasing the likelihood that one's _____ will be passed on to future generations.

57. Social-learning approaches claim that aggression is largely a _____ behavior. Bandura illustrated the power of _____ in a classic study on aggression in preschool-age children. It made clear that exposure to aggressive models _____ the likelihood that aggression on the part of observers will follow. Because of its _____ content, television can have a powerful influence on the subsequent aggressive behavior of viewers. Exposure to nonaggressive models can _____ aggression.

58. _____ television programs contain higher levels of violence than other types of programs,. In an average hour, these programs contain more than _____ as many violent incidents than other types of programs.

59. The cognitive approach to aggression suggests that the key to understanding moral development is to examine preschoolers' _____ of others' behavior and of the environmental _____. Some children are more prone than others to assume that actions are _____ motivated. They are unable to pay attention to appropriate _____.

60. Methods for encouraging preschoolers' moral conduct and reducing the incidence of aggression include providing opportunities to _____ others acting in a cooperative, helpful prosocial manner. It is important not to _____ aggressive behavior, and children should be helped to devise _____ explanations for others' behavior. Television viewing should be _____. Children should be helped to understand their _____ and parents must teach _____ and _____.

CRITICAL THINKING QUESTIONS

To further your mastery of the topics in this chapter, write out your answers to the following essay questions from your text in the spaces provided.

1. Is an individual's self-concept fully formed by the time he or she reaches adulthood? What processes might influence an adult's self-concept?

2. How does the issue of secure attachment discussed in an earlier chapter relate to Erikson's stages of trust versus mistrust, autonomy versus shame and doubt, and initiative versus guilt?

3. What are the distinctions among gender differences, gender expectations, and gender stereotypes? How are they related?

4. Beyond physical characteristics, do significant racial and ethnic differences exist? Is it important to teach young children about racial and ethnic differences? Why or why not?

5. Are the styles and strategies of preschool-age children's play, such as parallel play and onlooker play, mirrored in adult life in realms of interaction other than play?

6. Why might the children of authoritative and of permissive parents equally tend to have sociability problems as adults?

7. Some people believe that researching and identifying personality traits of abused children, such as fussiness or failure to adapt to new situations, contributes to a tendency to blame the victim. What do you think? Why are such studies conducted?

8. Resilience seems to have positive benefits for both the child and the members of the social community with which he or she interacts. Would there be an ethical objection to teaching resilience skills as a part of standard public education? Why or why not?

9. If high-prestige models of behavior are particularly effective in influencing moral attitudes and actions, are there implications for individuals in such industries as sports, advertising, and entertainment?

10. If television and aggression are ever conclusively linked, what will be the social-policy implications? Why do children enjoy watching acts of aggression and violence on television?

PRACTICE TEST – POST TEST

Circle the correct answer in each of the following Multiple Choice questions and check your answers with the Answer Key at the end of this chapter.

1. Awareness of racial identity is greater in preschoolers who
    a. are bilingual.
    b. have older siblings.
    c. have a good self-concept.
    d. belong to the dominant culture.

2. A gender role that includes characteristics believed to be typical of both men and women is called
    a. androgynous.
    b. gender role adaptation.
    c. gender role orientation.
    d. gender schema reversal.

3. In psychoanalytic theory a young girl's sexual attraction to her father is accompanied by the experience of
    a. heteronomous morality.
    b. homonomous morality.
    c. castration anxiety.
    d. penis envy.

4. When the rules in a house are too lenient and are inconsistently enforced, the parents would be classified as
    a. permissive.
    b. disoriented.
    c. authoritative.
    d. authoritarian.

5. Children who are independent, self-assertive, and socially competent have parents who have most likely adopted what parenting style?
    a. permissive
    b. disoriented
    c. authoritative
    d. authoritarian

6. A child has been hit repeatedly by her parents. What is the most likely age of this child?
   a. 6-12 months   c. 3-4 years
   b. 1-2 years   d. 5-6 years

7. What percent of people who were abused or neglected as children abuse their own children?
   a. 13 percent   c. 33 percent
   b. 23 percent   d. 53 percent

8. Heteronomous morality is best described as a belief that
   a. rules are made to be broken.
   b. rules and laws are created by people.
   c. rules are unchangeable, and beyond people's control.
   d. each person needs to make up his or her own rules to live by.

9. According to the American Academy of Pediatrics, what is the best way to discipline a child?
   a. spanking   c. ignoring the undesired behavior
   b. time-out   d. discipline is never appropriate

10. In Bandura's experiment involving children watching a film of an adult playing aggressively with a Bobo doll, the preschoolers
    a. were less aggressive after being frustrated.
    b. were equally aggressive whether or not they had been frustrated.
    c. who had seen an aggressive model were less aggressive.
    d. who had seen the aggressive model were more aggressive.

11. Children's preferences for violent TV shows at age eight were studied through longitudinal methodology and found to be related to
    a. college grades.
    b. the amount of schooling completed.
    c. cooperative behaviors in adulthood.
    d. the seriousness of criminal convictions by age 30.

12. Which society is most likely to have a collectivistic orientation?
    a. Chinese   c. British
    b. German   d. American

13. What is the earliest age at which children consistently label themselves and those around them as male or female?
    a. one year old   c. three years old
    b. two years old   d. four years old

14. According to Freud, by age six
    a. boys have developed penis envy.
    b. girls have experienced castration anxiety.
    c. boys and girls have been through the phallic stage.
    d. all children identify with their mother.

15. Sylvester has the ability to overcome circumstances that would place the average child at high risk for psychological or physical damage. He displays
    a. authoritarian parenting.   c. spiritual strength.
    b. gender identity.   d. resilience.

16. Who argued that pretend play is an important means of expanding preschoolers' cognitive skills?
    a. Bandura   c. Vygotsky
    b. Freud   d. Werner

17. Children are best off if their parents are
    a. authoritarian.   c. permissive.
    b. authoritative.   d. uninvolved.

18. Freud believed that morality was linked to
    a. the superego.   c. identification.
    b. empathy.   d. autonomy.

19. In order to increase moral behavior and reduce aggression in preschoolers, parents should
    a. ignore aggressive behavior.
    b. allow the child to assume reasons for the behavior of others.
    c. help preschoolers understand their own feelings.
    d. allow preschoolers to develop self-control on their own.

20. Who was the first to study moral development in children?
    a. Kolberg   c. Piaget
    b. Bandura   d. Erikson

ANSWER KEYS

Practice Test – Pretest (with text page numbers)

1. d 265	6. d 280	11. b 288	16. d 292
2. b 288	7. b 284	12. a 295	17. b 274
3. d 278	8. d 283	13. c 265	18. a 278
4. a 274	9. b 287	14. a 267	19. c 290
5. d 278	10. c 286	15. b 269	20. b 291

Key Names

1. k	4. i	7. d	10. e
2. f	5. g	8. f	11. h
3. a	6. c	9. b	12. j

Key Vocabulary Terms

1. Gender identity is the perception of oneself as male or female; gender constancy is the belief that people are permanently males or females, depending on fixed, unchangeable biological factors.

2. Functional play involves simple, repetitive activities typical of three-year-olds; constructive play is when children manipulate objects to produce or build something; parallel play is play with similar toys, in a similar manner, but children do not interact with each other; and cooperative play is play in which children genuinely play with one another taking turns, playing games, or devising contests.

3. Authoritative parents are firm, setting clear and consistent limits, but try to reason with their children giving explanations for why they should behave in a particular way; authoritarian parents are controlling, punitive, rigid, and cold, and they value strict and unquestioning obedience, not tolerating expressions of disagreement form their children.

4. Permissive parents provide lax and inconsistent feedback; uninvolved parents show no interest in their children and indifferent, rejecting behavior.

5. Instrumental aggression is motivated by the desire to obtain a concrete goal; relational aggression is non-physical and is intended to hurt another's psychological well-being.

6.   Androgynous, Uninvolved, Temperament, Heteronomous, Onlooker, Race, Individualistic, Teratogen, Abstract, Resilience, Identification, Aggression, Neonate (Authoritarian)

7.   Self-concept, Collectivistic, History, Empathy, Moral, Associative (Schema)

Programmed Review

1.   psychosocial, society, behavior
2.   autonomy versus shame and doubt, independent, exploration, restricted
3.   initiative versus guilt, persons, decisions
4.   identity, accurate, overestimate
5.   culture, collectivistic, interdependence, social, individualistic, identity, uniqueness, autonomous, competition
6.   racial, ethnic, awareness, meaning
7.   3 or 4, group, membership
8.   ambivalence, dissonance
9.   Ethnic, bilingual
10. birth, Gender, anatomy, behavior, perception, label
11. rough and tumble, organized, role-playing, same-sex, ethnic
12. behavior, flexible, males, females
13. Hormones, androgens, female
14. corpus callosum, women, men, biological
15. biological, phallic, genital, Oedipal, mothers, fathers, castration, father, Identification, incorporating
16. fathers, penis, mothers, gender
17. scientific
18. observation, traditional, direct, expectations
19. gender, schema, cognitive, Kohlberg
20. appearance, behavior, constancy
21. androgynous
22. 3, companionship, play, entertainment, continuing, relationship, future
23. shared, abstract
24. Functional, active, constructive, physical, cognitive, fine, sequence, cooperate
25. parallel, onlooker, associative, cooperative
26. preschool, social, unrealistic
27. social, cognitive
28. parallel, pretend
29. beliefs, perspectives, mental, physical, motives, social, make-believe
30. 3, false belief, Autism
31. Brain, language, social, make-believe, cultural
32. 10, 21, 35, 55
33. Authoritarian, obedience, Permissive, Authoritative, reason, independent, Uninvolved
34. withdrawn, dependent, hostile, dependent, self-control, authoritative, supportive, uninvolved, Western
35. chiao shun, respect, directive
36. five, 140,000, 3
37. stressful, Stepfathers, violence
38. control, adaptable, 3 and 4, 15 to 17
39. violence, any
40. Spanking, Culture
41. age, cycle-of-violence, neglect, abuse, discipline
42. Psychological, neglect
43. self-esteem, underachievement, criminal, suicide
44. overcome, temperaments, affectionate, soothed, care, pleasant, communication, intelligent, independent, developmental
45. authoritative, Spanking, time-out, characteristics, routines
46. justice, behavior
47. Piaget, heteronomous, 4, 7, rigidly, cooperation, social, rules, autonomous, modified
48. intention, immanent

49. underestimated, 3
50. environment, prosocial, models, norms, abstract
51. empathy
52. Freud, superego, Oedipal
53. intentional, declines, Emotional, intensity
54. Emotional, Instrumental, Relational
55. death, hostility, instinct, territory, food
56. sociobiologists, reproductive, genes
57. learned, models, increases, violent, reduce
58. Children's, twice
59. interpretations, context, aggressively, cues
60. observe, ignore, alternative, monitored, feelings, reasoning, self-control

PRACTICE TEST – POST TEST

1.	a 267	6.	c 280	11.	d 293	16.	c 274
2.	a 271	7.	c 283	12.	a 266	17.	a 278
3.	d 270	8.	c 286	13.	b 267	18.	a 289
4.	a 278	9.	b 285	14.	c 270	19.	c 296
5.	c 278	10.	d 292	15.	d 284	20.	c 286

Chapter 9

Physical and Cognitive Development in Middle Childhood

CHAPTER OUTLINE

- Physical Development
    - The Growing Body
    - Motor Development
    - Health During Middle Childhood
    - Psychological Disorders
    - Children with Special Needs
    - Attention-Deficit Hyperactivity Disorder

- Intellectual Development
    - Piagetian Approaches to Cognitive Development
    - Information Processing in Middle Childhood
    - Vygotsky's Approach to Cognitive Development and Classroom Instruction
    - Language Development: What Words Mean
    - Bilingualism: Speaking in Many Tongues

- Schooling: The Three Rs (And More) of Middle Childhood
    - Schooling Around the World and Across Genders: Who Gets Educated?
    - Reading: Learning to Decode the Meaning of Words
    - Educational Trends: Beyond the Three Rs
    - Intelligence: Determining Individual Strengths
    - Intelligence Benchmarks: Differentiating the Intelligent from the Unintelligent
    - Group Differences in IQ
    - Below and Above Intelligence Norms: Mental Retardation and the Intellectually Gifted

LEARNING OBJECTIVES

After you have read and studied this chapter, you should be able to answer the following questions.

1. In what ways do children grow during the school years, and what factors influence their growth?
2. What are the main health concerns of school-age children?
3. What sorts of special needs may become apparent in children at this age, and how can they be met?
4. In what ways do children develop cognitively during these years, according to major theoretical approaches?
5. How does language develop during the middle childhood period?
6. What are some trends in schooling today?
7. How can intelligence be measured, and how are children with exceptionalities educated?

PRACTICE TEST - PRETEST

Circle the correct answer for each of the following multiple choice questions and check your answers with the Answer Key at the end of this chapter.

1. A child is given Protropin. This child is probably receiving medical treatment to
   a. increase height.
   b. decrease weight.
   c. hasten pubertal changes.
   d. reduce hyperactivity.

2. Obesity is defined as body weight that is more than _____ above the average for a person of a given age and height.
   a. 5 percent
   b. 10 percent
   c. 20 percent
   d. 30 percent

3. According to the American Academy of Pediatrics, when should we separate the sexes in physical exercise and sports?
   a. at infancy
   b. at puberty
   c. in early childhood
   d. in middle childhood

4. If someone's visual acuity is less than 20/200 after correction, the diagnosis would be
   a. myopia.
   b. dyslexia.
   c. blindness.
   d. partial sightedness.

5. A child with attention-deficit hyperactivity disorder will have difficulty with all of the following EXCEPT
   a. physical activity.
   b. self-control.
   c. staying on task.
   d. distraction.

6. A child in the concrete operational stage is less egocentric and can take in several aspects of a situation. This ability is known as
   a. seriating.
   b. conserving.
   c. decentering.
   d. reversibility.

7. From Piaget's perspective, the preschooler thinks
   a. operationally.
   b. preoperationally.
   c. concretely.
   d. formally.

8. Who proposed the zone of proximal development?
   a. Piaget
   b. Binet
   c. Gardner
   d. Vygotsky

9. Which of the following is used in teaching bilingual children?
   a. immersion
   b. reciprocal teaching
   c. conservation
   d. cooperative learning

10. The Wechsler scales consists of
    a. verbal skills only.
    b. a total IQ score only.
    c. nonverbal skills only.
    d. both verbal and nonverbal skills.

11. Robert Sternberg's definition of intelligence involves several aspects of mental functioning. Which of the following is NOT included?
    a. nonverbal intelligence
    b. contextual intelligence
    c. experiential intelligence
    d. componential intelligence

12. A friend of yours is excellent at problem solving and applying information she has learned over the years in novel ways. According to Sternberg's theory she would be high in
    a. practical intelligence.
    c. experiential intelligence.
    b. contextual intelligence.
    d. componential intelligence.

13. Your child tested at the gifted level and was allowed to skip from sixth grade to eighth grade. This approach to helping the gifted student is called
    a. acceleration.
    c. mainstreaming.
    b. enrichment.
    d. least restrictive environment.

14. If someone has an IQ of 35 with problems in muscle control and speech, and requires assistance for everyday tasks, that person would be classified as
    a. mildly retarded.
    c. profoundly retarded.
    b. severely retarded.
    d. moderately retarded.

15. Research in the United States has shown that from age 6 to 18 years, boys decrease their physical activity by _____ percent and girls by _____ percent.
    a. 24; 36
    c. 36; 24
    b. 40; 20
    d. 20; 40

16. Bernadette is a child with bipolar disorder, which antidepressant will she most likely be treated with?
    a. Ritalin
    c. Wellbutrin
    b. Adderral
    d. Aspirin

17. A reading disability resulting in the misperception of letters during reading and writing, confusion between left and right, and difficulties in spelling is
    a. dyslexia.
    c. Prozac.
    b. ADHD.
    d. asthma.

18. Which of the following is NOT a memory process?
    a. encoding
    c. retrieval
    b. storage
    d. control

19. An understanding of one's own use of language is
    a. metamemory.
    c. metalinguistic awareness.
    b. proximal development.
    d. bilingualism.

20. The model that states that the diverse, coequal cultural groups of American society should preserve their individual cultural features is the
    a. cultural assimilation model.
    c. bicultural identity model.
    b. pluralistic society model.
    d. componential model.

KEY NAMES

Match the following names with the most accurate description and check your answers with the Answer Key at the end of this chapter.

1. ___ Alfred Binet   a. concrete operational stage

2. ___ Howard Gardner   b. mental age

3. ___ Jean Piaget   c. eight intelligences

4. ___ Robert Sternberg   d. triarchic theory of intelligence

5. ___ Lev Vygotsky   e. zone of proximal development

KEY VOCABULARY TERMS

Differentiate between the following pairs.

1. Mental age; Chronological age
2. Stanford Binet Intelligence Scale; Kaufman Assessment Battery for Children (K-ABC)
3. Fluid intelligence; Crystallized intelligence
4. Acceleration; Enrichment

In the following puzzles, fill in the blanks with the term that fits each definition. The first letters of the terms (from top to bottom) will spell the term for the last definition. (NOTE: Some terms may be from previous chapters.)

5. _ _ _ _ _ _   The process by which information is initially recorded, stored, and retrieved.

   _ _ _ _ _ _   A chronic condition with periodic attacks of wheezing, coughing, and shortness of breath.

   _ _ _ _ _ _ _ _ _ _ _ _   The capacity to understand the world, think with rationality, and use resources effectively.

   _ _ _ _ _ _ _ _ _ _ _   Observation of behavior without intervention.

   _ _ _ _ _ _   Retardation in which IQ scores range from around 20 or 25 to 35 or 40.

   _ _ _ _ _ _ _ _   A theory of intelligence consisting of componential, experiential, and contextual elements.

   _ _ _ _ _ _ _ _   A trait that is present but not expressed.

   _ _ _ _ _ _ _ _ _   An approach in which students are kept at grade level but enrolled in special programs and given individual activities to allow greater depth of study on a topic.

   _ _ _ _ _ _ _ _   An impairment that involves the loss of hearing or some aspect of hearing.

   _ _ _ _ _ _ _ _ _   An understanding of processes that underlie memory.

   _ _ _ _ _ _ _ _ _ _ _   A measure that takes into account a student's mental and chronological age is the _____ quotient.

   _ _ _ _ _   Average performance of a large sample of children.

   _ _ _ _ _ _   Children with high performance capability in various areas such as intelligence and creativity are _____ and talented.

An educational approach in which exceptional children are integrated to the extent possible into the traditional educational system and are provided with a broad range of educational alternatives is _ _ _ _ _ _ _ _ _ _ _ _ _.

6. _ _ _ _ _ _ _ _   IQ from 35 or 40 to 50 or 55 indicate _____ retardation.

   _ _ _ _ _ _ _ _ _ _ _   WAIS is the Wechsler Adult _____ Scale.

   _ _ _ _ _ _ _   _____disabilities are difficulties in the acquisition and use of listening, speaking, reading, writing, reasoning, or mathematical abilities.

_ _ _ _ _ _ _ _ _ _ _   The ability to take multiple aspects of a situation into account.

Retardation in which IQ scores fall in the range of 50 or 55 to 70 are _ _ _ _.

7. _ _ _ _ _ _ _ _   Retardation in which IQ scores fall below 20 or 25.

_ _ _ _ _   The setting that is most similar to that of children without special needs is the _ _ _ _ _ restrictive environment.

_ _ _ _ _ _ _ _ _ _   A prenatal test that uses sound waves.

_ _ _ _ _ _ _ _ _ _   Mental _ _ _ _ is a significantly subaverage level of intellectual functioning and related limitations in two or more areas.

_ _ _ _ _ _ _ _ _ _ _   Special programs that allow gifted students to move ahead at their own pace, including skipping to higher grades.

_ _ _ _ _ _ _   A systematic meaningful arrangement of symbols for communication.

_ _ _ _ _ _ _ _   Visual _ _ _ _ _ is a difficulty in seeing that may include blindness or partial sightedness.

_ _ _ _ _ _ _ _ _   Substantial disruption in rhythm and fluency of speech.

_ _ _ _ _ _ _ _ _ _   Speech using only the critical elements of sentences.

_ _ _ _ _ _ _ _ _ _ _   WISC is Wechsler _ _ _ _ Scale for Children.

_ _ _ _ _ _ _ _   A period of cognitive development characterized by active appropriate use of logic is _ _ _ _ operational.

The _ _ _ _ _ _ _ _ _ _ _ _ society model is the concept that American society is made up of diverse, coequal cultural groups that should preserve their individual cultural features.

Look up the definitions for each of the following terms and give a specific example of each.

8. Attention-deficit hyperactivity disorder
9. Metalinguistic awareness
10. Bilingualism
11. Multicultural education
12. Cultural assimilation model
13. Bicultural identity
14. Auditory impairment
15. Visual impairment

PROGRAMMED REVIEW

Fill in the blanks in the following Programmed Review and check your answers with the Answer Key at the end of this chapter.

Physical Development

The Growing Body

1. While they are in elementary school, children in the United States grow, on average, _____ inches a year. This is the only time during the life span when _____ are, on average, taller than _____. Girls start their adolescent growth spurt around the age of _____.

2. During middle childhood, both boys and girls gain around _____ pounds a year and weight also becomes _____ as the rounded look of baby fat disappears. These average height and weight averages disguise significant _____ differences.

3. Most children in North America receive _____ nutrition. In other parts of the world, inadequate _____ and _____ produce children who are shorter and weigh less than those with sufficient nutrients. In the United States, most variations in height and weight are the result of _____ inheritance.

4. Tens of thousands of children who have insufficient natural _____ hormones are taking drugs that promote growth. The drug may lead to the premature onset of _____, which may restrict later growth.

5. Longitudinal studies show that children's nutritional backgrounds are related to several dimensions of _____ and _____ functioning at school age. Children who had received more nutrients were more involved with their _____, showed more positive _____, had less _____, and had more moderate _____ levels than their peers who had less adequate nutrition. The children with a better nutritional history were more eager to _____ new environments, showed more _____ in frustrating situations, were more _____ on some types of activities, and generally displayed higher _____ levels and more self-confidence.

6. Nutrition is also linked to _____ performance. Well-nourished children performed better on a test of _____ abilities and on other cognitive measures.

7. Overnutrition, the intake of too many _____, presents problems, particularly when it leads to childhood _____, defined as body weight that is more than _____ percent above the average for a person of a given age and height. By this definition, some _____ percent of all children are obese—a proportion that is _____.

8. Obesity is caused by a combination of _____ and _____ characteristics. _____ factors also enter into children's weight problems. Parents who are particularly _____ and directive regarding their children's eating may produce children who lack _____ controls to regulate their own food intake.

9. School-age children tend to engage in relatively little _____. Fitness surveys reveal that children in the United States have shown little or no _____ in the amount of exercise they get despite national efforts to increase the level of fitness. Many children are inside their homes, watching _____. The _____ between television viewing and obesity is significant because children also tend to _____ while watching television.

Motor Development

10. One important improvement in gross motor skills is in the realm of _____ coordination. Traditionally, developmentalists have concluded that _____ differences in gross motor skills become increasingly pronounced during these years, but when comparisons are made between boys and girls who regularly take part in similar activities, gender variations are _____. Performance differences were probably found in the first place because of differences in _____ and _____.

11. One of the reasons for advances in fine motor skills is that the amount of _____ in the brain increases significantly between the ages of 6 and 8. It provides protective _____ that surrounds parts of nerve cells and raises the _____ at which electrical impulses travel between neurons.

Health During Middle Childhood

12. For most children, middle childhood is a period of robust _____. Routine _____ during childhood have produced a considerably lower incidence of life-threatening illnesses. Illness is not uncommon, more than _____ percent of children are likely to have at least one serious medical condition during middle childhood. Most children have a short-term illness, but _____ has a chronic condition.

13. _____ is a chronic condition characterized by periodic attacks of coughing, wheezing, and shortness of breath. More than _____ children suffer from the disorder in the U.S. and the number is _____ worldwide. Some researchers have indicated that increased air _____ has led to the rise, other feel that the diagnosis was _____ earlier, or exposure to asthma _____ have led to the rise. Children living in poverty have a higher incidence probably due to poorer _____ care and less _____ living conditions.

14. Between the ages of _____ and _____ the rate of injury for children increases. _____ are more apt to be injured than _____ because their overall level of activity is greater. The increased mobility of school-age children is a source of several kinds of _____. The most frequent source of injury to children is _____ accidents.

15. The newest threat to safety for school-age children comes from _____ and _____. Although claims that Cyberspace is overrun with _____ and child _____ are exaggerated, there is still material that parents find objectionable.

Psychological Disorders

16. _____ disorder is diagnosed when a person cycles back and forth between two emotional states. For years people neglected the symptoms of such psychological disorders in _____. _____ children and adolescents has a psychological disorder that produces at least some impairment.

17. Advocates for the increased use of _____ for children suggests psychological disorders can be treated successfully using _____ therapies. Critics contend that there is little evidence for _____ effectiveness. There is some evidence linking the use of these substances with an increased risk of _____.

Children with Special Needs

18. Children with special needs differ significantly from typical children in terms of _____ attributes or _____ abilities.

19. _____ is visual acuity of less than 20/200 after correction, whereas _____ sightedness is visual acuity of less than 20/70 after correction. The legal criterion pertains solely to _____ vision, while most _____ tasks require close-up vision.

20. Auditory impairments can cause _____ problems, and they can produce _____ difficulties as well, since considerable _____ interaction takes place through informal conversation. In some cases of hearing loss, only a limited range of _____ or pitches is affected. The _____ of onset of a hearing loss is critical in determining the degree to which a child can adapt to the impairment. If the loss of hearing occurs in _____, the effects will probably be much more severe. The reason relates to the critical role that hearing plays in the development of _____. Severe and early loss of hearing is also associated with difficulties in _____ thinking.

21. Auditory difficulties are sometimes accompanied by _____ impairments, speech that deviates so much from the speech of others that it calls _____ to itself, interferes with _____, or produces _____ in the speaker. _____, which entails substantial disruption in the rhythm and fluency of speech, is the most common speech impairment.

22. Learning disabilities are characterized by difficulties in the ____ and use of listening, speaking, reading, writing, reasoning, or mathematical abilities. They are diagnosed when there is a _____ between children's actual performance and their apparent _____ to learn.

23. Some children suffer from ____, a reading disability that can result in the misperception of letters during reading and writing, unusual difficulty in sounding out _____, confusion between _____ and _____, and difficulties in _____. Learning disabilities are generally attributed to some form of ____ dysfunction, probably due to ____ factors.

Attention-Deficit Hyperactivity Disorder

24. Attention-deficit _____ disorder, or ADHD, is marked by inattention, impulsiveness, a low tolerance for _____, and a great deal of inappropriate activity.

25. It is hard to know how many children have the disorder, but most estimates put the number between _____ percent of those under the age of 18.

26. Doses of _____ or _____, which are _____, reduce activity levels in hyperactive children.

27. To encourage children to become more physically active, make exercise _____, be an exercise role _____, gear activities to the child's _____ level and _____ skills, encourage the child to find a _____, start _____, urge participation in _____ sports, don't use physical activity as _____, encourage children to participate in an organized physical _____ program.

Intellectual Development

Piagetian Approaches to Cognitive Development

28. The _____ operational stage, occurring between 7 and 12 years of age, is characterized by the active and appropriate use of _____. This thought involves applying logical _____ to concrete problems. Because they are less _____, children can now take multiple aspects of a situation into account, an ability known as _____. They attain the concept of _____, which is the notion that processes that transform a stimulus can be reversed, returning it to its original form.

29. Concrete operational thinking also permits children to understand concepts such as the relationship between _____ and speed. They remain tied to concrete, physical _____, and are unable to understand truly ____ or _____ questions, or ones that involve _____ logic.

30. Piaget's theories have powerful _____ implications, but many researchers argue that Piaget _____ children's capabilities. He seems to have misjudged the ____ at which children's cognitive abilities emerge, but he was right when he argued that concrete operations were _____ achieved during middle childhood The progress of cognitive development cannot be understood without looking at the nature of a child's _____.

Information Processing in Middle Childhood

31. _____ in the information-processing model is the ability to encode, store, and retrieve information. During middle childhood, short-term memory _____ improves significantly.

32. _____, an understanding about the processes that underlie memory, also emerges and improves during middle childhood. School-age children's understanding of memory becomes more sophisticated as they increasingly engage in _____ strategies—conscious, intentionally used tactics to improve cognitive processing. School-age children are aware that _____, the repetition of information, is a useful strategy for improving memory. They progressively make more effort to _____ material into coherent patterns.

33. Children can be _____ to be more effective in the use of control strategies. In the _____ strategy, one word is paired with another that sounds like it.

<u>Vygotsky's Approach to Cognitive Development and Classroom Instruction</u>

34. Vygotsky proposed that cognitive advances occur through exposure to information within a child's zone of _____ development. He suggested that education should focus on activities that involve _____ with others. _____ learning, in which children work together in groups to achieve a common goal, incorporates several aspects of Vygotsky's theory. _____ teaching is a technique to teach reading comprehension strategies.

<u>Language Development: What Words Mean</u>

35. Vocabulary continues to _____ during the school years, and mastery of _____ improves. Over the course of middle childhood, the use of both _____ voice and _____ sentences increases and children's understanding of _____, the rules that indicate how words and phrases can be combined to form sentences, grows. School-age children may have difficulty decoding sentences when the meaning depends on _____ or tone of voice.

36. Children also become more competent during the school years in their use of _____, rules governing the use of language to communicate in a social context.

37. One of the most significant developments in middle childhood is the increasing _____ awareness of children, the understanding of one's own use of language. Such awareness helps children achieve _____ when information is fuzzy or incomplete.

38. The growing sophistication of the language helps school-age children _____ and _____ their behavior.

<u>Bilingualism: Speaking in Many Tongues</u>

39. One approach to educating non-English speakers is _____ education, in which children are initially taught in their native language, while at the same time learning English. An alternative approach is to _____ students in English, teaching solely in that language.

40. Speakers of two languages show greater cognitive _____. They can solve problems with greater _____ and versatility and some research suggests that learning in one's native tongue is associated with higher _____ in minority students. Bilingual students often have greater _____ awareness, and even may score higher on tests of _____. Instruction in a native language may enhance instruction in a _____ language.

Schooling: The Three Rs (and More) of Middle Childhood

<u>Schooling Around the World: Who Gets Educated?</u>

41. In the United States, as in most developed countries, a primary school education is both a _____ right and a _____ requirement. In almost all developing countries, fewer _____ than _____ receive formal education and even in developed countries, women lag behind men in their exposure to _____ and _____ topics.

<u>Reading: Learning to Decode the Meaning Behind Words</u>

42. Development of reading skill generally occurs in several broad, frequently _____ stages. In Stage 0, which lasts from birth to the start of first grade, children learn the essential _____ for reading. Stage 1 brings the first real type of reading, but it is largely _____ recoding skill, that is, children can sound out words by blending the letters together. In Stage 2, typically around second and third grades, children learn to read _____ with fluency; however, they do not attach much _____ to the words. Stage 3 extends from fourth to eighth grades and children use reading to _____ about the world, but they are able to comprehend information only when it is presented from a _____ perspective. In the final stage, Stage 4, children are able to read and process information that reflects _____ points of view. This ability begins during the transition into _____ school.

43. According to proponents of _____ approaches to reading, reading should be taught by presenting the basic skills that underlie reading. These approaches emphasize the components of reading such as _____. In _____ approaches to reading, reading is viewed as a natural process, similar to the acquisition of _____ language. Children should learn to read through exposure to _____ writing. The National Research Council argued that the optimum approach was to use a _____ of elements of code-based and whole-language approaches.

Educational Trends: Beyond the Three Rs

44. U.S. schools are experiencing a definite return to the educational _____, and an emphasis on educational _____ is strong. Elementary school classrooms today also stress individual _____. Dissatisfaction with public schools has led to growth of _____. Education pays increased attention to issues involving student _____ and multiculturalism.

Developmental Diversity: Multicultural Education

45. Margaret Mead said that in its broadest sense, education is a _____ process, the way in which newborn infants are transformed into full members of a specific human _____. Culture can be thought of as a set of behaviors, beliefs, values, and _____ shared by members of a particular society. Multicultural education is a form of education in which the goal is to help _____ students develop competence in the culture of the majority group, while maintaining positive group _____ that build on their original cultures.

46. Multicultural education developed in part as a reaction to a cultural _____ model which fostered the view of American society as the melting pot. According to this view, the goal of education was to _____ individual cultural identities into a unique, _____ American culture.

47. In the early 1970s, educators and members of minority groups began to suggest that the cultural assimilation model ought to be replaced by a _____ society model. According to this conception, American society is made up of diverse, coequal cultural groups that should _____ their individual cultural features. Educators began to argue that the presence of students representing diverse cultures _____ and broadened the educational experience of all students.

48. Most educators agree that minority children should be encouraged to develop a _____ identity. They recommend that children be supported in _____ their original cultural identities while they _____ themselves into the dominant culture.

Intelligence: Determining Individual Strengths

49. Intelligence is the capacity to _____ the world, think with _____, and use _____ effectively when faced with challenges.

Intelligence Benchmarks: Differentiating the Intelligent from the Unintelligent

50. Binet's pioneering efforts in intelligence _____ left three important legacies. The first was his _____ approach to the construction of intelligence tests. The second stems from his focus on linking intelligence and _____ success. Finally, Binet developed a procedure of linking each intelligence test score with a _____ age, the age of the children taking the test who, on average, achieved that score.

51. An intelligence _____, or IQ score, is a measure of intelligence that takes into account a student's mental and _____ age. Scores today are calculated in a more mathematically sophisticated manner and are known as _____ IQ scores. The average deviation IQ score remains set at _____, and tests are now statistically constructed so that approximately _____ of children of a given age fall within 15 points of the average score.

52. The _____-Binet intelligence scale began as an American revision of Binet's original test. The _____ Intelligence Scale for Children-Revised and its adult version, the _____ Adult Intelligence Scale-Revised

provide separate measures of _____ and _____ (or nonverbal) skills. The Kaufman Assessment Battery for Children tests children's ability to integrate different kinds of _____ simultaneously and to use step-by-step _____.

53. The intelligence tests used most frequently in school settings today share an underlying premise that intelligence is composed of a single, unitary mental ability commonly called _____. Some psychologists suggest that there are two kinds of intelligence: _____ intelligence reflects information processing capabilities, reasoning, and memory; and _____ intelligence is the accumulation of information, skills, and strategies that people have learned through experience.

54. Gardner suggests that we have _____ distinct intelligences. Vygotsky contends that assessment should involve _____ interaction between the individual and the person doing the assessment, a process called _____ assessment. Sternberg suggests that intelligence is best thought of in terms of _____ processing. His _____ theory of intelligence states that intelligence consists of three components. The _____ aspect of intelligence reflects how efficiently people can process and analyze information. The _____ element is the insightful component of intelligence and the _____ element of intelligence concerns practical intelligence.

Group Differences in IQ

55. Cultural _____ and _____ have the potential to affect intelligence test scores.

56. The question of how to interpret _____ in intelligence scores across cultures lies at the heart of the major controversies in child development. The issue is important because of _____ implications.

57. Herrnstein and Murray argue that the average 15-point IQ difference between whites and African Americans is due primarily to _____ rather than environment. They argue that this IQ difference accounts for the higher rates of _____, lower _____ and higher use of _____ among minority groups.

58. Most developmentalists and psychologists responded by arguing that the differences between races in measured IQ can be explained by _____ differences between the races. When a variety of indicators of economic and social factors are statistically taken into account simultaneously, mean IQ scores of black and white children turn out to be actually quite _____.

Below and Above Intelligence Norms: Mental Retardation and the Intellectually Gifted

59. In 1975, Congress passed Public Law 94-142, the Education for All _____ Children Act. The intent of the law was to ensure that children with special needs received a full education in the least _____ environment. This educational approach to special education is called _____. Full _____ is the integration of all students, even those with the most severe disabilities, into regular classes.

60. Approximately _____ percent of the school-age population is considered to be mentally retarded, substantial _____ in present functioning characterized by significantly _____ intellectual functioning, existing concurrently with related limitations in adaptive _____ areas. Mental retardation manifests before age _____.

61. The vast majority of the mentally retarded have relatively low levels of deficits and are classified with _____ retardation, scoring in the range of 50 or 55 to 70 on IQ tests. People whose IQ scores range from around 35 or 40 to 50 or 55 are classified with _____ retardation. They compose between _____ percent of the mentally retarded, are slow to develop _____ skills, and their _____ development is also affected. Those who are classified with _____ retardation (IQs from 20 or 25 to 35 or 40) and _____ retardation (IQ below 20 or 25) are severely limited in ability to function.

62. The federal government considers the term gifted to include children who give evidence of high performance capability in areas such as _____, creative, artistic, _____ capacity, or specific academic fields and who require _____ or activities not ordinarily provided by the school. In one study, gifted students were found to be _____, better _____, and psychologically better _____ than their less intelligent classmates.

124

63. Two main approaches to educating the gifted and talented are _____, which allows gifted students to move ahead at their own pace, and _____, through which children are kept at grade level but are enrolled in special programs.

CRITICAL THINKING QUESTIONS

To further your understanding of the topics covered in this chapter, write out your answers to the following essay questions from your text in the space provided.

1. Under what circumstances would you recommend the use of a growth hormone such as Protropin? Is shortness primarily a physical or a cultural problem?

2. Do proven links among affluence, nutrition, and the development of cognitive and social skills provide insight into the notion of "the cycle of poverty"? How might the cycle be broken?

3. In general, are social attitudes toward people with speech impairments supportive? How would you advise children to treat a youngster with a noticeable speech impairment?

4. An increasing number of children are being diagnosed with and treated for ADHD every year. What factors might attribute to the increase in diagnosis and treatment?

5. We infer that two rules of pragmatics, which govern the social uses of language, are (1) that speakers should take turns, and (2) that speakers should address the same topic. Name other rules of pragmatics.

6. What method of education would you prefer for your gifted child? For your challenged child? Why?

7. Is an educational focus on the basic academic skills appropriate? How does the theory that there are multiple intelligences relate to this issue?

8. How do fluid intelligence and crystallized intelligence interact? Which of the two is likely to be more influenced by genetic factors, and which by environmental factors? Why?

9. What are the advantages of mainstreaming? What challenges does it present? Are there situations in which you would not support mainstreaming? Explain your answer.

10. Some people argue that expending additional resources on gifted and talented children is wasteful, because these children will succeed anyway. What is your opinion of this suggestion, and why?

PRACTICE TEST – POST TEST

Circle the correct answer for each of the following multiple choice questions and check your answers with the Answer Key at the end of this chapter.

1. Robby has been diagnosed with attention-deficit hyperactivity disorder. He is part of what percent of school-age children with the same diagnosis?
   a. 1 percent
   b. 2-4 percent
   c. 3-5 percent
   d. 5-10 percent

2. Children with chronic wheezing, coughing, and shortness of breath may have
   a. asthma.
   b. the flu.
   c. emotional problems.
   d. attention-deficit disorder.

3. There is a significant increase of myelin in the brain between the ages of
   a. 1 and 2.
   b. 2 and 4.
   c. 5 and 6.
   d. 6 and 8.

4. Keith has a substantial disruption in the rhythm and the fluency of his speech. He most likely suffers from
   a. stuttering.
   b. learning disability.
   c. ADHD.
   d. visual impairment.

5. According to Piaget, children in elementary school are in the cognitive development stage of
   a. sensorimotor.
   b. preoperational thought.
   c. concrete operational thought.
   d. formal operational thought.

6. All of the following are ways to keep children fit EXCEPT
   a. urge participation in organized sports.
   b. be an exercise role model.
   c. encourage the childe to exercise alone.
   d. make exercise fun.

7. You are preparing for an exam in your life span development class and you begin to make flash cards and other review tools which you have found useful for memorizing material. In doing this you show an understanding of memory called
   a. sequencing.
   b. meta-memory.
   c. semantic elaboration.
   d. metalinguistic awareness.

8. You are visiting your sister and her very polite son, when you overhear him playing outside with his friends. You hear him talking to his friends in a way that is very different from the way he speaks to you. This difference is an aspect of language called
   a. syntax.
   b. semantics.
   c. phonology.
   d. pragmatics.

9. Which of the following does NOT belong with the others?
   a. phonics
   b. code-based
   c. basic skills
   d. whole-language

10. Alfred Binet developed an intelligence test which comes up with one score. Other researchers have developed theories that propose intelligence is a complex combination of numerous areas. Who proposed that we have at least eight distinct intelligences?
    a. Alfred Binet
    b. Arthur Jensen
    c. Robert Sternberg
    d. Howard Gardner

11. Over the years Mitch has had to overcome several obstacles and he developed what some people might call "street smarts." He is practical and uses a great deal of common sense. According to Sternberg's theory he would be high in
    a. nonverbal intelligence.
    b. contextual intelligence.
    c. experiential intelligence.
    d. componential intelligence.

12. School-age children may have difficulty decoding sentences if the meaning depends upon
    a. intonation.
    b. phonemes.
    c. syntax.
    d. grammar

13. What percent of the school-age population has been tested as mentally retarded?
    a. 1 to 3 percent
    b. 4 to 6 percent
    c. 8 to 10 percent
    d. 10 to 12 percent

14. Which of the following statements about growth in childhood is accurate?
    a. Girls are taller than boys throughout childhood and adolescence.
    b. Children grow on average 4 to 5 inches a year.
    c. Girls start their adolescent growth spurt around the age of 10.
    d. There are few individual differences in height during childhood.

15. Sam is an average 8-year-old. He should be able to
    a. run 17 feet per second.
    b. achieve a jump of 3 feet.
    c. grip objects with 12 pounds of pressure.
    d. throw a small ball 41 feet.

16. Which of the following is an approach to teaching non-English speakers to speak English?
    a. bilingual enrichment
    b. bilingual acceleration
    c. bilingual literacy
    d. bilingual education

17. Critics of Piaget claim that
    a. he failed to accurately describe cognitive development.
    b. he overestimated children's capabilities.
    c. he misjudged the age at which cognitive abilities emerge.
    d. his approach should be dismissed.

18. The average 6-year-old has a vocabulary of from
    a. 8,000 to 14,000 words.   c. 13,000 to 19,000 words.
    b. 5,000 to 10,000 words.   d. 9,000 to 11,000 words.

19. Research has shown that bilingual children
    a. have lower metalinguistic awareness.
    b. score lower on tests of intelligence.
    c. have lower self-esteem.
    d. show greater cognitive flexibility.

20. A child with a mental age of 10 and a chronological age of 8 has an IQ of
    a. 8.   c. 80.
    b. 12.5   d. 125.

ANSWER KEYS

Practice Test – Pretest (with text page numbers)

1.	a 303	6.	c 316	11.	a 337	16.	c 310
2.	c 305	7.	b 316	12.	c 337	17.	a 312
3.	b 306	8.	a 320	13.	a 344	18.	d 319
4.	c 311	9.	a 323	14.	b 342	19.	c 322
5.	a 313	10.	d 334	15.	a 303	20.	b 330

Key Names

1. b   2. c   3. a   4. d   5. e

Key Vocabulary Terms

1. Mental age is the typical intelligence level found for people at a given chronological age; chronological age is the actual age of the child taking the intelligence test.

2. The Stanford-Binet Intelligence Scale is a test that consists of a series of items that vary according to the age of the person being tested; the Kaufman Assessment Battery for Children (K-ABC) is an intelligence test that measures children's ability to integrate different stimuli simultaneously and step-by-step thinking.

3. Fluid intelligence reflects information processing capabilities, reasoning, and memory; crystallized intelligence is the accumulation of information, skills, and strategies that people have learned through experience and that they can apply in problem-solving situations.

4. Acceleration is special programs that allow gifted students to move ahead at their own pace, even if it means skipping to a higher grade level; enrichment is an approach through which students are kept at grade level but are enrolled in special programs and given individual activities to allow greater depth of study on a given topic.

5. Memory, Asthma, Intelligence, Naturalistic, Severe, Triarchic, Recessive, Enrichment, Auditory, Metamemory, Intelligence, Norms, Gifted (Mainstreaming)

6. Moderate, Intelligence, Learning, Decentering (Mild)

7. Profound, Least, Ultrasound, Retardation, Acceleration, Language, Impairment, Stuttering, Telegraphic, Intelligence, Concrete (Pluralistic)

Programmed Review

1. 2 to 3, girls, boys, 10
2. 5 to 7, redistributed, individual
3. sufficient, nutrition, disease, genetic
4. growth, puberty
5. social, emotional, peers, emotion, anxiety, activity, explore, persistence, alert, energy
6. cognitive, verbal
7. calories, obesity, 20, 10, growing
8. genetic, social, Social, controlling, internal
9. exercise, improvement, television, correlation, snack
10. muscle, gender, minimized, motivation, expectations
11. myelin, insulation, speed
12. health, immunizations, 90, one in nine
13. Asthma, 15 million, 150 million, pollution, missed, triggers, medical, sanitary
14. 5, 14, boys, girls, accidents, automobile
15. Internet, World Wide Web, pornography, molesters
16. Bipolar, children, One in five
17. antidepressants, long-term, suicide
18. physical, learning
19. Blindness, partial, distance, educational
20. academic, social, peer, frequencies, age, infancy, language, abstract
21. speech, attention, communication, maladjustment, Stuttering
22. acquisition, discrepancy, potential
23. dyslexia, letters, left, right, spelling brain, genetic
24. hyperactivity, frustration
25. 3 to 7
26. Ritalin, Dexadrine, stimulants
27. fun, model, physical, motor, partner, slowly, organized, punishment, fitness
28. concrete, logic, operations, egocentric, decentering, reversibility
29. time, reality, abstract, hypothetical, formal
30. educational, underestimated, age, universally, culture
31. Memory, capacity
32. Metamemory, control, rehearsal, organize
33. trained, keyword
34. proximal, interaction, Cooperative, Reciprocal
35. increase, grammar, passive, conditional, syntax, intonation
36. pragmatics
37. metalinguistic, comprehension
38. control, regulate
39. bilingual, immerse
40. flexibility, creativity, self-esteem, metalinguistic, intelligence, second
41. universal, legal, females, males, science, technological
42. overlapping, prerequisites, phonological, aloud, meaning, learn, single, multiple, high
43. code-based, phonics, whole-language, oral, complete, combination
44. fundamentals, basics, accountability, home-schooling, diversity
45. cultural, society, expectations, minority, identities
46. assimilation, assimilate, unified

47. pluralistic, preserve, enriched
48. bicultural, maintaining, integrate
49. understand, rationality, resources
50. testing, pragmatic, school, mental
51. quotient, chronological, deviation, 100, two-thirds
52. Stanford, Wechsler, Wechsler, verbal, performance, stimuli, thinking
53. g, fluid, crystallized
54. eight, cooperative, dynamic, information, triarchic, componential, experiential, contextual
55. background, experience
56. differences, social
57. heredity, poverty, employment, welfare
58. environmental, similar
59. Handicapped, restrictive, mainstreaming, inclusion
60. 1 to 3, limitation, subaverage, skill, 18
61. mild, moderate, 5 and 10, language, motor, severe, profound
62. intellectual, leadership, services, healthier, coordinated, adjusted
63. acceleration, enrichment

Practice Test – Post Test (with text page numbers)

1.	c 313	6.	c 315	11.	b 334	16.	d 323
2.	a 308	7.	b 320	12.	a 322	17.	c 317
3.	d 307	8.	d 322	13.	a 341	18.	a 321
4.	a 312	9.	d 327	14.	c 303	19.	d 323
5.	c 316	10.	d 332	15.	c 307	20.	d 332

Chapter 10

Social and Personality Development in Middle Childhood

CHAPTER OUTLINE

◆ The Developing Self
  ◆ Psychosocial Development in Middle Childhood: Industry versus Inferiority
  ◆ Understanding One's Self: A New Response to "Who Am I?"
  ◆ Self-Esteem: Developing a Positive – or Negative – View of Oneself
  ◆ Moral Development

◆ Relationship: Building Friendship in Middle Childhood
  ◆ Stages of Friendship: Changing Views of Friends
  ◆ Individual Differences in Friendship: What Makes a Child Popular?
  ◆ Gender and Friendships: The Sex Segregation of Middle Childhood
  ◆ Cross-Race Friendships: Integration In and Out of the Classroom

◆ Family and School: Shaping Children's Behavior in Middle Childhood
  ◆ Family: The Changing Home Environment
  ◆ School: The Academic Environment

LEARNING OBJECTIVES

After you have read and studied this chapter, you should be able to answer the following questions.

1. In what ways do children's views of themselves change during middle childhood?
2. Why is self-esteem important during these years?
3. How does children's sense of right and wrong change as children age?
4. What sorts of relationships and friendships are typical of middle childhood?
5. How do gender and ethnicity affect friendships?
6. How do today's diverse family and care arrangements affect children?
7. How do children's social and emotional lives affect their school performance?

PRACTICE TEST - PRETEST

Circle the correct answer for each of the following multiple choice questions and check your answers with the Answer Key at the end of this chapter.

1. Comparing ourselves to others in the areas of behavior, abilities, expertise, and opinions is called
   a. attributions.
   b. social comparison.
   c. social competence.
   d. social problem solving.

2. Vera's belief that she is a good soccer player, but not good at singing refers to her
   a. self-esteem.
   b. status.
   c. coregulation.
   d. social reality.

3. Reward and punishment are most important to people in which of Kohlberg's levels of morality?
   - a. preconventional
   - b. conventional
   - c. postconventional
   - d. formal operational thought

4. A student who decides not to cheat on an exam because he thinks he would feel guilty reasons at the _____ level of morality.
   - a. preconventional
   - b. conventional
   - c. postconventional
   - d. formal operational thought

5. Higher status children are more likely to
   - a. form cliques.
   - b. play with younger children.
   - c. play with less popular children.
   - d. interact with fewer children.

6. What theory provides an explanation of the complex relationship between self-esteem and minority group status?
   - a. information-processing approach
   - b. peer identity theory
   - c. social cognitive theory
   - d. social identity theory

7. Social problem solving begins with
   - a. choosing a response.
   - b. finding and identifying relevant social cues.
   - d. determining possible problem-solving responses.
   - d. evaluating responses and their probable consequences.

8. What percent of children in the United States will pass through childhood living with both of their parents, each of whom has been married only one time?
   - a. 25 percent
   - b. 50 percent
   - c. 75 percent
   - d. 85 percent

9. According to Weiner, attributions have all of the following dimensions EXCEPT
   - a. internal-external.
   - b. rigid-flexible.
   - c. stable-unstable.
   - d. controllable-uncontrollable.

10. When an expectation helps bring about the predicted event, which then strengthens the expectation, a _____ has occurred.
   - a. motivation
   - b. expectation
   - c. goal strategy
   - d. self-fulfilling prophecy

11. The cycle of behavior in which a teacher transmits an expectation about a child and thereby actually brings about the expected behavior is called
   - a. social comparison.
   - b. social competence.
   - c. teacher expectancy effect.
   - d. maladaptive attributional pattern.

12. Children who let themselves into their homes after school and wait alone until their caretakers return from work are known as
   - a. dropoff children.
   - b. self-care children.
   - c. workforce children.
   - d. empty nest children.

13. During middle childhood, there is a shift in self-understanding to a
   - a. more external view.
   - b. greater emphasis on physical attributes.
   - c. greater emphasis on psychological traits.
   - d. concern for intellectual abilities.

14. Children tend to make downward social comparisons
    a. until six years of age.
    b. throughout childhood.
    c. to avoid being asked to achieve.
    d. to protect their self-image.

15. According to social identity theory, members of a minority group
    a. traditionally prefer members of the majority group to those of their own group.
    b. have similar self-esteem as the majority group if they blame society for the prejudice they experience.
    c. typically blame themselves for the prejudice they experience.
    d. usually identify most strongly with the majority group.

16. According to Kohlberg's theory the fifth stage of development is
    a. good-boy morality.
    b. morality of contract, individual rights, and democratically accepted laws.
    c. reward orientation.
    d. obedience and punishment orientation.

17. According to Gilligan, the second state of moral development is
    a. postconventional morality.
    b. orientation toward individual survival.
    c. goodness as self-sacrifice.
    d. morality of nonviolence.

18. Given their dominance hierarchy, what type of play do many school-age boys engage in?
    a. parallel
    b. nonsocial play
    c. restrictive play
    d. constructive play

19. According to Carol Beal, the motivation of girls to solve social conflicts indirectly stems from
    a. a lack of self-confidence.
    b. apprehension over the use of direct approaches.
    c. an inability to be confrontational.
    d. a goal to maintain equal status relationships.

20. The good adjustment of children whose parents both work is related to
    a. the psychological adjustment of the mother.
    b. family finances.
    c. whether the family lives in a rural or urban environment.
    d. the number of children in the family.

KEY NAMES

Match the following names with the most accurate description and check your answers with the Answer Key at the end of this chapter.

1. ___ William Damon   a. Asian academic success

2. ___ Kenneth Dodge   b. attributions

3. ___ Erik Erikson   c. emotional intelligence

4. ___ Leon Festinger   d. industry versus inferiority

5. ___ Carol Gilligan   e. moral development in girls

6. ___ Daniel Goleman   f. preconventional morality

7. ___ Lawrence Kohlberg   g. social problem solving

8. ___ Harold Stevenson   h. social reality

9. ___ Bernard Weiner   i. stages of friendship

KEY VOCABULARY TERMS

Differentiate among the following pairs.

1. Preconventional morality; Conventional morality; Postconventional morality
2. Social competence; social problem solving

Fill in the blanks for the term next to each definition. The first letters of each term (from top to bottom) will spell out the term for the last definition. (NOTE: Some terms may be from previous chapters.)

3. _ _ _ _ _ _ _ _ _ _ _ _ _ _ _ .   The desire to evaluate one's own behavior, abilities, and opinions by comparing them to those of others.

    _ _ _ _ _ _   When a teacher transmits an expectation about a child and thereby actually brings about the expected behavior the ____ expectancy effect has occurred.

    _ _ _ _ _ _ _ _ _ _ _ _   People's explanations for reasons for their behavior.

    _ _ _ _ _ _ _ _ _ _   Agents that cause birth defects.

    _ _ _ _ _ _ _ _ _   A method of prenatal testing that uses sound waves.

    _ _ _ _ - _ _ _ _ _   An individual's overall and specific positive and negative self-evaluation.

The evaluation of a role or person by other relevant members of a group. _ _ _ _ _ _

4. _ _ _ _ - _ _ _ _   Children who let themselves into their home after school and wait alone until their caretakers return from work; previously known as latchkey children.

    _ _ _ _ _ _ _   A type of conditioning in which behavior is controlled by its consequences.

    _ _ _ _ _ _ _ _ _ _ _   A period in which parents and children jointly control children's behavior.

    _ _ _ _ _ _ _ _   Erikson's stage that lasts from 6 to 12 years of age is _____ vs. inferiority.

    _ _ _ _ _ _ _ _ _ _   The positive emotional bond between a child and an adult.

    _ _ _ _ _ _ _ _ _ _ _ _   Research that follows a group of people over a period of time.

The collection of individual social skills that permit individuals to perform successfully in social settings is _ _ _ _ _ _ competence.

Look up the definition for each of the following terms and give a specific example of each.

5. Status
6. Dominance hierarchy
7. Blended families
8. Emotional intelligence
9. Coregulation
10. Self-care children
11. Industry-versus-inferiority stage
12. Self-esteem

PROGRAMMED REVIEW

Fill in the blanks in the following Programmed Review and check your answers with the Answer Key at the end of this chapter.

The Developing Self

Psychosocial Development in Middle Childhood: Industry versus Inferiority

1. According to _____, middle childhood encompasses the industry versus inferiority stage. This stage lasts from roughly age _____ to age _____ and is characterized by a focus on efforts to attain _____ in meeting the challenges presented by parents, peers, and school. Success in this stage brings feelings of _____ and _____ and a growing sense of _____. Difficulties in this stage lead to feelings of _____ and _____.

Understanding One's Self: A New Response to "Who Am I?"

2. During middle childhood, children begin to view themselves less in terms of external _____ attributes and more in terms of _____ traits. The use of inner traits to determine self-concept results from the child's increasing _____ skills.

3. Children's views of self become more _____, divided into personal and _____ spheres. The nonacademic self-concept includes the components of physical _____, peer _____, and physical _____. The separate self-concepts are not always _____, although there is overlap among them.

4. Social _____ is the desire to evaluate one's own behavior, abilities, expertise, and opinions by comparing them to those of others. According to Festinger, when concrete, objective measures of ability are lacking, people turn to social _____ to evaluate themselves. Downward social comparison protects _____, and helps to explain why some students in elementary schools with low achievement levels are found to have _____ academic self-esteem than very capable students.

Self-Esteem: Evaluating the Self

5. Self-esteem is an individual's overall and specific positive and negative _____. It is more _____ oriented. As children progress into the middle childhood years, their self-esteem becomes _____.

6. The self-esteem of most children tends to _____ during middle childhood, with a brief decline around the age of _____. The main reason for this appears to be school _____. Children with chronically low self-esteem face a tough road, in part because their self-esteem becomes enmeshed in a cycle of _____ that grows increasingly difficult to break. Parents can help break the cycle through the use of a _____ child-rearing style.

7. Early research found that _____ had lower self-esteem than _____; however, subsequent research has found these early assumptions to be _____. According to social _____ theory, members of a minority group are likely

to accept the negative views held by a majority group only if they perceive that there is little realistic possibility of _____ the power and status differences between the groups.

8. In the United States, more than _____ children are either foreign born or the children of immigrants. They tend to show _____ levels of self-esteem to nonimmigrant children, although they do report feeling less _____ and less in _____ of their lives.

Moral Development

9. Kohlberg contends that people pass through a series of stages in the evolution of their sense of _____ and in the kind of _____ they use to make moral judgments. He suggests that moral development can best be understood within the context of a _____-level sequence that is further subdivided into _____ stages.

10. At the lowest level, _____ morality (Stages 1 and 2), people follow unvarying rules based on _____ and _____. In the next level, that of _____ morality (Stages 3 and 4), people approach moral problems in terms of their own position as good, responsible members of society. Finally, individuals using _____ morality (Stages 5 and 6), invoke universal moral _____ that are considered broader than the rules of the particular society in which they live.

11. Kohlberg's theory proposes that people move through the periods of moral development in a fixed _____ and that they are unable to reach the highest stage until _____ due to deficits in _____ development. Although this theory provides a good account of the development of moral _____, it is less adequate in predicting moral _____. Kohlberg's theory has been criticized because it was based solely on observations of members of _____ cultures. Another problematic aspect of Kohlberg's theory is its difficulty explaining _____ moral behaviors.

12. Gilligan suggests that differences in the ways boys and girls are _____ in our society lead to basic distinctions in how men and women view moral behavior. Boys view morality primarily in terms of broad principles such as _____ or fairness, whereas girls see it in terms of _____ toward individuals and willingness to _____ themselves to help specific individuals within the context of particular relationships. _____ for individuals is a more prominent factor in moral behavior for women than it is for men.

13. Gilligan views morality as developing among females in a _____ stage process. In the first stage, orientation toward individual _____, females first concentrate on what is practical and best for them. In the second stage, goodness as _____, females begin to think that they must sacrifice their own wishes to what other people want. Finally, in the third stage, morality of _____, women come to see that hurting anyone is immoral, including hurting themselves.

14. Gilligan's sequence of stages is quite different from Kohlberg's and some suggest that _____ differences are not as _____ as first thought.

Relationships: Building Friendship in Middle Childhood

15. During middle childhood, children grow progressively more sensitive to the importance of _____. Friendships provide children with _____ about the world and other people, as well as about themselves. Friends provide _____ support that allows children to respond more effectively to stress, teaches children how to manage and _____ their emotions, and helps them to _____ their own emotional experiences. Friendships also provide a training ground for _____ and interacting with others, and they can foster _____ growth. Friendships allow children to practice their skills in forming close _____ with others.

Stages of Friendship: Changing Views of Friends

16. According to Damon, a child's view of friendship passes through _____ distinct stages. In the first stage, which ranges from _____ years of age, children see friends as others who like them and with whom they share _____ and other activities. In the next stage, lasting from age _____, children take others' personal _____ and traits into consideration. The third stage of friendship begins toward the end of middle childhood, from _____

years of age, and the main criteria for friendship shift toward _____ and _____. Children also develop clear ideas about which _____ they seek in their friends and which they dislike.

Individual Differences in Friendship: What Makes a Child Popular?

17. Status is the _____ of a role or person by other relevant members of a group and is an important determinant of children's _____. Children who have _____ status have greater access to _____.

18. Higher status children are more likely to be viewed as _____ by other children. They are more likely to form _____, groups that are viewed as exclusive and desirable, and they tend to _____ with a greater number of other children. Children of lower status are more likely to play with _____ or less _____ children.

19. Popular children are usually _____, cooperating with others on joint projects. They are also _____, tending to have a good sense of humor and to appreciate others' attempts at humor. They are better able to understand others' _____ experiences by more accurately reading their nonverbal behavior. Popular children are high in social _____, the collection of individual social skills that permit individuals to perform successfully in social settings.

20. Social _____ refers to the use of strategies for solving social conflicts in ways that are satisfactory both to oneself and to others, and according to Dodge, it proceeds through a series of steps that correspond to children's _____ strategies. The manner in which children solve social problems is a consequence of the _____ that they make at each point in the sequence.

21. Several programs have been developed to _____ children a set of social skills that seem to underlie general social competence. They were taught ways to _____ material about themselves, to learn about others by asking _____, and to offer help and suggestions to others in a _____ way.

Gender and Friendships: The Sex Segregation of Middle Childhood

22. Avoidance of the opposite _____ becomes quite pronounced, to the degree that the social networks of most boys and girls consist almost entirely of _____ groupings. The segregation of friendships according to gender occurs in almost all _____.

23. Behavior termed _____ work helps to emphasize the clear boundaries that exist between the two sexes. It may pave the way for future interactions that involve _____ or _____ interests when children reach _____.

24. Boys typically have _____ networks of friends than girls and they tend to play in _____. The status _____ is usually fairly blatant, with an acknowledged _____ and members falling into particular levels of status. Because of the fairly rigid ranking, known as the _____ hierarchy, members of higher status can safely question and _____ children lower in status. Boys tend to be concerned with their _____ in the status hierarchy and this makes for a style of play known as _____, in which interactions are interrupted when a child feels that his status is challenged. Consequently, boys' play tends to come in _____ rather than in more extended episodes.

25. School-age girls focus on one or two _____ friends, who are of relatively equal status. Girls profess to _____ differences in status, preferring to maintain friendships at _____ status levels. Conflicts among school-age girls are solved through _____, by _____ the situation, or by giving in. The goal is to smooth over _____, making social interaction easy and _____. Girls are more apt to use _____ that is less confrontational and directive and to use _____ forms of verbs.

26. According to the National Association of School Psychologists, _____ U.S. schoolchildren stay home from school each day because they are afraid of being bullied. The victims of bullies are _____ who are fairly passive. They often _____ easily, and they tend to lack the _____ skills that might otherwise defuse a bullying situation with humor. Some _____ percent of middle school students report being bullied at some point in their time at school.

27. About _____ percent of students bully others at one time or another. About half of all bullies come from _____ homes. They tend to watch more _____ containing violence. When their bullying gets them into trouble, they may try to _____ their way out of the situation, and they show little _____ for their victimization of others. Bullies are more likely to break the _____ as adults. They are often relatively _____ among their peers.

28. Victims of bullying can be taught skills that help them _____ difficult circumstances that might otherwise lead to being victimized. They also need to increase their _____, understanding that they should not get upset by a bully's taunts and realizing they are not _____ for the bully's behavior. Social _____ on bullies can help to keep their bullying in check.

Cross-Race Friendships: Integration In and Out of the Classroom

29. Children's closest friendships tend largely to be with others of the same _____. As children age, there is a _____ in the number and depth of friendships outside their own racial group. By the time they are 11 or 12, it appears that _____ children become particularly aware of and sensitive to prejudice and discrimination directed toward members of their race. Whites and African Americans, as well as members of other minority groups, can show a high degree of mutual _____, particularly in schools with ongoing _____ efforts.

30. To increase children's social competence, encourage social _____, teach _____ skills, make children aware that people display emotions and moods _____, teach _____ skills, and don't ask children to choose teams or groups _____.

Family and School: Shaping Children's Behavior in Middle Childhood

Family: The Changing Home Environment

31. Middle childhood is a period of _____ in which children and parents jointly _____ behavior. Although children spend significantly _____ time with their parents, parents remain the major influence in their lives.

32. Siblings can provide support, companionship, and a sense of _____, but sibling _____ can occur, and parents may intensify it by being perceived as _____ one child over another.

33. Only children are, in some ways, _____ adjusted, often having higher _____ and stronger motivation to _____.

34. Children whose working parents are loving, are _____ to their children's needs, and provide appropriate _____ care develop no differently from children in families in which one of the parents does not work. In general, women who are satisfied with their lives tend to be more _____ with their children. When work provides a high level of satisfaction, mothers who work outside of the home may be more psychologically _____ of their children. Children with mothers and fathers who work full-time spend essentially the same amount of _____ with family, in class, with friends, and alone as children in families where one parent stays at home.

35. _____ children let themselves into their homes after school and wait alone until their parents return from work. Such children were previously called _____ children. Although many children report negative experiences while at home by themselves, they seem emotionally _____ by the experience. Children may develop an enhanced sense of _____ and competence. Research has identified _____ differences between self-care children and children who return to homes with parents.

36. Only around _____ of children in the United States spend their entire childhood living in the same household with both their parents.

37. Immediately after a divorce, the results can be quite _____. Both children and parents may show several types of psychological _____ for a period that may last from 6 months to 2 years. Even though children most often live with their _____ following a divorce, the quality of the mother-child relationship _____ in the majority of cases.

38. During the early stage of middle childhood, children whose parents are divorcing often tend to blame _____ for the breakup. By the age of 10, children feel pressure to choose _____, and experience some degree of divided _____. Twice as many children of divorced parents require psychological _____ as children from intact families.

39. Factors that relate to how children react to divorce include the _____ standing of the family the child is living with. In many cases, divorce brings a _____ in both parents' standard of living. In other cases, the negative consequences of divorce are less severe than they might otherwise be because the divorce reduces the _____ and _____ in the home.

40. About _____ of all children under the age of 18 in the United States live with only one parent. For _____ children the numbers are even higher. In the vast majority of cases, the single parent is the _____. The _____ status of the single-parent family plays a role in determining the consequences on children.

41. Overall _____ percent of all children in the U.S. live in blended families. More than 5 million remarried coupes have at least one stepchild living with them in what has come to be called _____ families. There often is a fair amount of role _____ in which roles and expectations are unclear.

42. In comparison to _____, who have more difficulties, school-age children often adjust relatively _____ to blended arrangements. The family's _____ situation is often improved after a parent remarries. In a blended family more people are available to share the burden of household _____. And the fact that the family contains more individuals can increase the opportunities for _____ interaction. Generally, the _____ the children, the easier the transition is within a blended family.

43. An increasing number of children have two _____ or two _____. Relatively little research has been done on the effects of _____ parenting, and the results are not definitive.

44. Members of _____ families are frequently willing to offer welcome and support to extended family members in their homes. _____ families often stress the importance of family life, as well as community and religious organizations. In keeping with the more collectivist orientation of _____ cultures, children tend to believe that family needs have a higher priority than personal needs.

45. The term orphanage has been replaced by _____ home or _____ treatment center. Group care has _____ significantly in the last decade. From 1995 to 2000, the number of children in _____ care increased by more that 50 percent. About _____ of the children in group care are victims of neglect and abuse. Most of them can be returned to their homes following _____ with their families by social service agencies.

The School: The Academic Environment

46. Weiner has proposed a theory of motivation based on people's _____, their understanding of the reasons behind their behavior. He suggests that people attempt to determine the causes of their academic success or failure by considering whether the cause is internal (_____) or external (_____), whether the cause is _____ or _____, and whether the cause is _____ or _____.

47. How people feel about their performance is a factor of the _____ they make for that performance. The internal-external dimension is related to _____ related emotions. When a success is attributed to internal factors, students tend to feel _____, but failure attributed to internal factors causes _____. The stability dimension determines future _____. The controllability dimension affects _____.

48. Among the strongest influences on people's attributions are their race, ethnicity, and _____ status. African Americans are _____ likely than whites to attribute success to internal rather than external causes.

49. An attributional pattern that overemphasizes the importance of _____ causes can cause problems. Attributions to external factors reduce a student's sense of personal _____ for success or failure. But when attributions are based on _____ factors, they suggest that a change in behavior can bring about a change in success. Women

often attribute their unsuccessful performance to _____ ability, but they do not attribute successful performance to _____ ability.

50. Stevenson's research suggests that teachers, parents, and students in the United States are likely to attribute school performance to stable _____ causes, whereas people in Japan, China, and other East Asian countries are more likely to see temporary, _____ factors as the cause of their performance. The Asian view tends to accentuate the necessity of hard _____ and _____. Because Asian students tend to assume that academic success results from hard _____, they may put greater _____ into their schoolwork than American students who believe that their _____ ability determines their performance.

51. Teachers seem to treat children for whom they have expectations of _____ differently from those for whom they have no such expectations. The teacher _____ effect is the cycle of behavior in which a teacher transmits an expectation about a child and actually brings about the expected behavior. This is a special case of the _____ prophecy.

52. Generally four major factors relate to the transmission of expectations: classroom social-emotional _____, _____ to children, _____ from teachers, and _____. Children who encounter a _____ social-emotional climate, who are given more _____ to complete, who have more _____ with teachers, and who are the recipients of more _____ from their teachers are going to develop more positive _____, be more _____, and _____ harder than those who receive negative treatment or neglect.

53. Educators in many elementary schools throughout the United States are being taught techniques to increase students _____ intelligence, the set of skills that underlies the accurate assessment, evaluation, expression, and regulation of emotions. Goleman argues that emotional _____ should be a standard part of the school curriculum. Programs to increase emotional intelligence have not been met with _____ acceptance.

CRITICAL THINKING QUESTIONS

To improve your understanding of the topics covered in the chapter, write out your answers to the following essay questions in the spaces provided.

1. Does the fact that students in low-achievement schools often have higher academic self-esteem than students in high-achievement schools argue against high-achievement schools? Why or why not?

2. What is an example of the relationship between low self-esteem and the cycle of failure in an area other than academics? How might the cycle of failure be broken?

3. Kohlberg and Gilligan each suggest three levels of moral development. Are any of their levels comparable? In which level of either theory do you think that the largest discrepancy between males and females would be observed?

4.   Do you think the stages of friendship are a childhood phenomenon, or do adult friendships display similar stages?

5.   How does the increasing sophistication of cognitive skills contribute to social competence? Does social competence relate to any of Howard Gardner's eight intelligences?

6.   Children are given hormones to regulate their growth, stimulant drugs to regulate their activity levels, and medication to regulate their moods. What (if any) would be the point at which parents and society let "nature take its course"?

7.   How might the development of self-esteem in middle childhood be affected by a divorce? By a family situation characterized by constant hostility and tension between parents?

8.   What do you think the major influences on your personal "moral development" have been? Do they agree or conflict with the theories presented in this chapter?

9.   Identify ways in which the attributions people apply to others may work to confirm stereotypes along racial or gender lines.

10.   Do expectancies operate outside the classroom, among adults? How?

Circle the correct answer for each of the following multiple choice questions and check your answers with the Answer Key at the end of this chapter.

1. The psychosocial stage of middle childhood is
    a. trust-versus-mistrust.
    b. initiative-versus-guilt.
    c. industry-versus-inferiority.
    d. autonomy-versus-shame-and-doubt.

2. The self-esteem of most children tends to increase during middle childhood, with a brief decline around the age of
    a. 7.
    b. 8.
    c. 10.
    d. 12.

3. A group of students participate in sit-in demonstrations to support a belief about which they feel very strongly. They believe the quality of life for everyone in the world is impacted. They are operating at what stage of moral development?
    a. reward and punishment
    b. obedience and punishment orientation
    c. authority and social-order-maintaining morality
    d. morality of individual principles and conscience

4. Gilligan's research on women's moral reasoning indicates that it is based on the concept of
    a. justice.
    b. equality.
    c. punishment.
    d. compassion.

5. Which of the following is NOT a way to deal with schoolyard bullies?
    a. teaching verbal skills to diffuse situations
    b. encourage victims to take responsibility for the bullying behavior
    c. encourage involvement with activities with other students
    d. encourage the development of self-confidence

6. Sarah has developed a collection of social skills that permit her to perform successfully in social settings. She has achieved
    a. social status.
    b. social identity.
    c. social competence.
    d. social comparisons.

7. Compared to girls during middle childhood, boys tend to
    a. have less concern for their status.
    b. have a smaller network of friends.
    c. play more often in pairs.
    d. develop a dominance hierarchy.

8. A family that includes a husband and wife and at least one stepchild living with them is called a
    a. mixed family.
    b. neutral family.
    c. blended family.
    d. full nest family.

9. All of the following are ways to increase social competence EXCEPT
    a. encouraging social interactions.
    b. teaching conversational skills.
    c. asking children to choose teams and groups publicly.
    d. teaching listening skills.

10. In what country are people more likely to attribute school performance to stable, internal causes?
    a. Japan
    b. China
    c. England
    d. United States

11. What dimension is related to esteem-related emotions?
    a. nature-nurture
    b. stable-unstable
    c. internal-external
    d. controllable-uncontrollable

12. A group of unpopular fifth and sixth graders were taught the skills that underlie social competence. Compared with a group of children who did not receive such training, the children who were in the experiment were
    a. less accepted by their peers than before training.
    b. more accepted by their peers than before training.
    c. accepted by their peers in the same way as before training.
    d. accepted by their teachers in the same way as before training.

13. Middle childhood marks a period of _____ in which children and parents jointly control behavior.
    a. coregulation
    b. autonomy
    c. initiative
    d. self-care

14. Which parenting style is most likely to promote a child's self-esteem?
    a. authoritative
    b. authoritarian
    c. permissive
    d. uninvolved

15. In the United States, children in middle childhood from immigrant families
    a. tend to emphasize individualism.
    b. have negative adjustment.
    c. feel an obligation to their families to succeed.
    d. pick up undesirable American behaviors.

16. Kohlberg's theory has been criticized because his research subjects were primarily
    a. female.
    b. from Western cultures.
    c. below the age of 10 years.
    d. minority groups.

17. In the second stage of friendship, children
    a. see friends as others who like them and share toys and activities.
    b. are 4 to 7 years of age.
    c. believe that mutual trust is the centerpiece of friendship.
    d. hold intimacy and loyalty as the main criteria of friendship.

18. Gender segregation of friendships during middle childhood
    a. is rarely found in nonindustrialized societies.
    b. only occurs when boys are assigned different activities than girls.
    c. helps to emphasize the clear boundaries that exist between the two sexes.
    d. is something parents should discourage.

19. Which of the following siblings will experience the most intense sibling rivalry?
    a. Moisha who is 5 years old and her 9-year-old brother
    b. Sharon who is 7 years old and Sara who is 8 years old
    c. Roger and Cathy who are treated equally by their parents
    d. Miguel who is 12 years old and his 5-year-old sister

20. Which of the following is an accurate statement concerning children's reaction to their parents' divorce?
    a. Severe maladjustment will last from 2 to 4 years.
    b. The quality of the mother-child relationship improves.
    c. Children often blame themselves for the breakup.
    d. Children under the age of eight years feel they must take sides.

ANSWER KEYS

Practice Test – Pretest (with page numbers)

1.	b 352	6.	d 355	11.	c 381	16.	b 357
2.	a 353	7.	b 364	12.	b 371	17.	c 360
3.	a 357	8.	b 371	13.	c 351	18.	c 366
4.	b 357	9.	b 377	14.	d 352	19.	d 368
5.	a 363	10.	d 381	15.	b 355	20.	a 371

Key Names

1. i		3. d		5. e		7. f		9. b
2. g		4. h		6. c		8. a		

Key Vocabulary Terms

1. In preconventional morality the concrete interests of the individual are considered in terms of rewards and punishments; in conventional morality people approach moral problems as members of society; in postconventional morality people use principles which are seen as broader than those of any particular society.

2. Social competence is the collection of social skills that permit individuals to perform successfully in social situations; social problem solving is the use of strategies for solving social conflicts in ways that are satisfactory both to oneself and others.

3. Social comparison, Teacher, Attributions, Teratogens, Ultrasound, Self-esteem (Status)

4. Self-care, Operant, Coregulation, Industry, Attachment, Longitudinal (Social)

Programmed Review

1. Erikson, 6, 12, competence, mastery, proficiency, competence, failure, inadequacy
2. physical, psychological, cognitive
3. differentiated, academic, appearance, relations, ability, correlated
4. comparison, reality, self-image, stronger
5. self-evaluation, emotionally, differentiated
6. increase, 12, transition, failure, authoritative
7. African American, whites, overstated, identity, changing
8. 13 million, similar, popular, control
9. justice, reasoning, three, six
10. preconventional, rewardsm punishment, conventional, postconventional, principles
11. order, adolescence, cognitive, judgments, behavior, Western, girls'
12. raised, justice, responsibility, sacrifice, Compassion
13. three, survival, self-sacrifice, nonviolence
14. differences, pronounced
15. friends, information, emotional, control, interpret, communicating, intellectual, relationships
16. three, 4 to 7, toys, 8 to 10, qualities, 11 to 15, intimacy, loyalty, behaviors
17. evaluation, friendships, higher, resources
18. friends, cliques, interact, younger, popular
19. helpful, funny, emotional, competence
20. problem solving, information-processing, decisions
21. teach, disclose, questions, nonthreatening
22. Sex, same-sex, societies
23. border, romantic, sexual, adolescence
24. larger, groups, hierarchy, leader, dominance, oppose, place, restrictive, bursts

25. best, avoid, equal, compromise, ignoring, disagreements, nonconfrontational, language, indirect
26. 160,000, loners, cry, social 90
27. 15, abusive, television, lie, remorse, law, popular
28. defuse, tolerance, responsible, pressures
29. race, decline, African-American, acceptance, integration
30. interaction, listening, nonverbally, conversational, publicly
31. coregulation, control, less
32. security, rivalry, favoring
33. better, self-esteem, achieve
34. sensitive, substitute, nurturing, supportive, time
35. Self-care, latchkey, undamaged, independence, few
36. half
37. devastating, maladjustment, mothers, declines
38. themselves, sides, loyalty, counseling
39. economic, decline, hostility, anger
40. one-quarter, minority, mother, economic
41. 17, blended, ambiguity
42. adolescents, smoothly, financial, chores, social, younger
43. mother, father, same-sex
44. African American, Hispanic, Asian
45. group, residential, grown, foster, three-quarters, intervention
46. attributions, dispositional, situational, stable, unstable, controllable, uncontrollable
47. attributions, esteem, pride, shame, expectations, emotion
48. socioeconomic, less
49. external, responsibility, internal, low, high
50. internal, situational, work, perseverance, work, effort, inherent
51. improvement, expectancy, self-fulfilling
52. climate, input, output, feedback, warm, material, contact, feedback, self-concepts, motivated, work
53. emotional, literacy, universal

Practice Test - Post Test (with page numbers)

1. c 351	6. c 364	11. c 377	16. b 359
2. d 353	7. d 366	12. b 364	17. c 362
3. d 357	8. c 373	13. a 370	18. c 366
4. d 360	9. c 369	14. a 354	19. b 372
5. b 367	10. d 379	15. c 356	20. c 373

Chapter 11

Physical and Cognitive Development in Adolescence

CHAPTER OUTLINE

- Physical Maturation
    - Growth During Adolescence: The Rapid Pace of Physical and Sexual Maturation
    - Puberty: The Start of Sexual Maturation
    - Body Image: Reactions to Physical Changes in Adolescence
    - Nutrition, Food, and Eating Disorders: Fueling the Growth of Adolescence
    - Brain Development and Thought: Paving the Way for Cognitive Growth

- Cognitive Development and Schooling
    - Piagetian Approaches to Cognitive Development: Using Formal Operations
    - Information-Processing Perspectives: Gradual Transformations in Abilities
    - Egocentrism in Thinking: Adolescents' Self-Absorption
    - School Performance
    - Socioeconomic Status and School Performance: Individual Difference in Achievement
    - Dropping Out of School
    - From Research to Practice: Preventing School Violence

- Threats to Adolescents' Well-Being
    - Illegal Drugs
    - Alcohol: Use and Abuse
    - Tobacco: The Dangers of Smoking
    - Sexually Transmitted Diseases: One Risk of Sex

LEARNING OBJECTIVES

After you have read and studied this chapter, you should be able to answer the following questions.

1. What physical changes do adolescents experience?
2. What are the consequences of early and late maturation?
3. What nutritional needs and concerns do adolescents have?
4. In what ways does cognitive development proceed during adolescence?
5. What factors affect adolescent school performance?
6. What dangerous substances do adolescents use and why?
7. What dangers do adolescent sexual practices present, and how can these dangers be avoided?

PRACTICE TEST - PRETEST

Circle the correct answer for each of the following multiple choice questions and check your answers with the Answer Key at the end of this chapter.

1. The developmental stage that comes after childhood is called
    a.   latency.
    b.   puberty.
    c.   adolescence.
    d.   young adulthood.

2. On the average, girls start puberty at about age 11 or 12, but that can vary from as early as
    a.   5 to as late as 20.
    b.   6 to as late as 18.
    c.   7 or 8 to as late as 16.
    d.   10 to as late as 14.

3. A boy has just entered high school but looks several years older. He is more likely to
    a.   succeed in school and avoid delinquency.
    b.   have difficulties in school but avoid delinquency.
    c.   succeed in school but be involved in delinquency.
    d.   have difficulties in school and be involved in delinquency.

4. How many calories does the average teenage male require?
    a.   1,500 calories per day
    b.   2,000 calories per day
    c.   2,500 calories per day
    d.   2,800 calories per day

5. Piaget suggested that _____ is achieved at the beginning of adolescence.
    a.   preoperational thought
    b.   operational thought
    c.   concrete operational thought
    d.   formal operational thought

6. When people think about the way they think, it is called
    a.   meta-memory.
    b.   metacognition.
    c.   memory capacity.
    d.   concrete operations.

7. Many adolescents are very concerned about their appearance and go to great lengths to have their hair and clothes perfect. This is the result of the
    a.   personal fable.
    b.   adolescent myth.
    c.   imaginary audience.
    d.   confounding variable.

8. According to anthropologist John Ogbu, members of certain minority groups have low academic achievement due to
    a.   uninvolved parents.
    b.   perception of school success as relatively unimportant.
    c.   a low socioeconomic status.
    d.   the belief that they can succeed despite poor school performance.

9. What in cigarettes produces a pleasant emotional state that smokers seek to maintain?
    a.   trichomoniasis
    b.   STD
    c.   nicotine
    d.   tar

10. According to the World Health Organization, what percent of the world's population will die because of smoking?
    a.   2 percent
    b.   5 percent
    c.   10 percent
    d.   15 percent

11. What percent of adolescents contract a sexually transmitted disease before graduating from high school?
    a.   5 percent
    b.   10 percent
    c.   20 percent
    d.   25 percent

12. What is the most common sexually transmitted disease?
    a. syphilis   c. genital herpes
    b. chlamydia   d. pelvic inflammatory disease

13. The information-processing approach argues that cognitive development is
    a. epigenetic.   c. discontinuous.
    b. continuous.   d. stage-like.

14. On the average, how many calories should adolescent girls eat each day?
    a. 1,400   c. 1,800
    b. 1,600   d. 2,200

15. What percent of high school seniors report having had an alcoholic drink in the last year?
    a. 76 percent   c. 88 percent
    b. 82 percent   d. 95 percent

16. Which of the following is an accurate statement concerning physical changes in adolescence?
    a. Girls react to menarche with anxiety.
    b. Boys tend to brag about their first ejaculation.
    c. Early maturation is best for both boys and girls.
    d. Girls are often unhappy with their bodies.

17. Which of the following was indicated as adolescent identification with drug culture?
    a. memory lapses   c. increased absenteeism or tardiness
    b. collection of beer cans   d. reduced motivation

18. An evaluation of Piaget's approach indicates that he was correct in stating that
    a. development proceeds in universal, step-like advances.
    b. cognitive growth is typified by relatively rapid shifts between stages.
    c. formal operations represents the epitome of thinking.
    d. children actively construct and transfer information about their world.

19. Which of the following countries has the highest high school graduation rate?
    a. Austria   c. South Korea
    b. New Zealand   d. United States

20. What percent of college students have consumed at least one alcoholic drink during the last 30 days?
    a. 25 percent   c. 75 percent
    b. 50 percent   d. 100 percent

KEY NAMES

Match the following names with the most accurate description and check your answers with the Answer Key at the end of this chapter.

1. ___ Elliot Aronson   a. anthropologist

2. ___ Gisela Labouvie-Vief   b. formal operations

3. ___ John Ogbu   c. postformal thinking

4. ___ Jean Piaget   d. school bullies

KEY VOCABULARY TERMS

Compare the terms in each of the following pairs.

1. Imaginary audience; Personal fables

2. Primary sex characteristics; Secondary sex characteristics

3. Anorexia, Bulimia

4. Chlamydia; Genital herpes

Define each term and give a specific example of each.

5. Secular trend
6. STD
7. Metacognition

In the following puzzles, fill in the blanks for the terms for each of the definitions. The first letter of each term (from top to bottom) will spell the term for the last definition in the puzzle. (NOTE: Some terms may be from previous chapters.)

8. _ _ _ _ _ _ _ _ _   Persons with alcohol problems who have learned to depend on alcohol and cannot control their drinking.

    _ _ _ _ _ _   A sexually transmitted ___ is spread through sexual contact.

    _ _ _ _ _ _ _ _   The stage at which people develop the ability to think abstractly is the formal _____ period.

    _ _ _ _ _ _ _ _ _ _   Research that studies a group of people over a period of time.

    _ _ _ _ _ _ _ _ _   Adolescent ____ is a state of self-absorption in which the world is viewed from one's own point-of-view.

    _ _ _ _ _ _   A statistical tendency observed over several generations is a _____ trend.

    _ _ _ _ _ _ _ _   The most common sexually transmitted disease, caused by a parasite.

    _ _ _ _ _ _ _ _   In the ecological approach, influences encompassing societal institutions.

    _ _ _ _ _ _   Anorexia ____ is a severe eating disorder in which individuals refuse to eat, while denying their behavior and appearance are out of the ordinary.

    _ _ _ _ _ _ _ _ _ _ _   The fibers connecting the two hemispheres of the brain.

    _ _ _   According to Freud, the rational part of the personality.

The developmental stage between childhood and adulthood is _ _ _ _ _ _ _ _ _ _ _.

9. _ _ _ _ _ _   The period during which the sexual organs mature.

    _ _ _ _ _ _ _ _ _   Socialization is a process in which infants invite further responses from others and vice versa.

149

_ _ _ _ _ _ _ _ _ _ _ _   Processing perspective seeks to identify changes in the way that individuals take in, use, and store information.

_ _ _ _ _ _ _ _   The onset of menstruation.

_ _ _ _ _ _ _ _ _   Drugs produce a biological or psychological dependence in users, leading to increasingly powerful cravings for them.

_ _ _ _ _ _ _ _ _ _   The ability to overcome circumstances that put one at risk.

_   The male chromosome on the 23rd pair.

_ _ _ _ _ _ _ _ sex characteristics are associated with the development of the organs and structures of the body that directly relate to reproduction.

PROGRAMMED REVIEW

Fill in the spaces in the following Programmed Review and check your answers with the Answer Key at the back of this chapter.

Physical Maturation

1. Members of Western cultures have their own rites of _____ into adolescence such as bar mitzvahs and bat mitzvahs at age 13 for Jewish boys and girls and _____ ceremonies in many Christian denominations. Their underlying purpose tends to be symbolically _____ the onset of the _____ changes that take a child to the doorstep of adulthood.

Growth During Adolescence: The Rapid Pace of Physical and Sexual Maturation

2. The dramatic changes during adolescence constitute the adolescent growth _____, a period of very rapid growth when height and weight increase as quickly as they did during _____.

3. On average, girls start their spurts _____ years earlier than boys, at around age _____, whereas boys start at about age _____. For the 2-year period starting at age 11, girls tend to be a bit _____ than boys.

Puberty: The Start of Sexual Maturation

4. Puberty, the period during which the _____ organs mature, begins earlier for _____ than for _____. Puberty begins when the _____ gland signals other glands to produce _____ (male hormones) or _____ (female hormones) at adult levels. Girls start puberty at around age _____ and boys begin at around age _____.

5. _____, the onset of menstruation, varies greatly in different parts of the world. In poorer, developing countries, menstruation begins _____ than in more economically advantaged countries. It appears that girls who are better _____ and _____ are more apt to start menstruation at an earlier age. Environmental _____ can bring about an early onset. The earlier start of puberty is an example of a significant _____ trend.

6. _____ sex characteristics are associated with the development of the organs and structures of the body that directly relate to reproduction. In contrast, _____ sex characteristics are the visible signs of sexual maturity that do not involve the sex organs directly.

7. Girls experience the development of primary sex characteristics through changes in the _____ and _____ as a result of maturation. Secondary sex characteristics include the development of _____ and pubic _____.

8. In terms of primary sex characteristics in boys, the _____ and _____ begin to grow at an accelerated rate around the age of 12 and by the age of about 13, a boy is usually able to have his first _____, known as _____.

Pubic _____ begins to grow, followed by the growth of _____ and facial hair, and boys voices _____ as the vocal cords become longer and the larynx larger. The surge in production of hormones that trigger the start of adolescence also may lead to rapid swings in _____.

Body Image: Reactions to Physical Changes in Adolescence

9. Some of the changes of adolescence do not show up in _____ changes but carry _____ weight. Menarche is typically accompanied by an increase in _____, a rise in _____ and greater _____. A boy's first _____ is roughly equivalent to menarche in a girl, and both generally occur _____.

10. For boys, _____ maturation is largely a plus because they tend to be more successful at _____ because of their larger size, to be more _____ and to have a more positive _____. Boys who mature early are more apt to have difficulties in _____, and they are more likely to become involved in _____ and substance _____.

11. Early maturers are more responsible and _____ in later life, and are also more conforming and lacking in _____.

12. _____ norms regarding how women should look play a big role in how girls experience early maturation. Early-maturing girls may have to endure _____ from their less mature classmates. They tend to be sought after more as potential _____ and their popularity may enhance their _____. Whether girls face difficulties with early maturation depends in part on _____ norms and standards.

13. As with early maturation, the situation with late maturation is _____, although in this case _____ fare worse than _____. Boys who are smaller and lighter than their more mature peers tend to be viewed as less _____, and they are at a disadvantage when it comes to _____ activities. The _____ lives of late-maturing boys may suffer and this may lead to a decline in _____. Late-maturing boys grow up to have several positive qualities such as _____ and _____, and they are more creatively _____.

14. Girls who mature later may be overlooked in _____ and other mixed-sex activities during junior high school and middle school, and they may have relatively low _____ status. By the time they are in tenth grade and have begun to mature visibly, their satisfaction with themselves and their bodies may be _____ because they are more apt to fit the societal _____ of a slender body type.

Nutrition, Food, and Eating Disorders: Fueling the Growth of Adolescence

15. The rapid physical growth of adolescence is fueled by an increase in _____ consumption. During the teenage years, the average girl requires some _____ calories a day, and the average boy _____ calories a day.

16. Several key nutrients are essential, including in particular _____ and _____, which helps prevent the later development of _____ and helps prevent iron-deficiency _____, an ailment that is not uncommon among teenagers.

17. The most common nutritional concern during adolescence is _____. One in _____ adolescents is overweight and one in _____ can be formally classified as obese. The _____ consequences for obesity are particularly severe during this time of life. Lack of _____ is one of the main culprits of obesity.

18. _____ is a severe eating disorder in which individuals refuse to eat, while denying that their behavior and appearance are out of the ordinary. This is a severe _____ disorder; some 15 to 20 percent starve themselves to _____. It primarily afflicts _____ between the ages of 12 and 40; those most susceptible are intelligent, successful, and attractive _____ adolescent girls from _____ homes.

19. _____ is characterized by binges on large quantities of food followed by purges of the food through vomiting or the use of _____. Although the weight remains fairly _____ this disorder is quite hazardous.

20. Girls who mature earlier than their peers and who have a higher level of body _____ are more susceptible to eating disorders during later adolescence. Adolescents who are clinically _____ are more likely to develop

eating disorders as well. Some theorists suggest that a _____ cause lies at the root of both anorexia nervosa and bulimia. There appear to be _____ components to the disorders and in some cases doctors have found _____ imbalances in sufferers. Anorexia nervosa is found only in cultures that idealize _____ female bodies and is not prevalent outside the _____.

Brain Development and Thought: Paving the Way for Cognitive Growth

21. The number of _____ continue to grow, and their _____ become more complex. The brain produces an oversupply of _____ matter during adolescence which is pruned back at the rate of _____ percent per year.

22. The _____ cortex is not fully developed until age 20. It allows people to think, evaluate, and make complex _____ and provides for _____ control. Adolescent brain development also produces changes in regions involving _____ sensitivity and production.

Cognitive Development and Schooling

23. Adolescents are able to keep in their heads a variety of _____ possibilities and they can understand issues in _____ as opposed to absolute terms.

Piagetian Approaches to Cognitive Development: Using Formal Operations

24. The _____ operational stage is the stage at which people develop the ability to think abstractly. Most people reach it at the start of _____, around the age of 12. Adolescents in this period are able to consider problems in the _____ rather than in concrete terms. They are able to test their understanding by systematically carrying out rudimentary _____ on problems and situations.

25. Adolescents in the formal operational stage use _____ reasoning in which they deduce _____ for specific situations from a general theory. They can also employ _____ thought that uses abstract _____ in the absence of concrete examples.

26. According to Piaget, adolescents are not fully settled in the formal operational stage until about the age of _____. Some evidence suggests that a sizable proportion of people hone their formal operational skills at a _____ age. Most studies show that only _____ percent of college students and adults fully achieve formal operational thinking. The scientific reasoning that characterizes this stage is not equally _____ in all societies.

27. Piaget suggests that cognitive development proceeds in _____ steplike advances that occur at particular stages, yet we find significant _____ in cognitive abilities from one person to another. The stage point of view implies that cognitive growth is typified by relatively _____ shifts from one stage to the next, but many developmentalists argue that cognitive development proceeds in a more _____ fashion. Because of the nature of the _____ that Piaget employed to measure cognitive abilities, critics suggest that he _____ the age at which certain capabilities emerge. It is now widely accepted that infants and children are more _____ at an earlier age than Piaget asserted. Piaget had a relatively _____ view of what is meant by thinking and knowing. Developmentalists such as Gardner suggest that we have many kinds of _____ and Labouvie-Vief suggests a stage called _____ thinking. Piaget made momentous contributions to our understanding of _____ development.

Information-Processing Perspectives: Gradual Transformation in Abilities

28. Proponents of information-processing approaches to cognitive development argue that growth in mental abilities proceeds _____ and continuously. Developmental advances are brought about by progressive changes in the ways people _____ their thinking about the world, develop _____ for dealing with new situations, sort facts, and achieve advances in _____ capacity and _____ abilities.

29. During adolescence, dramatic improvements evolve in the specific mental abilities that underlie _____. Verbal, mathematical, and spatial abilities _____, memory _____ grows, and adolescents become more adept at effectively _____ their attention across more than one stimulus at a time. Adolescents become increasingly

sophisticated in their _____ of problems, their ability to grasp _____ concepts and to think _____, and their comprehension of the _____ inherent in situations. Their store of _____ increases as the amount of material to which they are exposed grows and their memory capacity enlarges. They have _____, knowledge about their own thinking processes and their ability to monitor their cognition.

Egocentrism in Thinking: Adolescents' Self-Absorption

30. Adolescent egocentrism is a state of _____ in which the world is viewed from one's own point of view. Egocentrism makes adolescents highly _____ of authority figures, unwilling to accept _____, and quick to find _____ with others' behavior. Adolescents may develop what has been called an _____ audience, the perception that they are the focus of others' attention. Adolescents develop personal _____, the view that what happens to them is unique, exceptional, and shared by no one else. This gives them the feeling that they are _____.

School Performance

31. On average, students' grades _____ during the course of schooling. The nature of the material to which the students are exposed becomes increasingly _____ and _____ over the course of adolescence. Teachers grade older adolescents more _____ than younger ones.

32. Only _____ percent of high school students graduate. The performance of students in the United States on _____ and _____ is poor when compared to that of students in other industrialized countries, and performance in _____ is only average.

Socioeconomic Status and School Performance: Individual Differences in Achievement

33. Middle and high SES students earn higher _____, score higher on standardized tests of _____, and complete more years of _____ than students from lower SES homes. The same findings hold for children in _____ grades.

34. Children living in poverty lack _____ and _____ care may be less adequate. Often living in _____ conditions, they may have few places to do _____. Their homes may lack the _____ and _____ commonplace in more economically advantaged households. Some researchers point to _____ factors as a source of SES differences but there is substantial _____ in school performance within a particular SES, often _____ than the variation between students of different SES.

35. Achievement differences between ethnic and racial groups are _____. On average, African-American and Hispanic students tend to perform at _____ levels, and score lower on standardized tests of _____ than Caucasian students. In contrast, Asian-American students tend to receive _____ grades than Caucasian students.

36. Much of ethnic differences in achievement is due to _____ factors. Ogbu argues that members of certain minority groups may perceive school success as relatively _____ and they may believe that societal _____ in the workplace will dictate that they will not succeed, no matter how much _____ they expend. Members of minority groups who enter a new culture _____ are more likely to be successful.

37. Students from many Asian cultures tend to view achievement as the consequence of temporary _____ factors, such as how hard they work. African-American students are more apt to view success as the result of _____ causes over which they have no control.

38. Adolescents' _____ about the consequences of not doing well in school may account for ethnic and racial differences in school performance. African-American and Hispanic students tend to believe that they can succeed _____ poor school performance. Asian-American students tend to believe that if they do not do well in school, they are unlikely to get good _____ and be successful.

153

Dropping Out of School

39. Some half _____ students each year drop out of school. The consequences for dropping out are _____. High school dropouts earn _____ percent less than high school graduates, and the unemployment rate for dropouts is _____ percent.

40. Some adolescents leave because of _____ or problems with the _____ language. Some leave for _____ reasons, needing to support themselves or their families. Hispanics and African Americans are _____ likely to leave school; Asians drop out at a _____ rate.

41. There has been a _____ in overall violence and school is one of the _____ places for children. Individuals who are at risk for carrying out violence in schools have a low tolerance for _____, poor _____ skills, a lack of _____, failed _____ relationships, resentment over perceived _____, depression, _____, and alienation. They frequently were the targets of _____ or have been _____ in some way.

42. In response to the potential of violence, what works best is programs that moderate the _____ of schools. Programs involving cooperative _____, peer _____, and _____ skills training appear to be helpful. Teaching students, parents, and educators to take _____ seriously is important.

Threats to Adolescent Well-Being

Illegal Drugs

43. Almost a _____ of eighth graders and _____ percent of high school seniors report using marijuana within the past year. Adolescents use drugs for the perceived _____ experience drugs may provide and others want the _____ from the pressure of everyday life that drugs temporarily permit, or simply the thrill of doing something _____. Adolescents are particularly susceptible to the perceived standards of their _____ groups.

44. _____ drugs produce a biological or psychological dependence in users leading to increasingly powerful cravings for them. If drugs are used as an escape they may prevent adolescents from confronting and potentially solving the _____ that led them to use drugs in the first place. Even casual users of less hazardous drugs can _____ to more dangerous forms of substance use.

Alcohol Use and Abuse

45. One of the most troubling patterns is the frequency of _____ drinking in college students, defined for men as drinking _____ or more drinks in one sitting, for women as _____ drinks in one sitting.

46. _____ drinking affects those who do not drink or drink very little. Male athletes' rate of drinking tends to be _____ than that of the adolescent general population. Many adolescents begin to drink because of the conspicuous examples of drunkenness strewn around campus convince them to assume that everyone is drinking heavily, know as the false _____ effect.

47. Alcoholics become increasingly immune to the _____ of drinking and therefore need to drink ever larger amounts of liquor to bring about the _____ effects they crave. Alcoholism runs in _____, and it may be triggered by efforts to deal with environmental _____.

Tobacco: The Dangers of Smoking

48. Overall, a _____ proportion of adolescents smoke than in prior decades, but smoking is _____ prevalent among girls. Smoking among _____ males of high school age is significantly greater than among _____ males in high school. Nicotine can produce biological and psychological _____.

49. In addition to seeking new converts in the United States, tobacco companies aggressively recruit _____ smokers abroad. In many developing countries, the number of smokers is still _____. According to the World Health

Organization smoking will prematurely kill some _____ of the world's children and adolescents, and overall _____ percent of the world's population will die because of smoking.

Sexually Transmitted Disease: One Risk of Sex

50. Acquired _____ syndrome or AIDS is one of the leading causes of death among young people. AIDS is transmitted through the exchange of bodily _____ including semen and blood. AIDS is classified as a _____ transmitted disease. African Americans and Hispanics account for some _____ percent of AIDS cases although they make up only _____ percent of the population. _____ million have died due to AIDS, and the number of people living with the disease numbers _____ million worldwide.

51. The use of _____ during sexual intercourse has increased and people are less likely to engage in _____ sex with new acquaintances. On the other hand, the use of safe sex practices is far from _____. Adolescents are prone to risky behavior due to feelings of _____.

52. Although AIDS is the _____ of sexually transmitted diseases, others are far more _____. _____, a disease caused by a parasite, is the most common STD and can lead to _____ inflammation and even to _____. Genital _____ is a virus and the first symptoms are often small _____ or sores around the _____. There is no _____ for this disease. Trichomoniasis, an infection of the vagina or penis, is caused by a _____. _____ and _____ are STDs that have been recognized for the longest time and both can be treated effectively.

CRITICAL THINKING QUESTIONS

To further your understanding of the topics covered in this chapter, write out your answers to the following essay questions in the spaces provided.

1. Why is the passage to adolescence regarded in many cultures as such a significant transition that it calls for unique ceremonies?

2. What are some of the educational implications of the variations in maturation rate that adolescents experience? How can a teacher help students deal with the wide variety of changes they are witnessing and in which they are participating?

3. In what ways might the popularity of early developing boys and girls offer both benefits and threats?

4. How can societal and environmental influences contribute to the emergence of an eating disorder?

5. Why must the treatment of eating disorders typically involve multiple therapies rather than simply a change in diet?

6. When faced with complex problems do you think most adults spontaneously apply formal operations like those used to solve the pendulum problem? Why or why not?

7. In what ways does adolescent egocentrism complicate adolescents' social and family relationships? Do adults entirely outgrow egocentrism and personal fables?

8. Do programs and/or methods exist to teach adolescents about the dangers of illicit drug use that are worth the investment in the time and resources? What do you think would be effective? How would you develop a program to teach adolescents about the risk of alcohol and illicit drug use?

9. Abstinence is the best defense against sexually transmitted diseases, yet many argue that programs that teach sexual health should include de-emphasize its importance and highlight more risky strategies. How would you develop a program to teach sexual health to adolescents?

10. Why do adolescents' increased cognitive abilities, including the ability to reason and to think experimentally, fail to deter them from irrational behavior such as drug and alcohol abuse, tobacco use, and unsafe sex practices?

PRACTICE TEST – POST TEST

Circle the correct answer for each of the following multiple choice questions and check your answers with the Answer Key at the end of this chapter.

1. Many cultures have rituals of entry into adolescence, such as bar mitzvah. These are known as
   a. training rituals.
   b. rites of passage.
   c. maturation landmarks.
   d. maturation ceremonies.

2. The changes that occur which result in a child's body taking on visible signs of sexual maturity are
   a. estrogens.
   b. androgens.
   c. primary sex characteristics.
   d. secondary sex characteristics.

3. Karla has a severe problem whereby she avoids eating and denies that her behavior and resulting appearance are a problem. She is mostly likely diagnosed with
   a. AIDS.
   b. obesity.
   c. anorexia nervosa.
   d. bulimia.

4. A teenage girl eats large amounts of food and then uses laxatives to get rid of the calories. What eating disorder does she have?
   a. pica
   b. bulimia
   c. body distortion
   d. anorexia nervosa

5. Your nephew is now an adolescent. How is his thinking different from when he was nine years old?
   a. He now may be able to think abstractly.
   b. He now understands the concept of time.
   c. He can remember ideas he had previously.
   d. He now can develop a sense of right and wrong.

6. A way of thinking that was prevalent during early childhood, and is once again seen in adolescence, is called
   a. centration.
   b. egocentrism.
   c. artificialism.
   d. irreversibility.

7. Sexually active adolescents often believe they will not get pregnant nor get a sexually transmitted disease, even though they do not use any protection. This dangerous thinking is the result of the
   a. personal fable.
   b. adolescent myth.
   c. imaginary audience.
   d. confounding variable.

8. The period during which the sexual organs mature is called
   a. adolescence.
   b. puberty.
   c. spermarche.
   d. menarche.

9. Which of the following is one of the leading causes of death among young people?
   a. AIDS
   b. alcoholism
   c. smoking
   d. chlamydia

10. How many people are living with AIDS?
   a. 5 million
   b. 10 million
   c. 20 million
   d. 34 million

11. What sexually transmitted disease is diagnosed by small blisters which break open, heal, and then recurs after a period of time?
   a. AIDS
   b. gonorrhea
   c. chlamydia
   d. genital herpes

12. AIDS is spread through
   a. casual contact.
   b. exchange of body fluids.
   c. airborne molecules.
   d. contaminated food.

13. The prefrontal cortex is not fully developed until age
   a. 10.
   b. 15.
   c. 20.
   d. 25.

14. The onset of menstruation
   a. occurs at the same age in all cultures.
   b. is called puberty.
   c. occurs later in girls who are malnourished.
   d. is a secondary sex characteristic.

15. Which of the following is a primary sex characteristic?
   a. spermarche
   b. development of breasts
   c. growth of pubic hair
   d. growth of underarm hair

16. What is the impact of early or late maturation?
    a. Early maturation is both good and bad for boys and girls.
    b. Early maturation is the most harmful for boys.
    c. Late maturation is preferable for girls.
    d. Late maturation raises self-concept.

17. All of the following abilities first appear with the formal operational stage EXCEPT
    a. hypothetico-deductive reasoning.   c. trial and error problem solving.
    b. propositional thought.   d. abstract thinking.

18. The chapter describes all of the following guidelines made by health psychologists and educators to help prevent the spread of AIDS EXCEPT
    a. consider abstinence.
    b. avoiding high risk behaviors.
    c. avoiding homosexual behaviors.
    d. use of condoms.

19. Which of the following is the best approach for preventing school violence?
    a. zero tolerance policies
    b. metal detectors and security cameras
    c. moderating the school culture
    d. surprise searches of student lockers

20. Which of the following adolescents is most likely to have started smoking earlier than the others?
    a. a white male   c. a white female
    b. an African-American female   d. an African-American male

ANSWER KEYS

Practice Test – Pretest (with text page numbers)

1.	c 390	6.	b 405	11.	d 417	16.	d 392
2.	c 392	7.	c 405	12.	b 417	17.	b 414
3.	d 395	8.	b 409	13.	b 404	18.	d 403
4.	d 396	9.	c 416	14.	d 396	19.	b 406
5.	d 401	10.	c 415	15.	a 413	20.	c 414

Key Names

1. d   2. c   3. a   4. b

Key Vocabulary Terms

1. Imaginary audience is an adolescent's belief that his or her own behavior is a primary focus of others' attentions and concerns; personal fable is the view held by some adolescents that what happens to them is unique, exceptional, and shared by no one else.

2. Primary sex characteristics are associated with the development of the organs and structures of the body directly related to reproduction; secondary sex characteristics are the visible signs of sexual maturity that do not directly involve the sex organs.

3. <u>Anorexia</u> is an eating disorder in which individuals refuse to eat, while denying that their behavior and appearance are out of the ordinary; <u>bulimia</u> is characterized by binges on large quantities of food followed by purging of the food.

4. <u>Chlamydia</u> is the most common sexually transmitted disease, which is a bacterial disease; <u>genital herpes</u> is a common sexually transmitted disease, which is a virus and not unlike cold sores that sometimes appear around the mouth.

8. Alcoholics, Disease, Operations, Longitudinal, Egocentrism, Secular, Chlamydia, Exosystem, Nervosa, Corpus callosum, Ego (Adolescence)

9. Puberty, Reciprocal, Information, Menarche, Addictive, Resilience, Y (Primary)

Programmed Review

1. passage, confirmation, celebrating, physical
2. spurt, infancy
3. 2, 10, 12, taller
4. sexual, girls, boys, pituitary, androgens, estrogens, 11 or 12, 13 or 14
5. Menarche, later, nourished, healthier, stress, secular
6. Primary, secondary
7. vagina, uterus, breasts, hair
8. penis, scrotum, ejaculation, spermarche, hair, underarm, deepen, mood
9. physical, psychological, self-esteem, status, self-awareness, ejaculation, privately
10. early, athletics, popular, self-concept, school, delinquency, abuse
11. cooperative, humor
12. Cultural, ridicule, dates, self-concept, cultural
13. mixed, boys, girls, attractive, sports, social, self-concept, assertiveness, insightfulness, playful
14. dating, social, greater, ideal
15. food, 2200, 2800
16. calcium, iron, osteoporosis, anemia
17. obesity, 5, 20, psychological, exercise
18. Anorexia nervosa, psychological, death, women, white, affluent
19. Bulimia, laxatives, normal
20. fat, depressed, biological, genetic, hormonal, slender, United States
21. neurons, interconnections, gray, 1-2
22. prefrontal, judgments, impulse, dopamine
23. abstract, relative
24. formal, adolescence, abstract, experiments
25. hypothetico-deductive, explanations, propositional, logic
26. 15, later, 40 to 60, valued
27. universal, differences, rapid, continuous, tasks, underestimated, sophisticated, narrow, intelligence, postformal, cognitive
28. gradually, organize, strategies, memory, perceptual
29. intelligence, increase, capacity, dividing, understanding, abstract, hypothetically, possibilities, knowledge, metacognition
30. self-absorption, critical, criticism, fault, imaginary, fables, invulnerable
31. decline, stringently, complex, sophisticated
32. 78, math, science, geography
33. grades, achievement, schooling, lower
34. nutrition, health, crowded, homework, books, computers, genetic, variation, more
35. significant, lower, achievement, higher
36. socioeconomic, unimportant, prejudice, effort, voluntarily
37. situational, external
38. beliefs, despite, jobs

39. million, severe, 42, 50
40. pregnancy, English, economic, more, lower
41. decline, safest, frustration, coping, resiliency, love, injustices, self-centeredness, bullying, rejected
42. cultures, learning, mediation, communication, threats
43. third, 40, pleasurable, escape, illegal, peer
44. Addictive, problems, escalate
45. binge, five, four
46. Binge, higher, consensus
47. consequences, positive, families, stress
48. smaller, more, white, African-American, dependence
49. adolescent, low, 200 million, 10
50. immunodeficiency, fluids, sexually, 40, 18, sixteen, 34
51. condoms, casual, universal, invulnerability
52. deadliest, common, Chlamydia, pelvic, sterility, herpes, blisters, genitals, cure, parasite, Gonorrhea, syphilis.

Practice Test - Post Test (with text page numbers)

1.	b 390	6.	b 405	11.	d 417	16.	a 394
2.	d 393	7.	a 405	12.	b 417	17.	c 401
3.	c 397	8.	b 391	13.	c 398	18.	c 418
4.	b 397	9.	a 417	14.	c 392	19.	c 410
5.	a 400	10.	d 417	15.	a 393	20.	c 415

Chapter 12

Social and Personality Development in Adolescence

CHAPTER OUTLINE

◆ Identity: Asking "Who Am I?"
- Self-Concept: What Am I Like?
- Self-Esteem: How Do I Like Myself?
- Identity Formation in Adolescence: Change or Crisis?
- Marcia's Approach to Identity Development: Updating Erikson
- Identity, Race, and Ethnicity
- Depression and Suicide: Psychological Difficulties in Adolescence

◆ Relationships: Family and Friends
- Family Ties: Reassessing Relations with Relations
- Relationships with Peers: The Importance of Belonging
- Popularity and Rejection
- Conformity: Peer Pressure in Adolescence
- Juvenile Delinquency: The Crimes of Adolescence

◆ Dating, Sexual Behavior, and Teenage Pregnancy
- Dating: Close Relationships in the 21st Century
- Sexual Relationships
- Sexual Orientation: Heterosexuality, Homosexuality, and Bisexuality

LEARNING OBJECTIVES

After you have read and studied this chapter, you should be able to answer the following questions.

1. How does the development of self-concept, self-esteem, and identity proceed during adolescence?
2. What dangers do adolescents face as they deal with the stresses of adolescence?
3. How does the quality of relationships with family and peers change during adolescence?
4. What are gender, race, and ethnic relations like in adolescence?
5. What does it mean to be popular and unpopular in adolescence, and how do adolescents respond to peer pressure?
6. What are the functions and characteristics of dating during adolescence?
7. How does sexuality develop in the adolescent years?

PRACTICE TEST – PRETEST

Circle the correct answer for each multiple choice question and check your answers with the Answer Key at the end of this chapter.

1. Research has shown that during early adolescence girls' self-esteem tends to be lower and more vulnerable than boys'. This appears to be related to the fact that girls are concerned
   a. more with social success.
   b. less with physical appearance.
   c. less with academic achievement.
   d. only with getting married.

2. Melissa is seventeen years old and really searching for a sense of who she is and what is unique about her. According to Erikson's theory, in what psychosocial stage is she?
   a. initiative versus guilt
   b. identity versus identity confusion
   c. intimacy versus isolation
   d. autonomy versus shame and doubt

3. A friend of yours did not get the opportunity to explore career choices on his own. His parents told him that he would be working in the family convenience store after graduation, which he agreed to do, although, he had wanted to look into other options also. Your friend experienced which identity status?
   a. identity foreclosure   c. identity diffusion
   b. identity achievement   d. psychological moratorium

4. What percent of adolescents experience major depression at one time or another?
   a. 3 percent   c. 53 percent
   b. 33 percent   d. 66 percent

5. Adolescent girls and boys use different methods to attempt suicide. Girls tend to use _____, while boys more often use _____.
   a. guns; drugs   c. drugs; hanging
   b. drugs; guns   d. hanging; auto accident

6. Adolescent autonomy is more likely to be found in
   a. Japan.   c. China.
   b. the United States.   d. Korea.

7. Julie, who is 14 years old, and her parents are likely to hold different views on matters of
   a. politics.   c. abortion.
   b. religion.   d. styles of dress.

8. When high school students belong to clubs that support many of their attitudes and ideals, the groups are functioning as
   a. peer groups.   c. self-identification.
   b. reference groups.   d. mutual regulation.

9. Adolescents who are liked by some and disliked by others are called
   a. controversial.   c. neglected.
   b. popular.   d. rejected.

10. According to the text, which of the following is NOT a warning sign of adolescent suicide?
    a. preoccupation with death in literature   c. writing a will
    b. illicit drug use   d. dramatic changes in behavior

11. Many researchers believe that sexual orientation develops from
    a. genetic factors.
    c. environmental factors.
    b. physiological factors.
    d. a combination of factors.

12. The teen pregnancy rate is higher in the United States than other developed countries. What is believed to contribute to this problem?
    a. frequent sexual activity
    b. lower standards of living
    c. earlier onset of sexual activity
    d. ineffective birth control and limited sex education

13. Amanda's peers call her and the 199 other band members in her school "geeks." This specifically refers to what type of adolescent group?
    a. clique
    c. crowd
    b. race cleavage
    d. sex cleavage

14. Jeb is psychologically normal but shoplifts when pressured by his peers. How would he be classified?
    a. prosocial delinquent
    c. socialized delinquent
    b. antisocial delinquent
    d. undersocialized delinquent

15. David has a more accurate understanding of who he is now that he is an adolescent. This is his
    a. self-esteem.
    c. reference group.
    b. self-concept.
    d. sense of autonomy.

16. According to Marcia, an adolescent who has explored alternatives but not yet made a commitment is in
    a. identity achievement.
    c. moratorium.
    b. identity foreclosure.
    d. identity diffusion.

17. What percent of arrests for serious crimes involve some under the age of 18?
    a. 3 percent
    c. 23 percent
    b. 16 percent
    d. 46 percent

18. If you suspect that a friend is contemplating suicide, you should
    a. avoid specific discussions about suicidal thought.
    b. leave the person alone to work out his or her problems.
    c. make a contract with the person.
    d. respect the person's privacy.

19. In traditional preindustrial cultures
    a. the amount of parent-child conflict is very high.
    b. individualism is not highly valued.
    c. adolescents are more inclined to risk independence.
    d. adolescents are more likely to engage in risky behavior.

20. For most adolescents, their initiation into sexuality comes from
    a. oral sex.
    c. sexual assault.
    b. masturbation.
    d. sexual intercourse.

KEY NAMES

Match the following names with the most accurate description and check your answers with the Answer Key at the end of this chapter.

1. ___ Erik Erikson   a. identification with parents

2. ___ Sigmund Freud   b. identity statuses

3. ___ Alfred Kinsey   c. womens's identity development

4. ___ James Marcia   d. sex researcher

5. ___ Carol Gilligan   e. identity versus identity confusion

KEY VOCABULARY TERMS

Explain the differences between each of the following pairs of terms.

1. Cliques; Crowd

2. Reference groups; Peer pressure

3. Undersocialized delinquents; Socialized delinquents

Fill in the blanks for the term for each definition. The first letters of the terms, from top to bottom, will spell the term for the last definition. (NOTE: Some terms may be from previous chapters.)

4. _ _ _ _ _ _ _ _ _   The status of adolescents who may have explored various identity alternatives to some degree, but have not yet committed themselves.

   _ _ _ _ _ _ _   Having independence and a sense of control over one's life.

   _ _ _ _ _ _ _ _ _   Adolescent delinquents who know and subscribe to the norms of society, and who are fairly normal psychologically.

   _ _ _ _ _ _ _ _   An agent that causes birth defects.

   _ _ _ _ _ _ _ _ _ _ _ _ _ _   Adolescent delinquents who are raised with little discipline, or with harsh, uncaring parental supervision.

   _ _ _ _ _ _ _   Children who are actually disliked and whose peers may react to them in an obviously negative manner.

   _ _ _ _ _ _ _ _   Someone who can speak two languages is _____.

   _ _ _ _ _ _ _ _ _ _   The status of adolescents who commit to a particular identity following a period of crisis during which they consider various alternatives.

   _ _ _ _ _ _ _ _   Sternberg's theory of intelligence.

   _ _ _ _ _ _ _   Diffusion is the status of adolescents who consider various identity alternatives, but never commit to one, or never even consider identity options in any conscious way.

_ _ _ _ _ _ _   A form of conditioning in which the response is determined by its consequences.

_ _ _ _ _ _ _ _ _   Children who receive relatively little attention from their peers in the form of either positive or negative interactions.

Sexual self-stimulation is _ _ _ _ _ _ _ _ _ _ _ _.

Write out the definitions for each of the following terms and give a specific example of each.

5. Identity versus identity confusion stage
6. Identity foreclosure
7. Cluster suicide
8. Identity achievement
9. Sex cleavage
10. Moratorium

PROGRAMMED REVIEW

Identity: Asking "Who Am I?"

1. Adolescents' _____ capacities become more adultlike. The dramatic physical changes during puberty make adolescents acutely aware of their own _____ and of the fact that others are _____ to them in ways to which they are unaccustomed.

Self-Concept: What Am I Like?

2. Adolescents' view of the self becomes more _____ and coherent and they can see various aspects of the self _____. They look at the self from a _____ perspective. During the early years of adolescence adolescents may be troubled by multiple aspects of their _____.

Self-Esteem: How Do I Like Myself?

3. Although adolescents become increasingly accurate in understanding who they are (their _____), this knowledge does not guarantee that they _____ themselves (their _____).

4. During early adolescence, girls' self-esteem tends to be _____ and more _____ than boys'. Girls are more highly concerned about _____ appearance and _____ success in addition to academic achievement. Society's stereotypical gender expectations may lead boys to feel that they should be _____, _____, and _____ all of the time.

5. Adolescents of higher _____ generally have higher self-esteem particularly during middle and later adolescence. Early studies argued that _____ status would lead to lower self-esteem, however most recent research suggests that African Americans differ _____ from whites in their levels of self-esteem. A stronger sense of racial _____ is related to a higher level of self-esteem in African Americans and Hispanics.

6. Teenagers in general focus their preferences and priorities on those aspects of their lives at which they are _____. Self-esteem may be influenced by a complex _____ of factors. Some developmental psychologists have considered race and gender simultaneously coining the germ _____ to refer to their joint influence.

Identity Formation in Adolescence: Change or Crisis?

7. According to Erikson, the search for identity inevitably leads some adolescents into substantial psychological _____ as they encounter the adolescent identity crisis. His theory suggests that adolescence is the time of the _____ stage.

8. Adolescents who stumble in their efforts to find a suitable identity may adopt _____ unacceptable roles or may have difficulty forming and maintaining long-lasting close personal _____ later on in life. Those who are successful in forging an appropriate identity learn their unique _____ and they develop an accurate _____ of who they are.

9. Societal _____ are high during this stage for adolescents. Adolescents increasingly rely on their friends and _____ as sources of information and their _____ on adults declines.

10. Erikson suggests that adolescents pursue a psychological _____, a period during which adolescents take time off from the upcoming responsibilities of adulthood and _____ various roles and possibilities. Many adolescents cannot, for practical reasons pursue this state, some for _____ reasons.

11. One criticism that has been raised against Erickson's theory is that he uses that _____ identity as the standard against which to compare _____ identity. _____ has suggested that women develop identity through the establishment of relationships.

Marcia's Approach to Identity Development: Updating Erikson

12. _____ suggests that identity can be seen in terms of two characteristics. _____ is a period of identity development in which an adolescent consciously chooses between various alternatives and makes decisions. _____ is psychological investment in a course of action or an ideology.

13. In identity _____, adolescents commit to a particular identity. They tend to be the most psychologically _____, higher in achievement _____, and _____ reasoning than adolescents of any other status. In identity _____, adolescents have committed to an identity but did not pass through a period of crisis. They tend to have a high need for social _____ and tend to be _____. Adolescents in _____ have explored various alternatives to some degree, but have not yet committed themselves. They show relatively high _____ and experience psychological _____. In identity _____, adolescents consider various alternatives, but never commit to one. They lack commitment, impairing their ability to form close _____ and are often socially _____.

Identity, Race and Ethnicity

14. Adolescents are told that society should be _____ blind. A traditional cultural _____ model holds that individual cultural identities should be assimilated into a unified culture in the United States. The _____ society model suggests that U.S. society is made up of diverse, coequal cultural groups that should _____ their individual cultural features. Identity in minority adolescents is facilitated by the formation of _____ identity in which adolescents draw from their own cultural identity while integrating themselves into the _____ culture.

Depression and Suicide: Psychological Difficulties in Adolescence

15. Only a small minority of adolescents, approximately ____ percent, experience _____ depression, a full-blown psychological disorder in which depression is severe and lingers for long periods. Adolescent _____ experience depression more often than _____.

16. In cases of severe long-term depression, _____ factors are often involved. Some adolescents seem to be _____ predisposed to experience depression. Environmental and _____ factors relating to the extraordinary changes in the social lives of adolescents are also an important cause.

17. Some psychologists speculate that _____ is more pronounced for girls than for boys in adolescence. They may be more apt than boys to react to stress by turning _____, thereby experiencing a sense of _____ and hopelessness. Boys more often react by externalizing the stress and acting more _____ or aggressively.

18. The rate of adolescent suicide in the United States has _____ in the last 30 years. Suicide is the _____ most common cause of death in the 15- to 24-year-old age group, after _____ and _____. The rate of suicide is higher for _____ than _____, although girls _____ suicide more frequently. Boys tend to use more _____ means, whereas girls are more apt to choose the more peaceful strategy of _____ overdose.

19. The risk of suicide is heightened by _____, _____ inhibition, perfectionism, and a high level of _____ and _____. The rate of suicide among drug and alcohol _____ is also relatively high. In _____ suicide, one suicide leads to attempts by others to kill themselves.

20. Warning signs of suicide include direct or indirect _____ about suicide, _____ difficulties, making _____ as if preparing for a long trip, writing a _____, loss of _____ or excessive _____, general _____, dramatic changes in _____, and preoccupation with _____ in music, art, or literature.

21. The U.S. Public Health Service makes several suggestions for dealing with someone contemplating suicide including _____ to the person; _____ without judging; talk specifically about _____ thoughts; evaluate the _____; be _____; take charge of finding _____; make the environment _____; do not keep suicide talk or threats _____; do not challenge, dare, or use verbal _____ treatment; make a _____ with the person; and beware of _____ moods and seemingly quick _____.

Relationships: Family and Friends

Family Ties: Reassessing Relations with Relations

22. Adolescents increasingly seek _____, independence, and a sense of control over their lives. Most parents intellectually realize that this shift is a _____ part of adolescence, representing one of the primary developmental tasks of the period, and in many ways they welcome it as a sign of their children's _____.

23. In most families, teenagers' autonomy grows _____ over the course of adolescence. Increasing autonomy leads them to perceive parents in less _____ terms and more as persons in their own right. Adolescents come to _____ more on themselves and to feel more like _____ individuals.

24. At the start of adolescence, the relationship tends to be _____ in that parents hold most of the _____ and influence over the relationship. By the end of adolescence, power and influence have become more _____.

25. In Western societies, which tend to value _____, adolescents seek autonomy relatively early. In contrast Asian societies are _____, promoting the idea that the well-being of the _____ is more important than that of the _____.

26. According to one argument, there is a _____ gap, a deep divide between parents and children in attitudes, values, aspirations, and worldviews. This gap, when it exists, is really quite _____. There is typically no gap in the value that parents and adolescents place on the _____ they have with one another. The majority of relationships are more _____ than _____ and they help adolescents avoid _____ pressure.

27. Parents and teens hold similar attitudes about social and _____ issues, but they often hold different views on matters of _____ taste. The newly sophisticated _____ of adolescents leads teenagers to think about parental rules in more complex ways. The argumentativeness and assertiveness of early adolescence at first may lead to an increase in _____.

28. The amount of parent-child conflict is lower in _____ preindustrial cultures. Individualism is not valued as _____ and adolescents are less inclined to seek _____.

Relationships with Peers: The Importance of Belonging

29. The seemingly compulsive need to _____ with friends demonstrates the role that peers play in adolescence. Peers provide the opportunity to compare and evaluate _____, abilities, and even physical changes—a process called social _____.

30. Adolescence is a time of _____, of trying out new roles and conduct. _____ groups are groups of people with whom one compares oneself. They present a set of _____ or standards against which adolescents can judge their social success.

31. Rather than defining people in _____ terms relating to what they do, adolescents use _____ terms packed with greater subtleties. Adolescent groups include _____, composed of from 1 to 12 people who have frequent social interactions with one another; and _____, that are larger, comprising individuals who share particular characteristics but may not interact with one another.

32. As children enter adolescence from middle childhood, their group of friends are composed almost universally of _____ individuals. This sex segregation is called the sex _____. Both the _____ surge that marks puberty and causes the maturation of the sex organs and the _____ pressures suggesting that the time is appropriate for romantic involvement lead to a change in the ways adolescents view the opposite sex. Cliques and crowds become less _____ at the end of adolescence.

33. The pattern of race segregation is repeated over and over in schools and _____ throughout the United States. During elementary school, and even during early adolescence, there is a fair amount of _____ among students of differing ethnicities.

34. Minority students actively seek support from others who share their minority _____. Socioeconomic status differences between people of different races and ethnicities may keep _____ at low levels. The lack of interaction between members of different racial and ethnic groups relates to differences in _____ performance.

35. Minority students may feel that the white majority is prejudiced, _____, and hostile, and they may prefer to stick to same-race groups. Majority students may assume that minority group members are _____ and unfriendly.

Popularity and Rejection

36. In contrast to popular adolescents, who are mostly liked, _____ adolescents are liked by some and disliked by others. _____ adolescents are uniformly disliked and _____ adolescents are neither liked nor disliked. Popular and controversial adolescents both have _____ overall status, more close _____, engage more frequently in activities with their _____, and _____ more about themselves to others. They are also more involved in _____ school activities.

Conformity: Peer Pressure in Adolescence

37. A prevalent view in the United States is that teenagers are highly _____ to peer pressure. When it comes to _____ matters, adolescents are more likely to turn to adults. In middle and late adolescence, teenagers turn to those they see as _____ on a given dimension. Adolescents conform less to both peers and adults as they develop increasing _____ over their lives.

Juvenile Delinquency: The Crimes of Adolescence

38. Adolescents, along with young _____, are more likely to commit crimes than any other age group. Some of the reasons for this have to do with the _____ of certain behaviors which are illegal for adolescents but not for older individuals, but adolescents are disproportionately involved in _____ crimes as well. Overall, _____ percent of all arrests for serious crimes involved a person under the age of 18.

39. _____ delinquents are adolescents who are raised with little discipline, or with harsh, uncaring parental supervision. These children have never been appropriately _____ and simply have not learned standards of _____ to regulate their own behavior. They tend to be relatively _____ and violent fairly early in life. They also are more likely to have been diagnosed with _____ as children and tend to be less _____ than average. As adults, they fit a psychological pattern called _____ personality disorder and are relatively unlikely to be successfully _____.

40. Most adolescents are _____ delinquents who know and subscribe to the norms of society. They are typically highly influenced by their _____ and their delinquency often occurs in _____.

Dating, Sexual Behavior, and Teenage Pregnancy

Dating: Close Relationships in the 21st Century

41. Society often encourages dating in adolescence, in part for adolescents to explore relationships that might eventually lead to _____. Some adolescents think that dating is outmoded and limiting, and favor _____ as more appropriate.

42. Dating is a way to learn how to establish _____ with another individual. It can provide _____ and _____. Dating can even be used to develop a sense of one's own _____.

43. Minority parents may try to control their children's dating behavior in an effort to preserve the minority group's _____ values.

Sexual Relationships

44. For most adolescents, their initiation into sexuality comes from _____, sexual self-stimulation. For males, it is most frequent in the _____ teens and then begins to decline, whereas females begin more slowly and reach a maximum _____. Experts on sexual behavior view masturbation as _____, healthy, and harmless.

45. The age at which adolescents first have sexual intercourse has been steadily _____ over the last 50 years. Around _____ of adolescents begin having intercourse between the ages of 15 and 18 and _____ percent have had intercourse by age 20.

46. The prevailing norm several decades ago was the _____ standard, in which premarital sex was considered permissible for males but not for females. Today it has been supplanted by _____ with affection. For some in our U.S. society premarital intercourse is viewed as permissible for both men and women if it occurs in the context of a long-term _____ or loving relationship.

Sexual Orientation: Heterosexuality, Homosexuality, and Bisexuality

47. The most frequent sexual orientation pattern is _____, sexual attraction and behavior directed toward the opposite sex. Some teenagers are _____, in which their sexual attraction and behavior is oriented to members of their own sex. Many homosexual males prefer the term _____ and female homosexual the term _____. Others find that they are _____, sexually attracted to people of both sexes.

48. Homosexuality and heterosexuality are not completely _____ sexual orientations. Kinsey argued that sexual orientation should be viewed as a _____.

49. Although sexual _____ relates to the object of one's sexual interests, gender _____ is the gender a person believes he or she is psychologically. _____ individuals feel that they have been born the wrong physical sex.

50. In the last 10 years teenage birthrate has dropped _____ percent. The overall pregnancy rate for teenagers is _____ births per 1,000. New initiatives have raised the awareness of the risks of _____ sex. The rate of sexual _____ amount teenagers has declined. The use of _____ and other forms of contraception has increased. Substitutes for sexual intercourse may be more _____.

51. Evidence suggests that _____ and _____ factors may play an important role. Research finds that various structures of the _____ are different in homosexuals and heterosexuals and _____ production also seems to be linked to sexual orientation. Freud argued that homosexuality was the result of inappropriate _____ with the opposite sex parent. Most experts believe that sexual orientation develops out of a complex _____ of genetic, physiological, and environmental factors.

52. Adolescents who find they are homosexuals are at greater risk for _____, and _____ rates are significantly higher for homosexual adolescents than heterosexual adolescents.

CRITICAL THINKING QUESTIONS

To test your understanding of the topics covered in this chapter, write out your answers to the following essay questions from the text in the spaces provided.

1. How might an adolescent's changing self-concept relate to changes in his or her cognitive development?

2. What are some consequences of the shift from reliance on adults to reliance on peers? Are there advantages? Dangers? Explain.

3. Do you believe that all four of Marcia's identity statuses can lead to reassessment and different choices later in life? Do you think some statuses are more likely than others to produce this type of rethinking? Why?

4. How would you design a high school program to reduce depression amongst adolescents? Would your tactics be the same or different for females and males? What would be the major barriers to implementing such a program?

5. In what ways do you think parents with different styles–authoritarian, authoritative, and permissive–tend to react to attempts to establish autonomy during adolescence?

6. Why does there appear to be no real generation gap in most attitudes, despite adolescents' need to question authority?

7. In what ways does membership in cliques or crowds constrain behavior? Do such groupings disappear in adulthood?

8. How do the findings about conformity and peer pressure reported in this chapter relate to adolescents' developing cognitive abilities?

9. Given what you learned in this chapter and your awareness of U.S. society, is it both healthy and normal for teenagers to engage in sexual intercourse? Why or why not. What arguments or concerns do people with the opposite opinion than yours raise?

10. How might the interplay of genetic, physiological, and environmental factors influence sexual orientation?

PRACTICE TEST – POST TEST

Circle the correct answer for each multiple choice question and check your answers with the Answer Key at the end of this chapter.

1. Carlos is a 17-year-old male who is sexually active. It is most probable that Carlos's sexual attraction and behavior is
   a. asexual.
   b. heterosexual.
   c. homosexual.
   d. bisexual.

2. Jeanne is an adolescent taking time of from both work and school to back-pack around Europe in an attempt to "find herself." What period of identity development is she experiencing?
   a. identity foreclosure   c. identity diffusion
   b. identity achievement   d. psychological moratorium

3. When people lack direction and avoid talking or thinking about the future, they tend to just hang out with friends and not move toward any particular goal. What identity status have they adopted?
   a. identity diffusion   c. identity moratorium
   b. identity foreclosure   d. identity achievement

4. What is the third most common cause of death in the 15-to-24-year-old age group?
   a. suicide   c. homicides
   b. accidents   d. infectious disease

5. Because Jackson heard about a classmate who committed suicide, he then attempted suicide. This is called
   a. mass suicide.
   b. cluster suicide.
   c. sympathetic suicide.
   d. self-fulfilling prophecy.

6. It is typical during the early teenage years for kids to hang out with a group of their same gender. This type of grouping is called
   a. sex cleavage.
   b. peer grouping.
   c. sex clustering.
   d. reference circle.

7. Adolescents will often evaluate their own personal abilities, behaviors, personality characteristics, appearance, and general sense of self against the characteristics of others. This process is called
   a. peer group evaluation.
   b. self-identification.
   c. mutual regulation.
   d. social comparison.

8. An adolescent clique consists of
   a. a highly cohesive group of 2 to 12 peers.
   b. a reference group that one aspires to be like.
   c. a group of any size with whom one shares a particular function or status.
   d. 15 to 30 peers that form the set of people with whom one sometimes interacts.

9. What percent of serious violent crimes are committed by adolescents?
   a. 25 percent
   b. 40 percent
   c. 65 percent
   d. 80 percent

10. The overall rate of teenager pregnancy is _____ per 1,000 births.
    a. 16
    b. 43
    c. 167
    d. 203

11. A couple believes that engaging in premarital intercourse is permissible because they are in a committed, long-term relationship. What society norm governing sexual conduct do they follow?
    a. don't ask, don't tell
    b. the double standard
    c. wait until commitment
    d. permissiveness with affection

12. When does true intimacy first become more common?
    a. mid-adolescence
    b. late adolescence
    c. early adulthood
    d. middle adulthood

13. Adolescents' view of the self differs from that of children in all of the following ways EXCEPT
    a. they view traits as concrete entities.
    b. they take both their views and those of others into account.
    c. their view of the self is more organized and coherent.
    d. they can see various aspects of the self simultaneously.

14. According to Marcia, an adolescent who has explored alternatives and made a commitment to a particular identity is in
    a. identity achievement.
    b. identity foreclosure.
    c. moratorium.
    d. identity diffusion.

15. Which of the following views holds that the United States is a "melting pot" of cultures?
    a. identity status model
    b. bicultural identity model
    c. pluralistic society model
    d. cultural assimilation model

16. Which of the following is an accurate statement about adolescent suicide?
    a. The rate is higher for girls than for boys.
    b. Girls attempt suicide more frequently than boys.
    c. It is the leading cause of death for adolescents.
    d. It has decreased over the past ten years.

17. Concerning the decline in teenage pregnancy, it would be most accurate to say that
    a. the rate of sexual intercourse has increased but rates of pregnancy have decreased.
    b. all high schools have comprehensive programs sexual education programs.
    c. the use of condoms has increased.
    d. oral and anal sex are used as alternatives to intercourse.

18. At the end of adolescence, cliques and crowds
    a. become more powerful.
    b. become more sex segregated.
    c. succumb to the increased male-female pairing.
    d. are still the center of adolescent social life.

19. Which two groups of adolescents have high status?
    a. popular and neglected   c. neglected and rejected
    b. controversial and rejected   d. popular and controversial

20. By age 20, what percent of adolescents have had sexual intercourse?
    a. 20 percent   c. 80 percent
    b. 50 percent   d. 100 percent

ANSWER KEYS

Practice Test – Pretest (with text page numbers)

1.	a 425	6.	b 437	11.	d 450	16.	a 429
2.	b 428	7.	d 438	12.	d 451	17.	b 446
3.	a 430	8.	b 441	13.	c 441	18.	b 435
4.	a 432	9.	a 443	14.	c 446	19.	a 440
5.	b 433	10.	b 434	15.	c 441	20.	b 449

Key Names

1. e   2. a   3. d   4. b   5. c

Key Vocabulary Terms

1. Cliques are groups of from two to twelve people whose members have frequent social interaction with one another; crowds are larger groups than cliques, composed of individuals who share particular characteristics but who may not interact with one another.

2. Reference groups are groups of people with whom one compares oneself; peer pressure is the influence of one's peers to conform to their behavior and attitudes.

3. Undersocialized delinquents are those adolescents raised with little discipline or with harsh, uncaring parental supervision; socialized delinquents are those adolescents who subscribe to the norms of society and are fairly normal psychologically.

4. Moratorium, Autonomy, Socialized, Teratogen, Undersocialized, Rejected, Bilingual, Achievement, Triarchic, Identity, Operant, Neglected (Masturbation)

Programmed Review

1. intellectual, bodies, reacting
2. organized, simultaneously, psychological, personality
3. self-concept, like, self-esteem
4. lower, vulnerable, physical, social, confident, fearless, and tough
5. SES, minority, little, identity
6. best, combination, ethgender
7. difficulties, identity versus identity confusion
8. socially, relationships, capabilities, sense
9. pressures, peers, dependence,
10. moratorium, explore, economic
11. male, female, Gilligan
12. Marcia, Crisis, Commitment,
13. achievement, healthy, motivation, moral, foreclosure, approval, authoritarian, moratorium, anxiety, conflict diffusion, relationships, withdrawn
14. color, assimilation, pluralistic, preserve, bicultural, dominant
15. 3, major, girls, boys
16. biological, genetically, social
17. stress, inward, helplessness, impulsively
18. tripled, third, accidents, homicide, boys, girls, attempt, violent, drug
19. depression, social, stress, anxiety, abusers, cluster
20. talk, school, arrangements, will, appetite, eating, depression, behavior, death
21. talk, listen, suicidal, situation, supportive, help, safe, secret, shock, contract, elevated, recoveries
22. autonomy, normal, growth
23. gradually, idealized, depend, separate
24. asymmetrical, power, balanced
25. individualism, collectivistic, group, individual
26. generation, narrow, relationship, positive, negative, peer
27. political, personal, reasoning, conflict
28. traditional, highly, independence
29. communicate, opinions, comparison
30. experimentation, Reference, norms
31. concrete, abstract, cliques, crowds
32. same-sex, cleavage, hormonal, societal, powerful
33. colleges, integration
34. status, integration, academic
35. discriminatory, antagonistic
36. controversial, Rejected, neglected, higher, friends, peers, disclose, extracurricular
37. susceptible, nonsocial, experts, autonomy
38. adults, definition, violent, 16
39. Undersocialized, socialized, conduct, aggressive, attention deficit disorder, intelligent, antisocial, rehabilitated
40. socialized, peers, groups
41. marriage, hooking-up
42. intimacy, entertainment, prestige, identity
43. traditional
44. masturbation, early, later, normal
45. declining, half, 80
46. double, permissiveness, committed
47. heterosexual, homosexual, gay, lesbian, bisexual
48. distinct, continuum
49. orientation, identity, Transgendered
50. 30, 43, unprotected, intercourse, condoms, prevalent
51. genetic, biological, brain, hormone, identification, interplay
52. depression, suicide

Practice Test - Post test (with text page numbers)

1.	b 450	6.	a 441	11.	d 449	16.	b 433
2.	d 429	7.	d 440	12.	b 448	17.	c 451
3.	a 431	8.	a 441	13.	a 424	18.	c 441
4.	a 433	9.	a 446	14.	a 429	19.	d 443
5.	b 433	10.	b 451	15.	d 431	20.	c 449

Chapter 13

Physical and Cognitive Development in Early Adulthood

CHAPTER OUTLINE

◈ Physical Development and Stress
- ♦ Physical Development and the Senses
- ♦ Motor Functioning, Fitness, and Health: Staying Well
- ♦ Eating, Nutrition, and Obesity: A Weighty Concern
- ♦ Physical Disabilities: Coping with Physical Challenge
- ♦ Stress and Coping: Dealing with Life's Challenges

◈ Cognitive Development
- ♦ Intellectual Growth in Early Adulthood
- ♦ Postformal Thought
- ♦ Schaie's Stages of Development
- ♦ Intelligence: What Matters in Early Adulthood?
- ♦ Life Events and Cognitive Development

◈ College: Pursuing Higher Education
- ♦ The Demographics of Higher Education
- ♦ The Changing College Student: Never Too Late to Go to College?
- ♦ College Adjustment: Reacting to the Demands of College Life
- ♦ Gender and College Performance
- ♦ Dropping Out of College

LEARNING OBJECTIVES

After you have read and studied this chapter, you should be able to answer the following questions.

1. How does the body develop during early adulthood, and to what risks are young adults exposed?
2. What are the effects of stress and what can be done about it?
3. Does cognitive development continue in young adulthood?
4. How is intelligence defined today, and what causes cognitive growth in young adults?
5. Who attends college today, and how is the college population changing?
6. What do students learn in college, and what difficulties do they face?

PRACTICE TEST – PRETEST

Circle the correct answer for each of the following multiple choice questions and check your answers with the Answer Key at the end of this chapter.

1. In young adulthood _____ have twice the death rate of _____
   a. Caucasians, African Americans
   b. Caucasians, Hispanics
   c. African Americans, Caucasians
   d. Hispanics, Caucasians

2. What is the most frequent cause of death for a young adult African American?
   a. AIDS
   b. cancer
   c. murder
   d. heart disease

3. Being exposed to long-term, continuous stress typically results in
   a. failure of the sympathetic nervous system.
   b. lowering of the heart rate and blood pressure.
   c. a reduction of the body's ability to deal with stress.
   d. a reduction in disease due to a constant secretion of white blood cells.

4. When people are faced with a difficult situation, they assess the degree to which they will be able to deal with the problem. This is called
   a. fact-finding.
   b. assessment.
   c. primary appraisal.
   d. secondary appraisal.

5. Piaget is to formal operations as Labouvie-Vief is to
   a. postformal thought.
   b. postraditional thought.
   c. postmodern thought.
   d. postoperational thought.

6. Acquisitive stage is to childhood and adolescence as the _____ stage is to young adulthood.
   a. executive stage
   b. achieving stage
   c. acquisitive stage
   d. responsible stage

7. According to Schaie, what is the central task of late adulthood?
   a. acquisition
   b. achievement
   c. reintegration
   d. social responsibility

8. Traditional intelligence tests tend to focus on what aspect of intelligence?
   a. contextual
   b. crystallized
   c. experiential
   d. componential

9. What percent of college students have gradated after six years?
   a. 37 percent
   b. 63 percent
   c. 87 percent
   d. 93 percent

10. What percentage of college students is 25 years of age or older?
    a. 15
    b. 20
    c. 25
    d. 33

11. What percent of all college students report having at least one significant psychological issue?
    a. 25 percent
    b. 50 percent
    c. 75 percent
    d. 100 percent

12. Eyesight changes sufficiently to be noticeable in the
    a. teen years.
    b. twenties.
    c. thirties.
    d. forties.

13. Which of the following is NOT a major cause of death for those 25 to 34?
    a. stroke
    b. heart disease
    c. cancer
    d. AIDS

14. Illness and disease overtake accidents as the leading cause of death at age
    a. 25.
    b. 35.
    c. 45.
    d. 55.

15. Between 1998 and 1999, obesity in the United States increased by
    a. 2 percent.
    b. 6 percent.
    c. 10 percent.
    d. 16 percent.

16. Researchers in the field of psychoneuroimmunology study the relationship of all of the following EXCEPT
    a. the brain.
    b. the immune system.
    c. psychological factors.
    d. the culture.

17. Selena works hard to keep a positive attitude about her job even though she has trouble with her boss. Selena is employing what type of coping?
    a. problem focused
    b. emotion focused
    c. social support
    d. defensive

18. Sternberg contends that success in a career necessitates which type of intelligence?
    a. emotional
    b. componential
    c. experiential
    d. practical

19. In which individuals does creativity peak at the latest age?
    a. architects
    b. poets
    c. novelists
    d. chamber musicians

20. Perry found that students entered schools using what type of thinking?
    a. multiple
    b. relativistic
    c. dualistic
    d. postformal

KEY NAMES

Match the following names with the most accurate description and check your answers with the Answer Key at the end of this chapter.

1. ____ Gisela Labouvie-Vief   a. academic dissatisfaction

2. ____ Arnold Lazarus   b. dualistic thinking

3. ____ William Perry   c. formal operations

4. ____ Jean Piaget   d. postformal thought

5. ____ K. Warner Schaie   e. stages of adult thinking

6. ____ Claude Steele   f. stages of stress

7. ____ Robert Sternberg   g. triarchic theory of intelligence

KEY VOCABULARY TERMS

Explain the relationship between the following pairs of terms.

1. Primary appraisal; Secondary appraisal

2. Executive stage; Reintegrative stage

Define the terms below and give a specific example for each term.

3. Stress
4. Senescence
5. Psychoneuroimmunology
6. Postformal thought
7. First-year adjustment reaction
8. Achieving stage
9. Practical intelligence
10. Creativity

Fill in the blanks for the term next to each definition. The first letters of the terms from top to bottom will spell out the last term in the puzzle. (NOTE: Some terms may be from previous chapters.)

11. _ _ _ _ _ _ _ _ _ _ _ _   Medical problems caused by the interaction of psychological, emotional, and physical difficulties and _____ disorders.

_ _ _ _ _ _ _ _ _ _   The stage where the major concerns of middle-aged adults relate to personal situations, including protecting and nourishing their spouses, families, and careers.

_ _ _ _ _ _ _ _ _ _   According to Schaie, the first stage of cognitive development, encompassing all of childhood and adolescence, in which the main developmental task is to acquire information.

_ _ _ _ _ _   The effort to control, reduce, or learn to tolerate the threats that lead to stress.

_ _ _ _ _ _ _ _   Sternberg's theory of intelligence.

_ _ _ _ _ _ _ _ _ _ _   The set of skills that underlie the accurate assessment, evaluation, expression, and regulation of emotions is emotional _____.

_ _ _ _ _ _ _ _ _   Combination of responses/ideas in novel ways.

_ _ _ _ _ _ _ _ _   The point reached by young adults in which intelligence is applied to specific situations involving the attainment of long-term goals regarding careers, family, and societal contributions.

_ _ _ _ _ _ _ _ _ _ _   Research following a group over time.

According to Sternberg, intelligence that is learned primarily by observing others and modeling their behavior is _ _ _ _ _ _ _ _ _ intelligence.

179

PROGRAMMED REVIEW

Fill in the blanks in the following programmed review and check your answers with the Answer Key at the end of this chapter.

Physical Development and Stress

Physical Development and the Senses

1. In most respects, physical development and maturation are _____ at early adulthood, and biological aging or _____ has begun. Some people, particularly late _____, continue to gain height in their early 20s. The _____ continues to grow in both size and weight, reaching its maximum during early adulthood.

2. There are changes in the _____ of the eye. Hearing is at its peak and women can detect _____ tones more readily than men. The other senses do not begin to deteriorate until the _____ or _____.

Motor Functioning, Fitness and Health: Staying Well

3. Less than _____ percent of Americans are involved in sufficient regular exercise to keep them in good physical shape, and less than a _____ engage in moderate regular exercise. People of _____ socioeconomic status often have neither the time nor the money to engage in regular exercise.

4. According to the recommendations from the American College of Sports Medicine and the Centers for Disease Control, people should accumulate at least _____ minutes of moderate physical activity at least _____ days per week. The time spent exercising can be continuous or occur in bouts of at least _____ minutes.

5. Exercise increases _____ fitness. Lung capacity increases, raising _____. Muscles become _____, and the body is more _____ and maneuverable. The range of movement is _____ and the muscles, tendons, and ligaments are more _____. Exercise during this period helps reduce _____, the thinning of the bones, in later life.

6. Exercise may also optimize the _____ response of the body, helping it fight off disease, and may even decrease _____ and anxiety and reduce _____. It can provide people with a sense of _____ over their bodies, as well as impart a feeling of _____. It also increases _____.

7. Health risks in general are relatively _____ during early adulthood. Adults in their 20s and 30s stand a higher risk of dying from _____. Lifestyle choices can hasten _____ aging physical decline brought about by environmental factors or individual behavior. African Americans have _____ the death rate of Caucasians. The _____ rate is significantly higher in the United States than in any other developed country and, although it is the _____ most frequent cause of death for young adult white Americans, it is the most likely cause of death for _____.

8. _____ are the least likely of any Western ethnic group to seek the help of a physician when they are ill. They, as well as members of some non-Western groups, are more likely to believe in _____ causes of illness. Members of these groups may attribute illness to a _____ from God, a lack of _____, or a _____. Demographic barriers, such as lower _____ status, also reduce the ability to rely on traditional medical care, which is expensive.

Eating, Nutrition, and Obesity: A Weighty Concern

9. According to guidelines provided by the U.S. Department of Agriculture, people can archive good nutrition by eating foods that are low in _____. In addition, whole _____ foods and cereal products, _____, and _____ are also beneficial. Milk and other sources of _____ are needed to prevent osteoporosis. People should reduce their _____ intake.

10. During adolescence, a poor _____ does not always present a significant problem. Young adults must reduce the _____ intake they were used to during adolescence.

11. Obesity, defined as body weight that is _____ percent or more above the average weight for a person of a given height, is on the rise in the United States. As age _____, more people are classified as obese.

Physical Disabilities: Coping with Physical Challenge

12. Some 50 million Americans are physically challenged, according to the official definition of _____, a condition that substantially limits a major life activity such as walking or vision. Despite the passage in 1990 of the landmark Americans with _____ Act (ADA) which mandates full access to public establishments, individuals with disabilities still face several kinds of barriers.

Stress and Coping: Dealing with Life's Challenges

13. Stress is the _____ and _____ response to events that threaten or challenge us. Events and circumstances that produce threats to our well-being are known as _____.

14. Researchers in the field of _____ have found that stress brings several outcomes, the most immediate typically being a _____ reaction, as certain hormones, secreted by the _____ glands, cause a rise in heart rate, blood pressure, respiration rate, and sweating. These immediate effects may be beneficial because they produce an _____ reaction in the _____ nervous system by which people are better able to defend themselves from a sudden, threatening situation. As stress-related hormones are constantly secreted, the heart, blood vessels, and other body tissues may _____. As a consequence, people become more susceptible to _____.

15. According to Lazarus and Folkman, people who are confronted with a stressor use _____ appraisal, an assessment of an event to determine whether its implications are positive, negative, or neutral. _____ appraisal is the individual's assessment of whether coping abilities and resources are adequate to overcome the harm, threat, or challenge posed by the potential stressor.

16. Some general principles that predict when an event will be appraised as stressful include events and circumstances that produce _____ emotions, situations that are _____ or _____, events or circumstances that are _____ and confusing, and people having to accomplish simultaneously many _____ that strain their capabilities.

17. Stress may also lead to _____ disorders, medical problems caused by the interaction of psychological, emotional, and _____ difficulties.

18. Some young adults are better than others at _____, the effort to control, reduce, or learn to tolerate the threats that lead to stress. Some people use _____ coping, by which they attempt to manage a stressful problem or situation by directly changing the situation to make it less stressful. Other people employ _____ coping, which involves the conscious regulation of emotion.

19. Coping is also aided by the presence of _____ support, assistance and comfort supplied by others. _____ coping involves unconscious strategies that distort or deny the true nature of a situation.

20. Some general guidelines that can help us to cope with stress include seeking _____ over the situation producing the stress, redefining threat as _____, getting _____ support, using _____ techniques, trying to maintain a _____ lifestyle, and keeping in mind that stress is a _____ part of life.

Cognitive Development

Intellectual Growth in Early Adulthood

21. Piaget argued that by the time people left adolescence, their thinking, at least _____, had largely become what it would be for the rest of their lives.

Postformal Thought

22. Labouvie-Vief suggests that adaptive thinking changes _____ during early adulthood and asserts that thinking based solely on _____ operations is insufficient to meet the demands placed on young adults. Young adults learn to use _____ and _____ to make comparisons, confront society's paradoxes, and become comfortable with a more subjective understanding.

23. _____ thought is thinking that acknowledges that adult predicaments must be sometime solved in relativistic terms. It encompasses _____ thinking, an interest in an appreciation for argument, counterargument, and debate.

24. Perry found that students entering college tended to use _____ thinking in their views of the world. As these students encountered new ideas and points of view they developed _____ thinking, which is characterized by a shift in they viewed authorities. Ultimately, according to Perry, they entered a stage in which knowledge and values were regarded as _____.

Schaie's Stages of Development

25. Schaie suggests that adults' thinking follows a set pattern of stages beginning with the _____ stage, which encompasses all of childhood and adolescence and has as its main cognitive developmental task the _____ of information. Young adults enter the _____ stage, in which intelligence is applied to specific situations involving the attainment of long-term _____ regarding careers, family, and societal contributions.

26. During the late stages of early adulthood and in middle adulthood, people move into the _____ stage, the major concerns of which are related to personal situations. Sometime later during middle adulthood, many people enter the _____ stage in which they take a broader perspective that includes concerns about the world. These people put energy into nourishing and sustaining _____ institutions. Old age marks entry into the _____ stage during which the focus is on tasks that have personal meaning. Information acquisition is directed toward particular issues that specifically _____ the person.

Intelligence: What Matters in Early Adulthood?

27. In his _____ theory of intelligence, Sternberg suggests that intelligence is made up of three major components. The _____ aspect relates to the mental components involved in analyzing data used in solving problems. The _____ component refers to the relationship among intelligence, people's prior experience, and their ability to cope with new situations. The _____ component involves the degree of success people demonstrate in facing the demands of their everyday, real-world environments. Traditional intelligence tests, which yield an IQ score, tend to focus on the _____ aspect of intelligence.

28. The IQ score that most traditional tests produce relates quite well to _____ success, but seems to be unrelated to other types of achievement such as _____ success.

29. Sternberg contends that success in a career necessitates a type of intelligence called _____ intelligence that is substantially different from that involved in traditional academic pursuits. _____ intelligence permits people to tune into other's feelings. It is of value to _____ and personal success.

30. People in early adulthood may be at the peak of their _____ because many of the problems they encounter on a professional level are novel. Productivity remains fairly _____ throughout adulthood, particularly in the _____.

31. _____ is defined as combining responses or ideas in novel ways and one important component is a person's willingness to take _____ that may result in potentially high payoffs.

Life Events and Cognitive Development

32. Some evidence suggests that major life events may lead to _____ growth. The ups and downs of life events may lead young adults to think about the world in novel, more _____ and sophisticated, and often less _____, ways. They apply the broader perspective of _____ thought.

College: Pursuing Higher Education

The Demographics of Higher Education

33. College students are primarily _____ and _____ class. The percentage of the minorities in college has _____ significantly. There are now more _____ than _____ enrolled in college.

The Changing College Student: Never Too Late to Go to College?

34. More than a _____ of students taking college courses for credit in the United States are 25 years old or older and the average age of community college students is _____.

35. One reason for increased numbers of nontraditional students is _____. In addition _____ reform a changing in attitude can reduce risk-taking behavior and make nontraditional students focus more on acquiring the ability to support their family.

College Adjustment: Reacting to the Demands of College Life

36. The _____ readjustment reaction is a cluster of psychological symptoms relating to the college experience. It is particularly likely to occur among students who have been unusually _____, either academically or socially, in high school. Male students are more likely to be concerned with their _____, social lives, and _____ decisions. Female students are concerned most with what to do with their _____, relationships, and the _____ of too much work.

37. Professional help is needed when psychological _____ lingers and interferes with a person's sense of well-being and ability to function. It is also needed when there are feelings that one is unable to _____ effectively with the stress, hopeless or _____ feelings for no apparent reason, an inability to build close _____ with others, and _____ symptoms that have no apparent underlying cause.

Gender and College Performance

38. Classes in education and the social sciences typically have a larger proportion of _____ and classes in engineering, the physical sciences, and mathematics tend to have more _____. The differences in gender distribution and attrition rates reflect the powerful influence of gender _____ that operate throughout the world of education.

39. Women expect to _____ less than men and these expectations fit with _____. Male and female college students also have different expectations regarding their areas of _____. Professors call on men in class more _____ and make more _____ contact with men. Males receive more _____ reinforcement.

40. Although some cases of unequal treatment of women represent _____ sexism, in other cases, women are the victims of _____ sexism in which they are placed in stereotyped and restrictive roles that seem to be positive.

41. Boys and girls perform virtually _____ on standardized math tests in elementary school and middle school. According to Steele, the reason behind the declining levels of performance for both women and African Americans is academic _____, a lack of personal identification with an academic domain. For women, it is specific to _____ and _____; for African Americans, it is more _____ across academic domains. In both cases, negative societal stereotypes produce a state of stereotype _____ in which members of the group fear that their behavior will indeed conform the stereotype. Evidence clearly suggests that women are vulnerable to _____

regarding their future success. When racial stereotypes are emphasized, the performance of African-American students is _____.

<u>Dropping Out of College</u>

42. Six years after starting college only _____ percent have graduated. Less than _____ of black and Hispanic students graduate in six years.

CRITICAL THINKING QUESTIONS

To further your understanding of the topics covered by this chapter, write out your answers to the following essay questions in the spaces provided.

1. If the advantages of exercise and proper nutrition are evident, why are obesity and poor physical fitness so widespread in the United States? Are these inevitable consequences of a high standard of living?

2. Why is violence so prevalent in the United States, compared with other societies?

3. What sorts of interpersonal barriers do people with disabilities face? How can those barriers be removed?

4. Why are there individual differences in people's reactions to stress? Do you think there are also cultural differences?

5. Given the economic and social benefits of obtaining a college degree, should all individuals go to college? Why or why not?

6. If practical intelligence depends on the environment and on observations of others, how might the nature of practical intelligence differ across cultural and socioeconomic environments?

7. Do you think that Perry's approach to postformal thinking can apply to individuals prior to attending college? What about to individuals who never attend college?

8. Some students are said to "disidentify" with academic success by downgrading its importance. Can you think of other situations in which people manifest this behavior?

9. Do college professors behave differently toward male and female students? How? What factors might contribute to this phenomenon? Should this situation be changed? Can this situation be changed?

10. Given what you know about human development, how are older students likely to affect the college classroom? Explain.

PRACTICE TEST - POST TEST

Circle the correct answer for each of the following multiple choice questions and check your answers with the Answer Key at the end of this chapter.

1. Some people experience a thinning of their bones as they age, which is called
    a. arthritis.
    b. leukemia.
    c. osteoporosis.
    d. atherosclerosis.

2. Which of the following is NOT a method of coping as discussed by the text?
    a. defensive coping
    b. offensive coping
    c. problem-focused coping
    d. emotion-focused coping

3. Obesity experts have reviewed successful dieting and some of the experts recommend that people should
    a. go on a weekly fast.
    b. avoid all red meat, alcohol, and high-fat foods.
    c. stop dieting and instead eat anything they want.
    d. avoid dieting and focus on eating what they really want in moderation.

4. Jamie finds that she is having problems finding enough time to study. Her part-time job and classes leave very little time. She is able to arrange with her boss to work fewer hours so that she can study. What coping strategy has Jamie used?
    a. social support
    b. emotion focused
    c. defensive coping
    d. problem-focused

5. According to Schaie, the first stage of cognitive development is the
    a. executive stage.
    b. achieving stage.
    c. acquisitive stage.
    d. responsible stage.

6. Schaie's first stage of development for middle-aged individuals is the
    a. executive stage.
    b. achieving stage.
    c. acquisitive stage.
    d. responsible stage.

7. Which of the following is NOT part of Sternberg's triarchic theory of intelligence?
   a. contextual
   b. crystallized
   c. experiential
   d. componential

8. One of our intelligences, according to the Sternberg, allows us to relate information to new situations in creative ways. Which of the following intelligences fosters this creativity?
   a. contextual
   b. crystallized
   c. experiential
   d. componential

9. The proportion of the minority population that enters college has _____ over the past decade.
   a. decreased
   b. gone up slightly
   c. remained steady
   d. increased

10. Most students experience an adjustment period when going from high school to college. Students who were unusually _____ in high school are particularly likely to experience this adjustment period.
    a. goal-oriented
    b. unsuccessful socially
    c. unsuccessful academically
    d. successful either academically or socially

11. A research study by Steele gave a group of male and female college students two math tests: one in which there were supposedly gender differences—women not performing as well on it—and a second math test in which there were no gender differences. Actually, the tests were drawn from the same group of questions. When the women were told there were gender differences in the test, they
    a. greatly outperformed the men.
    b. greatly underperformed the men.
    c. performed slightly better than the men.
    d. performed slightly worse than the men.

12. In young adulthood _____ are more adapt to die than _____.
    a. women, men
    b. men, women
    c. the rich, the poor
    d. the poor, the rich

13. According to recommendations from the American College of Sports Medicine and the Centers for Disease Control and Prevention, people should engage in moderate physical activity at least _____ for at least _____ days a week.
    a. 10 minutes; 5
    b. 20 minutes; 3
    c. 30 minutes; 5
    d. 60 minutes; 3

14. The least likely of any Western ethnic group to seek the help of a physician when they are ill are
    a. African Americans.
    b. Asians.
    c. Euro Americans.
    d. Latinos.

15. What federal legislation was passed in 1990 to mandate full access to public establishments?
    a. Equal Opportunity Act
    b. Civil Liberties Act
    c. No Child Left Behind Act
    d. Americans with Disabilities Act

16. Matt has applied for a new job with a higher salary and just found out he didn't get the job. His appraisal of this event as negative is a
    a. primary appraisal.
    b. secondary appraisal.
    c. stress reaction.
    d. coping mechanism.

17. In contrast to formal thought, postformal thought
    a. is based on purely logical processes.
    b. considers answers to problems as absolutely right or wrong.
    c. acknowledges that predicaments can be solved in relativistic terms.
    d. is based on concrete operations.

18. Keith just broke up from a long-term romantic relationship and is assessing his ability to move on with his life. He is engaged in _____ appraisal.
    a. primary
    b. secondary
    c. stress
    d. defensive

19. Total minority enrollment now comprises _____ of total college enrollment.
    a. a quarter   c. two-thirds
    b. half   d. three-quarters

20. White women earn what percent of doctorates?
    a. 5 percent   c. 22 percent
    b. 13 percent   d. 43 percent

ANSWER KEYS

Practice Test – Pretest (with text page numbers)

1.	c 461	6.	b 474	11.	b 482	16.	d 466
2.	c 462	7.	c 474	12.	d 459	17.	b 468
3.	c 466	8.	d 475	13.	a 460	18.	d 475
4.	d 466	9.	b 488	14.	b 460	19.	c 476
5.	a 473	10.	d 481	15.	b 463	20.	c 473

Key Names

1. d   2. f   3. b   4. c   5. e   6. a   7. g

Key Vocabulary Terms

1. Primary appraisal is the assessment of an event to determine whether its implications are positive, negative, or neutral; secondary appraisal is the assessment of whether one's coping abilities and resources are adequate to overcome the harm, threat, or challenge posed by the potential stressor.

2. The Executive stage is the period in middle adulthood when people take a broader perspective than earlier, including concerns about the world; the reintegrative stage is the period of late adulthood during which the focus is on tasks that have personal meaning.

11. Psychosomatic, Responsible, Acquisitive, Coping, Triarchic, Intelligence, Creativity, Achieving, Longitudinal (Practical)

Programmed Review

1. complete, senescence, maturers, brain
2. elasticity, higher, 40s, 50s
3. 10, quarter, lower

4. 30, 5, 10
5. cardiovascular, endurance, stronger, flexible, greater, elastic, osteoporosis
6. immune, stress, depression, control, accomplishment, longevity
7. slight, accidents, secondary, twice, murder, fifth, African Americans
8. Latinos, supernatural, punishment, faith, hex, socioeconomic
9. fat, grain, vegetables, fruit, calcium, salt
10. diet, caloric
11. 20, increases
12. disability, Disabilities
13. physical, emotional, stressors
14. psychoneuroimmunology, biological, adrenal, emergency, sympathetic, deteriorate, diseases
15. primary, Secondary
16. negative, uncontrollable, unpredictable, ambiguous, tasks
17. psychosomatic, physical
18. coping, problem-focused, emotion-focused
19. social, Defensive
20. control, challenge, social, relaxation, healthy, natural
21. qualitatively
22. qualitatively, formal, analogies, metaphors
23. Postformal, dialectical
24. dualistic, multiple, relativistic
25. acquisitive, acquisition, achieving, goals
26. responsible, executive, societal, reintegrative, interest
27. triarchic, componential, experiential, contextual, componential
28. academic, career
29. practical, Emotional, career
30. creativity, steady, humanities
31. Creativity, risks
32. cognitive, complex, rigid, postformal
33. white, middle, increased, women, men
34. third, 31
35. economic, maturation
36. first-year, successful, grades, vocational, lives, strain
37. distress, cope, depressed, relationships, physical
38. women, men, stereotypes
39. earn, reality, competence, frequently, eye, positive
40. hostile, benevolent
41. identically, disidentification, math, science, generalized, threat, expectations, depressed
42. 63, half

Practice Test - Post Test (with text page numbers)

1.	c 463	6.	d 474	11.	b 487	16.	a 466
2.	b 468	7.	b 475	12.	b 461	17.	c 473
3.	d 463	8.	c 475	13.	c 460	18.	b 466
4.	d 468	9.	d 480	14.	d 463	19.	a 480
5.	c 474	10.	d 482	15.	d 465	20.	b 481

Chapter 14

Social and Personality Development in Early Adulthood

CHAPTER OUTLINE

- Forging Relationships: Intimacy, Liking, and Loving During Early Adulthood
  - The Components of Happiness: Fulfillment of Psychological Needs
  - The Social Clocks of Adulthood
  - Seeking Intimacy: Erikson's View of Young Adulthood
  - Friendship
  - Falling in Love: When Liking Turns to Loving
  - Passionate and Companionate Love: The Two Faces of Love
  - Sternberg's Triangular Theory: The Three Faces of Love
  - Choosing a Partner: Recognizing Mr. or Ms. Right
  - Attachment Styles and Romantic Relationships: Do Adult Loving Styles Reflect Attachment in Infancy?

- The Course of Relationships
  - Marriage, POSSLQ, and Other Relationship Choices: Sorting Out the Options of Early Adulthood
  - What Makes Marriage Work?
  - Early Martial Conflict
  - Parenthood: Choosing to Have Children
  - The Impact of Children on Parents: Two's a Couple, Three's a Crowd
  - Gay and Lesbian Parents
  - Staying Single: I Want to Be Alone

- Work: Choosing and Embarking on a Career
  - Identity During Young Adulthood: The Role of Work
  - Picking an Occupation: Choosing Life's Work
  - Gender and Career Choices: Women's Work
  - Why Do People Work? More Than Earning a Living

LEARNING OBJECTIVES

After you have read and studied this chapter, you should be able to answer the following questions.

1. How do young adults form loving relationships, and how does love change over time?
2. How do people choose spouses, and what makes relationships work and cease working?
3. How does the arrival of children affect a relationship?
4. Why is choosing a career such an important issue for young adults, and what factors influence the choice of a career?
5. Why do people work, and what elements of a job bring satisfaction?

Circle the answers to the following multiple choice questions and then check your answers with the Answer Key at the end of this chapter.

1. A 24-year-old man has the developmental task of
    a. consolidating work identity.
    b. accepting the passage of time.
    c. accepting social responsibility.
    d. developing a capacity for intimacy with a partner.

2. All of the following are components of Sternberg's theory about the components of love EXCEPT
    a. passion.   c. infatuation.
    b. intimacy.   d. commitment.

3. When two people have a relationship full of commitment and intimacy, but lack passion, Sternberg calls this form of love
    a. empty love.   c. consummate love.
    b. fatuous love.   d. companionate love.

4. Men, more than women, prefer a potential marriage partner who is
    a. intelligent.   c. physically attractive.
    b. emotionally stable.   d. ambitious and industrious.

5. When a man marries a woman who shares similarity in leisure actives and role preferences he is adhering to a principle called
    a. the filtering model.   c. social homogamy.
    b. polygamy.   d. the marriage gradient.

6. Some relationships are characterized by overinvestment, repeated break-ups with the same partner, and the overly invested partner having relatively low self-esteem. The overly invested partner probably has the _____ attachment style.
    a. secure   c. dependent
    b. avoidant   d. anxious-ambivalent

7. The marriage gradient described tendencies of marriage based on all of the following factors EXCEPT
    a. status.   c. age.
    b. size.   d. race.

8. Women get married for the first time in the United States at the median age of
    a. 20.   c. 25.
    b. 22.   d. 26.

9. What percent of people in the U.S. spent their entire lives in singlehood?
    a. 2 percent   c. 25 percent
    b. 10 percent   d. 40 percent

10. Eli Ginzberg developed a theory in the area of
    a. marriage.   c. stimulus-value-role.
    b. career-choice.   d. labeling theory of passionate love.

11. Relationships proceed in a fixed order of three stages according to which theorist?
    a. Erikson   c. Murstein
    b. Vaillant   d. Ginzberg

12. Occupations associated with relationships are called
    a. social professions.
    c. communal professions.
    b. agentic professions.
    d. enterprising professions.

13. What type of motivation is involved when a person decides on a career based on prestige and money?
    a. remote
    c. extrinsic
    b. intrinsic
    d. immediate

14. The evaluation of a role or person by other relevant members of a group or society is called
    a. status.
    c. hierarchy.
    b. selection.
    d. social comparison.

15. Mario finds that he has to concentrate on remaining oriented to the present and future and avoid becoming preoccupied with the past. Mario is most likely
    a. 65 years old.
    c. 40 years old.
    b. 50 years old.
    d. 35 years old.

16. Most people choose their friends on the basis of all of the following EXCEPT
    a. proximity.
    c. personal qualities.
    b. similarity.
    d. influence.

17. Zoe and Carl are committed to their relationship even though they feel little passion for each other and are not intimate in any way. Their love is
    a. fatuous.
    c. empty.
    b. companionate.
    d. consummate.

18. Jack and Jill, a couple with a similarity in leisure activity and role preferences, are displaying
    a. social homogamy.
    c. heterosexuality.
    b. the marriage gradient.
    d. companionate love.

19. John Holland studied
    a. personality types.
    c. marriage conflicts.
    b. attachment styles.
    d. birth order.

20. According to research by Vaillant on people in the stage of career consolidation
    a. men remain under their parents' influence until age 40.
    b. people in this stage display strong independence.
    c. people in this stage are rule-followers.
    d. the stage begins at age 50.

KEY NAMES

Match the following names with the most accurate descriptions and check your answers with the Answer Key at the end of this chapter.

1. ___ David Buss   a. attachment styles

2. ___ Erik Erikson   b. career choice theory

3. ___ Eli Ginsberg   c. career consolidation

4. ___ Ravenna Helson   d. evolutionary perspective

5. ___ John Holland   e. intimacy vs. isolation

6. ___ Bernard Murstein   f. personality type theory

7. ___ Phillip Shaver   g. stimulus-value-role

8. ___ Robert Sternberg   h. social clocks

9. ___ George Vaillant   i. martial satisfaction

10. ___ John Gottman   j. triangular theory of love

KEY VOCABULARY TERMS

Distinguish between the following pairs of terms.

1. Passionate (or romantic) love; Companionate love

2. Passion component; Decision/commitment component

3. Intrinsic motivation; Extrinsic motivation

Define each of the following terms and give a specific example for each.

4. Homogamy
5. Marriage gradient
6. Stimulus-value-role theory
7. Fantasy period
8. Agentic professions
9. Social clock
10. Intimacy versus isolation stage
11. Status

Fill in the blanks for term next to each definition. When complete, the first letters of the terms from top to bottom will spell the last term in the puzzle.

12. _ _ _ _   Murstein's theory is stimulus, value, _____.

_ _ _ _ _ _ _ _   Motivation that drives people to obtain tangible rewards, such as money and prestige.

_ _ _ _ _ _ _   Occupations that are associated with getting things accomplished.

_ _ _ _ _ _ _ _   The theory that individuals experience romantic love when two events occur together: intense physiological arousal and situational cues suggesting that the arousal is due to love.

_ _ _ _ _ _ _ _   The component of love that encompasses feelings of closeness, affection, and connectedness.

_ _ _ _ _ _   The evaluation of a role or person by other relevant members of a group or society.

_ _ _ _ _ _ _ _   The second stage of Ginzberg's theory, which spans adolescence, when people begin to think in pragmatic terms about the requirements of various jobs and how their own abilities might fit with them.

_ _ _ _ _ _ _ _ _ _   Motivation that causes people to work for their own enjoyment, not for the rewards work may bring.

_ _ _ _ _ _ _ _ _ _ _   Couples living together without being married.

The third stage of Ginzberg's theory occurring in early adulthood when people begin to explore specific career options through actual experience on the job or through training for a profession, and narrow their choices and make a commitment is _ _ _ _ _ _ _ _ .

PROGRAMMED REVIEW

Fill in the blanks in the following programmed review and check your answers with the Answer Key at the end of this chapter.

Forging Relationships: Intimacy, Liking, and Loving During Early Adulthood

The Components of Happiness: Fulfillment of Psychological Needs

1. When asked to recall a time when they were happy, people in early adulthood focus on the satisfaction of _____ needs rather than _____ needs. Times when they were least satisfied were incidents in which basic _____ needs were left unsatisfied.

The Social Clocks of Adulthood

2. The social clock records the major _____ in people's lives. Our social clocks are _____ determined, and there is _____ in the social clocks of men and women.

3. Helson determined that _____ development is determined by proceeding according to a socially acceptable and _____ social-clock pattern.

Seeking Intimacy: Erikson's View of Young Adulthood

4. Erikson regards young adulthood as the time of the _____ stage. During this period, the focus is on developing close, intimate _____ with others. Intimacy comprises a degree of _____, involving the sacrifice of one's own needs to those of another; _____, the experience of a joint pleasure from focusing not just on one's own gratification but also on that of one's partner; and deep _____, marked by efforts to fuse one's identity with the identity of a partner.

5. Erikson's view of healthy intimacy was limited to adult _____, the goal of which was to produce children. He focused more on _____ development than on _____.

Friendship

6. People maintain relationships because of a basic need for _____. People become friends because of _____, accessibility, _____ of attitudes and values, and _____ qualities.

Falling in Love: When Liking Turns to Loving

7. The evolution of a relationship can be seen in terms of what Murstein calls _____ theory. In the _____ stage, relationships are built on surface, physical characteristics, such as the way a person looks. The _____ stage usually occurs between the second and the seventh encounter and the relationship is characterized by increasing similarity of values and _____. In the _____ stage, the relationship is built on specific roles played by the participants. One criticism of the SVR theory is that not every relationship follows a similar _____.

Passionate and Companionate Love: The Two Faces of Love

8. Love differs not only _____ from liking, but also _____. Love, at least in its early stages, involves relatively intense _____ arousal, an all-encompassing _____ in another individual, recurrent _____ about the other individual, and rapid swings of _____. Love includes elements of closeness, _____, and exclusivity.

9. _____ (or romantic) love is a state of powerful absorption in someone. It includes intense _____ interest and arousal, and caring for another's _____. In comparison, _____ love is the strong affection that we have for those with whom our lives are deeply involved.

10. In Hatfield and Berschied's _____ theory of passionate love, individuals experience romantic love when two events occur together: intense _____ arousal and _____ cues that indicate that love is the appropriate _____ for the feelings they are experiencing. This theory helps explain why people may feel deepened love even when they experience continual _____ or _____ from their assumed lover.

Sternberg's Triangular Theory: The Three Faces of Love

11. Sternberg suggests that love is made up of _____ components. The _____ component encompasses feelings of closeness, affection, and connectedness. The _____ component comprises the motivational drives relating to sex, physical closeness, and romance. The decision/_____ component embodies both the initial cognition that one loves another person and the longer-term determination to _____ that love.

12. _____ refers to people who have only the most casual of relationships. _____ develops when only intimacy is present; _____ love exists when only passion is felt; and _____ love exists when only decision/commitment is present. _____ love occurs when intimacy and passion are present, and _____ love when intimacy and decision/commitment occur jointly. _____ love exists when passion and decision/commitment are present without intimacy.

13. In _____ love, all three components of love are present. Many _____ and entirely satisfactory relationships are based on types of love other than consummate love. The type of love that predominates in a relationship _____ over time. In strong, loving relationships, the level of decision/commitment peaks and remains fairly _____. Passion tends to peak _____ in a relationship, but then declines and levels off. Intimacy also increases fairly _____, but can continue to grow over time. Sternberg's theory of love emphasizes both the _____ of love and its _____, _____ quality.

Choosing a Partner: Recognizing Mr. or Ms. Right

14. In the United States, most people have no hesitation in articulating that the major factor in choosing a spouse is _____. In other societies, love becomes a _____ consideration. _____ and mutual _____ are relatively highly desired across all cultures.

15. Certain gender differences in the preferred characteristics of a mate are _____ across cultures. Men prefer a potential marriage partner who is physically _____. In contrast, women prefer a potential spouse who is ambitious and _____.

16. One explanation for cross-cultural similarities in gender differences rests on _____ factors. Buss and colleagues claim that human beings seek out certain characteristics in order to maximize the availability of beneficial _____. Males in particular are genetically programmed to seek out mates with traits indicative of high _____ capacity. Consequently, physically attractive, _____ women might be more desirable because they are more capable of having _____ over a longer period of time. Women are genetically programmed to seek out men who have the potential to provide scarce _____ in order to increase the likelihood that their offspring will _____.

17. The filtering model assumes that people first filter for factors relating to broad determinants of _____. The end result is a choice based on _____ between two individuals. People often marry according to the principle of

_____, the tendency to marry someone who is _____ in age, race, education, religion, and other basic demographic characteristics.

18. The marriage _____ represents another societal standard, the tendency for men to marry women who are slightly younger, smaller, and lower in _____, and women to marry men who are slightly _____, larger, and higher in status. It limits the number of potential mates for _____, especially as they age, and allows _____ a wider choice. It makes finding a spouse particularly difficult for _____ African-American women.

<u>Attachment Styles and Romantic Relationships: Do Adult Loving Styles Reflect Attachment in Infancy?</u>

19. Attachment refers to the positive emotional _____ that develops between a child and a particular individual. Infants generally are seen as _____ attached (with healthy, positive, trusting relationships), _____ (relatively indifferent to caregivers and avoiding interactions with them), or _____ (showing great distress when separated from a caregiver but appearing angry on the caregiver's return). The influence of infants' attachment styles continues into adulthood and affects their _____ relationships. Attachment style is also related to _____ that adults give to their romantic partners. People who are having difficulty in relationships might look back to their _____ to identify the root of their problem.

20. Gay men describe successful relationships in ways that are similar to _____ couples' descriptions. The _____ preferences in the marriage gradient for heterosexuals also extend to partner preferences for homosexual men. The age preferences of lesbians fall somewhere _____ those of heterosexual women and heterosexual men. Most gays and lesbians seek loving, _____, and meaningful relationships that differ little qualitatively from those desired by heterosexuals.

The Course of Relationships

<u>Marriage, POSSLQ, and Other Relationship Choices: Sorting Out the Options of Early Adulthood</u>

21. The past three decades have seen a dramatic rise in couples living together without being married, a status known as _____. These people, whom the census bureau calls _____, or persons of the opposite sex sharing living _____, now make up around _____ percent of all couples in the United States. They tend to be _____. The chances of divorce are somewhat _____ for those who have previously cohabited.

22. A spouse can play an _____ role, providing security and financial well-being, and fill a _____ role, offering a means of sexual gratification and fulfillment that is fully accepted by society. Spouses provide a sounding board to discuss one another's _____ and act as partners for _____. Marriage also offers the only means of having _____ that is fully accepted by all segments of society. Finally marriage offers _____ benefits and _____.

23. Fewer U.S. citizens are married now than at any time since the late _____. The median age of first marriage in the United States is now _____ for men and _____ for women. Some _____ percent of people eventually marry. The delay in marriage age in part reflects _____ concerns and the commitment to establishing a _____.

<u>What Makes Marriage Work?</u>

24. Partners in successful marriages visibly show _____ to one another, communicate relatively little _____, and tend to perceive themselves as part of an _____ couple. They also experience social _____, a similarity in leisure activity and role preferences. Only about _____ of all marriages in the United States remain intact. Countries around the world, both rich and poor, have shown _____ in divorce during the last several decades.

<u>Early Martial Conflict</u>

25. According to some statistics, nearly _____ of newly married couples experience a significant degree of conflict. One of the major reasons is that partners may initially _____ one another. Husbands and wives may have difficulty making the status _____ from children of their parents to autonomous adults. Others have

difficulty developing an _____ apart from their spouses and some struggle to find a satisfactory allocation of _____ to share with the spouse. Most married couples view the early years of marriage as deeply _____.

Parenthood: Choosing to Have Children

26. Young adults typically cite _____ reasons for having children. They expect to derive _____ from watching their children grow, _____ from their children's accomplishments, _____ from seeing them become successful, and _____ from forging a close bond with their children. Parents-to-be may hope that their children will _____ for them in their old age, maintain a family _____ or farm, or simply offer _____. Others have children because to do so is such a strong _____ norm.

27. Unplanned pregnancies occur most frequently in _____, poorer, and less _____ couples. There has been a dramatic rise in the use and effectiveness of _____ and the incidence of undesired pregnancies has _____ in the last several decades.

28. Today, most families seek to have no more than _____ children. The _____ rate reached a post-World War II peak in the United States and began to decline to today's rate of below _____ children per woman, which is less than the _____ level, the number of children that one generation must produce to be able to replenish its numbers.

29. In addition to the availability of more reliable birth control methods, increasing numbers of women have joined the _____. Many women who work outside the home are choosing to have children _____ in their childbearing years in order to develop their careers. Some of the traditional incentives for having children, such as their potential for providing _____ support in old age, may no longer be as attractive.

30. Even when both spouses work similar hours, the wife generally spends _____ time taking care of the children than the husband does. Husbands tend to carry out chores that are more easily _____ in advance, whereas women's household chores tend to be devoted to things that need _____ attention. As a result, wives experience greater levels of anxiety and _____.

The Impact of Children on Parents: Two's a Couple, Three's a Crowd

31. The birth of a child brings about a dramatic shift in the _____ spouses must play. For many couples the strains accompanying the birth of a child produce the _____ level of marital satisfaction of any point in the marriage. This is particularly true for _____, who tend to be more _____ than men with their marriages after the arrival of children.

32. Three factors that permitted couples to deal with the increased stress after childbirth were: working to build fondness and _____ towards one partner; remaining aware of events in one's spouse life and _____ to those events; and considering problems as _____ and _____.

Gay and Lesbian Parents

33. Labor tends to be divided more _____ in homosexual households. Gay and lesbian couples cling more strongly to the ideal of an _____ allocation of household work. As in heterosexual unions, a _____ of roles develops. Although both partners usually say they share household tasks and decision making equally, _____ mothers are more involved in child care. Most research suggests that children raised in households in which the parents are homosexual show no differences in terms of eventual _____ from those raised in heterosexual households.

Staying Single: I Want to Be Alone

34. _____, living alone without an intimate partner, has increased significantly over the last several decades. One reason people chose to live alone is that they view _____ negatively. Others view marriage as too _____, and some never encounter someone with whom they wish to spend the _____ of their life.

196

Work: Choosing and Embarking on a Career

<u>Identity During Young Adulthood: The Role of Work</u>

35. According to Vaillant, young adulthood is marked by a stage of development called career _____, a stage that begins between the ages of 20 and 40, when young adults become centered on their careers. In his view, career concerns come to supplant the focus on _____. Critics point out that Vaillant's sample was unusually _____ and lacked ___ and societal ____ have changed since then as reasons that his conclusion are not fully _____.

<u>Picking an Occupation: Choosing Life's Work</u>

36. According to Ginzberg, people typically move through a series of stages in choosing a career, the first stage being the _____ period when choices are made solely on the basis of what sounds _____. During the _____ period, which spans adolescence, people begin to think in _____ terms about the requirements of various jobs and how their own abilities might fit with them. In early adulthood, people enter the _____ period when they explore specific career options either through actual _____ on the job or through _____ for a profession.

37. According to Holland, certain _____ types match particularly well with certain careers. _____ people are down to earth, practical problem solvers, and physically strong, but their social skills are mediocre. _____ types are oriented toward the theoretical and abstract and are not particularly good with people. The traits associated with the ____ personality type are related to verbal skills and interpersonal relations. _____ individuals prefer highly structured tasks and _____ individuals are risk takers and take-charge types. _____ types use art to express themselves and often prefer the world of art to interactions with people.

<u>Gender and Career Choices: Women's Work</u>

38. Traditionally, women were considered most appropriate for _____ professions, occupations associated with relationships. In contrast, men were perceived best suited for _____ professions associated with getting things accomplished. _____ professions typically have lower status and pay less than _____ professions.

39. Women make up _____ percent of the workforce. Women and minorities in high-status, visible professional roles may hit what has come to be called the _____ ceiling, an invisible barrier within an organization that prevents individuals from being _____ beyond a certain level.

<u>Why Do People Work? More Than Earning a Living</u>

40. _____ motivation drives people to obtain tangible rewards, such as money and prestige. _____ motivation causes people to work for their own enjoyment. People in many Western societies tend to subscribe to the _____ work ethic, the notion that work is important in and of itself. According to this view, working is a _____ act that brings _____ and even _____ well-being and satisfaction.

41. Work also brings a sense of personal _____ and may be a central element in people's _____ lives. The kind of work that people do is a factor in determining _____, the evaluation by society of the role a person plays. The higher the status of the job, the more _____ people tend to be. The status of the job of the major _____ can affect the status of the other members of the family.

42. Job satisfaction increases when workers have _____ into their jobs. People enjoy jobs that require several different types of _____ more than those that require only a minimal number. The more _____ employees have over others, the greater their job satisfaction.

43. Guidelines for at least starting to come to grips with the question of what occupational path to follow include systematically _____ a variety of choices, knowing _____, creating a _____ sheet listing the potential gains and losses, trying out different careers through paid or unpaid _____, remembering that one can _____ careers, and that a different career might be more _____ later in life.

CRITICAL THINKING QUESTIONS

In order to improve your understanding of the topics covered in this chapter, write out your answers to the following essay questions in the space provided.

1. How might a relationship that focuses first on values differ from one that focuses initially on external stimuli? Do any relationships focus first on roles?

2. What has to change for a relationship to move from passionate to companionate love? From companionate to passionate love? In which direction is it more difficult for a relationship to move? Why?

3. Through which of Sternberg's eight types of love do relationships tend to pass if they proceed from first acquaintance to a lifelong marriage?

4. How do the principles of homogamy and the marriage gradient work to limit options for high-status women? How do they affect men's options?

5. In what ways do you think cognitive changes in early adulthood (e.g., the emergence of postformal thought and practical intelligence) affect how young adults deal with questions of marriage, divorce, and childrearing?

6. Why do you think society is questioning its previous powerful norm in favor of marriage? How might our society be the same or different if the traditional marriage were no longer favored?

7. Do the changes that children bring to a relationship affect husbands and wives equally? Do they affect each partner in a gay or lesbian relationship equally? Why or why not?

8. If Vaillant's study were performed today on women, in what ways do you think the results would be similar to or different from those of the original study?

9. What sorts of unconscious behaviors and attitudes on the part of supervisors and coworkers contribute to the glass ceiling that affects women and minorities in the workplace?

10. In what aspects of your life are your behaviors intrinsically motivated? What types of tasks are accomplished only because of extrinsic motivation?

PRACTICE TEST - POST TEST

Circle the answers to the following multiple choice questions and then check your answers with the Answer Key at the end of this chapter.

1. In Murstein's SVR theory, the stage of a relationship in which initial judgments are formed on the other's physical characteristics is called the
    a. role stage.
    b. value stage.
    c. stimulus stage.
    d. response stage.

2. According to the labeling theory of passionate love, people experience romantic love when
    a. intimacy and passion occur together.
    b. infatuation and commitment occur together.
    c. intense physiological arousal and verbal commitment occur together.
    d. intense physiological arousal and situational cues occur together.

3. According to Erikson, young adulthood is the time to develop
    a. identity.
    b. trust.
    c. autonomy.
    d. intimacy.

4. If two people get married who are from the same background, including socioeconomic level and religion, their attraction is probably based on the principle of
    a. polyandry.
    b. polygamy.
    c. homogamy.
    d. the marriage gradient.

5. What percent of young adults display the secure style of attachment?
    a. 50 percent
    b. 70 percent
    c. 80 percent
    d. 90 percent

6. What is POSSLQ?
    a. The possibility of a high love quotient.
    b. Possibility of simultaneous interaction leading to a relationship.
    c. The U. S. Census Bureau's term for people cohabiting.
    d. None of these are correct.

7. What percent of female POSSLQS are under age 25?
    a. 10 percent
    b. 20 percent
    c. 40 percent
    d. 60 percent

8. What percent of marriages in the United States remain intact?
   a. 35 percent
   b. 50 percent
   c. 60 percent
   d. 80 percent

9. Upon examination of job duties and family responsibilities, it has been found that when men and women work the same number of hours on the job,
   a. the household chores are shared evenly.
   b. the child-care chores are shared evenly.
   c. men are more active in household chores.
   d. women spend more time in child-care activities.

10. Internships during the senior year of college would provide support for what stage of career-choice?
    a. fantasy
    b. realistic
    c. tentative
    d. consolidation

11. According to Holland, which personality type has excellent verbal and interpersonal skills?
    a. social
    b. artistic
    c. enterprising
    d. conventional

12. Many organizations currently have an invisible barrier which prevents some people from being promoted. This barrier is called the
    a. status level.
    b. glass ceiling.
    c. selective barrier.
    d. dominance hierarchy.

13. Which of the following was given as a reason that people chose to remain single?
    a. They do not want children.
    b. They do not posses the economic means to marry.
    c. Their sexual orientation does not permit marriage.
    d. They view marriage as too restrictive.

14. Which of the following is a developmental task of middle adulthood?
    a. living through illness and death of parents and contemporaries
    b. maintaining physical health
    c. adapting ethical and spiritual values
    d. continuing meaningful work and play

15. Today, the social clock
    a. is fairly uniform for both men and women.
    b. has changed dramatically for men.
    c. is more heterogeneous for both men and women.
    d. follows a set pattern for women.

16. The idea that people should marry for love
    a. is a universal criterion for marriage.
    b. was not invented until the middle ages.
    c. is more prominent in non-Western societies.
    d. has been accepted since the early Roman civilization.

17. According to Buss, genetic programming causes
    a. females to look for physically attractive mates.
    b. males to seek older women as mates.
    c. females to look for mates who will be good providers.
    d. males to seek females who are nurturing.

18. Ishmael attends college only because of the economic gains he hopes to reap in the further. In this instance Ishmael displays _____ motivation.
    a.   intrinsic
    b.   extrinsic
    c.   agentic
    d.   communal

19. According to studies comparing gay, lesbian, and heterosexual couples
    a.   labor tends to be more evenly divided in homosexual households than in heterosexual households.
    b.   heterosexual couples are more egalitarian.
    c.   lesbian couples divide child care equally between the biological and nonbiological mothers.
    d.   children are emotionally disturbed in lesbian and gay households.

20. Among the following professions, which would NOT be considered communal?
    a.   nurse
    b.   counseling psychologist
    c.   computer programmer
    d.   child-care worker

ANSWER KEYS

Practice Test – Pretest (with text page numbers)

1.	d 497	6.	d 504	11.	c 498	16.	d 497
2.	c 500	7.	d 504	12.	c 518	17.	c 500
3.	b 500	8.	c 508	13.	c 519	18.	a 509
4.	c 502	9.	b 515	14.	a 520	19.	a 517
5.	c 509	10.	b 517	15.	a 495	20.	c 516

Key Names

1. d		3. b		5. f		7. a		9. c	
2. e		4. h		6. g		8. j		10. i	

Key Vocabulary Terms

1. Passionate (or romantic) love is a state of powerful absorption in someone; companionate love is the strong affection for those with whom our lives are deeply involved.

2. The passion component is the component of love that comprises the motivational drives relating to sex, physical closeness, and romance; the decision/commitment component is the aspect of love that embodies both the initial cognition that one loves another person and the longer-term determination to maintain that love.

3. Intrinsic motivation causes people to work for their own enjoyment, not for the rewards that work may bring; extrinsic motivation drives people to obtain tangible rewards.

12. Role, Extrinsic, Agentic, Labeling, Intimacy, Status, Tentative, Intrinsic, Cohabitation (Realistic)

Programmed Review

1. psychological, material, psychological
2. milestones, culturally, heterogeneity
3. personality, justified,
4. intimacy vs. isolation, relationships, selflessness, sexuality, devotion
5. heterosexuality, men's, women's

6. belongingness, proximity, similarity, personal
7. stimulus-value-role, stimulus, value, beliefs, role, pattern
8. quantitatively, qualitatively, physiological, interest, fantasies, emotion, passion
9. Passionate, physiological, needs, companionate
10. labeling, physiological, situational, label, rejection, hurt
11. three, intimacy, passion, commitment, maintain
12. Nonlove, Liking, infatuated, empty, Romantic, companionate, Fatuous
13. consummate, long-lasting, varies, stable, early, rapidly, complexity, dynamic, evolving
14. love, secondary, Love, attraction
15. similar, attractive, industrious
16. evolutionary, genes, reproductive, younger, children, resources, survive
17. attractiveness, compatibility, homogamy, similar
18. gradient, status, older, women, men, well-educated
19. bond, securely, avoidant, anxious-ambivalent, romantic, caregiving, infancy
20. heterosexual, age, between, long-term
21. cohabitation, POSSLQ, quarters, 10, young, higher
22. economic, sexual, problems, activities, children, legal, protection
23. 1890s, 27, 25, 90, economic, career
24. affection, negativity, interdependent, homogamy, half, increases
25. half, idealize, transition, identity, time, satisfying
26. psychological, pleasure, fulfillment, satisfaction, enjoyment, provide, business, companionship, societal
27. younger, educated, contraceptives, declined
28. two, fertility, 2.1, replacement
29. workforce, later, economic
30. more, scheduled, immediate, stress
31. roles, lowest, women, dissatisfied
32. affection, responding, controllable, solvable
33. evenly, egalitarian, specialization, biological, adjustment
34. Singlehood, marriage, restrictive, remainder
35. consolidation, intimacy, bright, women, norms, generalizable
36. fantasy, appealing, tentative, pragmatic, realistic, experience, training
37. personality, Realistic, Intellectual, social, Conventional, enterprising, Artistic
38. communal, agentic, Communal, agentic
39. 55, less, glass, promoted
40. Extrinsic, Intrinsic, Puritan, meaningful, psychological, spiritual
41. identity, social, status, satisfied, wage-earner
42. input, skills, influence
43. evaluating, yourself, balance, internships, change, appropriate

Practice Test – Post Test (with text page numbers)

1.	c	498	6.	c	507	11.	a	517	16.	b	502
2.	d	499	7.	b	507	12.	b	519	17.	c	502
3.	d	497	8.	b	509	13.	d	515	18.	b	519
4.	c	504	9.	d	513	14.	a	496	19.	a	506
5.	a	504	10.	b	517	15.	c	496	20.	c	518

Chapter 15

Physical and Cognitive Development in Middle Adulthood

CHAPTER OUTLINE

◆ Physical Development
  ♦ Physical Transitions: The Gradual Change in the Body's Capabilities
  ♦ Height, Weight, and Strength: The Benchmarks of Change
  ♦ The Senses: The Sights and Sounds of Middle Age
  ♦ Reaction Time: Not-So-Slowing Down
  ♦ Sex in Middle Adulthood: The Ongoing Sexuality of Middle age

◆ Health
  ♦ Wellness and Illness: The Ups and Downs of Middle Adulthood
  ♦ Stress in Middle Adulthood
  ♦ The A's and B's of Coronary Heart Disease: Linking Health and Personality
  ♦ The Threat of Cancer

◆ Cognitive Development
  ♦ Does Intelligence Decline in Adulthood?
  ♦ The Development of Expertise: Separating Experts from Novices
  ♦ Memory: You Must Remember This

LEARNING OBJECTIVES

After you have read and studied this chapter, you should be able to answer the following questions.

1. What sorts of physical changes affect people in middle adulthood?
2. What changes in sexuality do middle-aged men and women experience?
3. Is middle adulthood a time of health or disease for men and women?
4. What sorts of people are likely to get coronary heart disease?
5. What causes cancer and what tools are available to diagnose and treat it?
6. What happens to a person's intelligence in middle adulthood?
7. How does aging affect memory, and how can memory be improved?

PRACTICE QUESTIONS - PRETEST

Circle the correct answers for each of the multiple choice questions and check your answers with the Answer Key at the end of this chapter.

1. A decline in height is experienced by more women than men because women have a
   a.   shorter stature.
   b.   longer lifespan.
   c.   greater risk of osteoporosis.
   d.   greater risk of rheumatoid arthritis.

2. What percent of maximum strength is lost by age 60?
   a. 10 percent
   c. 30 percent
   b. 20 percent
   d. 50 percent

3. When fluid cannot drain properly from the eye or if too much fluid is inside the eye, the condition is called
   a. cataracts.
   c. stigmatism.
   b. glaucoma.
   d. senile macular degeneration.

4. Research in declining motor skills in aging leads to the conclusion that
   a. reaction time remains the same throughout adulthood.
   b. motor skills remain constant throughout adulthood.
   c. motor skills actually improve throughout adulthood.
   d. practice and experience can compensate for declining motor skills.

5. What percent of all women experience severe distress during menopause?
   a. 10 percent
   c. 30 percent
   b. 20 percent
   d. 40 percent

6. How long does the female climacteric last?
   a. 6 to18 months
   c. 10 to 15 years
   b. 1 to 2 years
   d. 15 to 20 years

7. All of the following are potential health benefits of hormone replacement therapy for menopausal women, EXCEPT
   a. prevention of osteoporosis.
   b. reduced risk of breast cancer.
   c. reduction in the incidence of stroke.
   d. reduction in incidence of heart disease.

8. What is perimenopause?
   a. period when hormone production changes
   b. period when hormone production ends
   c. false menopause
   d. extended menopause

9. What is the most common cause of cancer death among women?
   a. lung cancer
   c. breast cancer
   b. skin cancer
   d. cervical cancer

10. Research has shown that the death rate after surgery for cancer varies according to a person's psychological reaction. The death rate was much lower for those who had
    a. felt hopeless and depressed.
    b. voiced no complaints and accepted their cancer.
    c. stoically accepted their cancer or felt hopeless.
    d. a fighting spirit or who had denied that they had the disease.

11. Dealing with situations by strategies learned through experience is
    a. fluid intelligence.
    c. crystallized intelligence.
    b. spatial intelligence.
    d. pragmatical intelligence.

12. Scientists are often more productive in their 50s than in their 20s. What form of intelligence helps explain why this might be true?
    a. fluid intelligence
    c. crystallized intelligence
    b. spatial intelligence
    d. pragmatical intelligence

13. Formal strategies for organizing material in ways that make it more likely to be remembered are called
    a. schemas.
    b. pragmatics.
    c. operations.
    d. mnemonics.

14. What mnemonic device includes paying attention when you are exposed to new information and purposefully thinking that you want to recall it in the future, and by practicing what you want to recall?
    a. rehearsal
    b. method of loci
    c. keyword technique
    d. encoding specificity phenomenon

15. What percent of men and women age 45-59 report having sexual intercourse about once a week or more?
    a. 25 percent
    b. 50 percent
    c. 75 percent
    d. 90 percent

16. What is a common aspect of hearing in middle adulthood?
    a. Women have more of a loss than men.
    b. Men have more of a loss than women.
    c. Hair cells increase in the inner ear.
    d. Sound localization increases in both ears.

17. Which of the following disorders is called the "silent killer"?
    a. digestive problems
    b. hypertension
    c. cancer
    d. arthritis

18. Which of the following drugs is NOT used to treat erectile dysfunction?
    a. Celexa
    b. Viagra
    c. Levitra
    d. Cialis

19. Those who argue against mammograms for women under the age of 50 base their objections on
    a. the incidence of false positives in younger women.
    b. the incidence of false negatives in younger women.
    c. the high cost of mammograms.
    d. all of the above.

20. According to Salthouse, overall IQ declines in middle age lead to no apparent decline in general cognitive competence for all of the following reasons EXCEPT
    a. traditional IQ measures do not measure the cognition required for occupational success.
    b. most successful middle-aged adults are not representative of middle aged adults in general.
    c. the degree of cognitive ability required for professional success to too high to be measured.
    d. older people are successful because they have developed specific kinds of expertise.

KEY NAMES

Match the following names with the most accurate description and check your answers with the Answer Key at the end of this chapter.

1. ___ Paul and Margaret Baltes

2. ___ Timothy Salthouse

3. ___ K. Warner Schaie

a. adult intelligence

b. cognition/IQ discrepancy

c. selective optimization

KEY VOCABULARY TERMS

Differentiate among the following terms:

1. Female climacteric; Male climacteric; Menopause

2. Fluid Intelligence; Crystallized intelligence

3. Type A behavior pattern; Type B behavior pattern

Define each of the following terms and give a specific example of each.

4. Glaucoma
5. Presbycusis
6. Selective optimization
7. Mnemonics

Fill in the blanks for the term next to each definition. When complete, the first letter of each term, from top to bottom, will spell the last term in this puzzle. (NOTE: Some terms may be from previous chapters.)

8. _ _ _ _ _ _ _ _ _ _   Another name for romantic love.

    _ _ _ _ _ _ _ _ _ _   A style of language use that primarily labels objects.

    _ _ _ _ _ _ _ _   The acquisition of skill or knowledge in a particular area.

    _ _ _ _ _ _   Organized bodies of information stored in memory.

    _ _ _ _ _ _ _   The type A _____ pattern is characterized by competitiveness, impatience, and a tendency toward frustration and hostility.

    _   The male chromosome on the 23rd chromosome pair.

    _ _ _ _ _ _ _ _ _ _ _   A condition in which the bones become brittle, fragile, and thin, often brought about by a lack of calcium in the diet.

    _ _ _ _ _ _   Behavior characterized by noncompetitiveness, patience, and a lack of aggression is the Type B Behavior _____.

    _ _ _ _ _ _ _ _ _ _ _   The accumulation of information, skills, and strategies that people have learned through experience, and that they can apply in problem solving strategies is crystallized _____.

    _ _ _ _ _ _ _ _ _ _ _   Understanding an experience in terms of current style of thinking.

A nearly universal change in eyesight during middle adulthood that results in some loss of near vision.

_ _ _ _ _ _ _ _ _ _

PROGRAMMED REVIEW

Fill in the blanks in the following programmed review and check your answers with the Answer Key at the end of this chapter.

Physical Development

Physical Transitions: The Gradual Change in the Body's Capabilities

1. People's _____ reactions to the physical changes of middle adulthood depend, in part, on their _____. For those whose self-image is tied closely to their _____ attributes, middle adulthood can be particularly difficult. Many middle-aged adults report no less _____ with their body image than do young adults.

Height, Weight, and Strength: The Benchmarks of Change

2. For most people, height reaches a maximum during their _____ and remains relatively stable until around age _____. At that point, people begin a settling process in which the bones attached to the _____ become less dense. Women are more prone to a decline in height because of their greater risk of _____, a condition in which the _____ become brittle, fragile, and thin, that is often brought about by a lack of _____ in the diet.

3. Both men and women continue to gain _____ during middle adulthood, and the amount of body _____ likewise tends to grow in the average person. These weight and fat gains lead to an increase in the number of people who are _____. People who maintain an _____ program during middle age tend to avoid obesity, as do individuals living in cultures in which the typical life is more _____ than that of many Western cultures. Changes in height and weight are also accompanied by declines in _____. By age 60 people have lost about _____ percent of their maximum strength.

The Senses: The Sights and Sounds of Middle Age

4. Starting at around age 40, visual _____, the ability to discern fine spatial detail in both close and distant objects, begins to decline. One major reason is a change in the shape and elasticity of the eye's _____, which makes it harder to focus images sharply onto the _____. The lens becomes less _____.

5. A nearly universal change in eyesight during middle adulthood is the loss of near vision, called _____. Declines occur in _____ perception, _____ perception, and the ability to view the world in _____ dimensions. Adaptation to _____ also declines. One of the most frequent causes of eye problems is _____ which occurs when pressure in the fluid of the eye increases.

6. Age brings a loss of _____, or hair cells in the inner ear, which transmit neural messages to the brain when vibrations bend them. The _____ becomes less elastic with age. The primary hearing loss is for sounds of high frequency, a problem called _____. _____ are more prone to hearing loss than _____, starting at around age 55. Because the two ears are not equally affected by hearing difficulties, sound _____, the process by which the origin of a sound is identified, is diminished.

Reaction Time: Not-So-Slowing Down

7. Although there is an _____ in reaction time, it is usually fairly mild and hardly noticeable. There are increases on _____ tasks such as reacting to a loud sound. _____ tasks which require the coordination of various skills show less of an increase. Increases in reaction time are largely produced by changes in the speed with which the _____ system processes nerve impulses.

Sex in Middle Adulthood: The Ongoing Sexuality of Middle Age

8. The frequency of sexual _____ declines with age, but sexual _____ remains a vital part of life. A man needs more time to achieve an _____ and it takes longer after an _____ to have another. The volume of fluid that is _____ declines, and production of _____, the male sex hormone, declines also.

9. For women, the walls of the _____ become thinner and less elastic. Starting at around age 45, women enter a period known as the _____ marking the transition from being able to bear _____ to being unable to do so. The most notable sign of this transition is _____, the cessation of menstruation, which marks the point at which a traditional _____ is no longer possible. In addition, the production of _____ and _____, the female sex hormones, begins to drop.

10. The female _____ marks the transition from being able to bear children to being unable to do so. _____ is the cessation of menstruation. After a year has gone by without a _____ period, menopause is said to have occurred.

11. The changes in hormone production in women may produce a variety of symptoms including _____, in which a woman senses an unexpected feeling of heat from the waist up. Headaches, feelings of _____, heart _____, and aching _____ are relatively common during this period. Only about _____ of all women experience severe distress during menopause and as many as _____ have no significant symptoms at all. _____ is the period beginning around ten years prior to menopause when hormone production begins to change. _____ -American women report relatively high levels of estrogen-related symptoms such as night sweats and hot flashes.

12. It now seems more reasonable to regard menopause as a _____ part of aging that does not produce psychological symptoms. Research indicates that the _____ women have make a significant difference in their experience of menopause.

13. In _____ replacement therapy, estrogen and progesterone are administered to alleviate the worst symptoms experienced by menopausal women. HRT reduces _____ flashes, loss of _____ elasticity, _____ heart disease, and thinning of _____. Some studies show the risk of _____ declines as well as _____ cancer. However, the risk of _____ cancer increases.

14. Men experience some changes during middle age that are collectively referred to as the male _____, the period of physical and psychological change that occurs during middle age. Despite progressive declines in the production of _____ and sperm, men continue to be able to father children throughout middle age. One physical change that does occur quite frequently is enlargement of the _____ gland. _____ dysfunction, a problem in which men are unable to achieve or maintain an erection, becomes more common.

Health

Wellness and Illness: The Ups and Downs of Middle Adulthood

15. People between the ages of _____ are less likely than younger adults to experience infections, allergies, respiratory diseases, and digestive problems. Their relative protection from such diseases is due to the fact that they may have already experienced them and built up _____.

16. During middle adulthood, people can become particularly susceptible to _____ diseases. Arthritis typically begins after the age of _____ and diabetes is most likely to occur in people between the ages of _____. _____ (high blood pressure) is one of the most frequent _____ disorders found in middle age. The _____ rate among middle-aged individuals is higher than it is in earlier periods of life.

17. The death rate for middle-aged African Americans in the United States is _____ the rate for Caucasians. The answer seems to lie in _____ status differences between majority and minority groups. The lower a family's income, the more likely it is that a member will experience a disabling _____. People living in lower SES households are more apt to work in occupations that are _____. Even though women's overall mortality rate is _____ than men's, the incidence of illness among middle-aged women is _____ than among men.

Stress in Middle Adulthood

18. According to _____, stress produces three main consequences. It has direct _____ outcomes, it leads people to engage in _____ behavior, and it has _____ effects on health-related behaviors.

The A's and B's of Coronary Heart Disease: Linking Health and Personality

19. More men die in middle age from diseases related to the _____ and _____ system than from any other cause. _____ are more likely to suffer from heart disease than _____ and the risk rises as people _____.

20. Some people are _____ predisposed to develop heart disease. Similarly _____ and _____ are factors. Cigarette smoking, a diet high in _____ and _____, and a relative lack of physical _____ all increase the likelihood of heart disease. Increasing evidence suggests that _____ factors may be associated with heart disease.

21. The _____ behavior pattern, is characterized by competitiveness, impatience, and a tendency toward frustration and _____. These people are driven to accomplish more than others, and they engage in _____ activities— multiple activities carried out simultaneously. They are easily _____ and become both verbally and nonverbally _____ if they are prevented from reaching a goal they seek to accomplish. The _____ behavior pattern is characterized by noncompetitiveness, patience, and a lack of _____.

22. Type A men have _____ the rate of coronary heart disease, a greater number of fatal _____ attacks, and five times as many heart problems overall. The most likely explanation is that when they are in stressful situations, they become excessively aroused _____. Undue wear and tear on the body's _____ system ultimately produces coronary heart disease. No definitive evidence has been found that Type A behavior _____ coronary heart disease. There is a growing consensus that the _____ and _____ related to the Type A behavior pattern may be the central link to coronary heart disease.

The Threat of Cancer

23. Many middle-aged individuals view a cancer diagnosis as a _____ sentence. Cancer is the _____ leading cause of death in the United States. Some kinds of cancer have clear _____ components. However, several _____ and _____ factors are also related to the risk of cancer.

24. Several forms of treatment are possible including _____ therapy, in which the tumor is the target of radiation designed to destroy it; _____ which is the controlled ingestion of toxic substances meant to poison the tumor, and _____ to remove the tumor.

25. In _____, a weak X-ray is used to examine breast tissue. The American Cancer Society suggests that women over the age of _____ routinely obtain one. However, there is the problem of false _____, in which the test suggests something is wrong when there is no problem, and false _____, in which it does not detect indications of cancer.

26. Some research indicates that the _____ responses of people with cancer can influence their recovery. Initial _____ is related to survival. The death rate of women who had a _____ spirit or who had _____ that they had the disease was much lower. Other studies suggest that the degree of _____ support people experience may be related. Some research finds that people with close _____ ties are less likely to develop cancer than those without them.

27. Cancer patients who are habitually _____ report less physical and psychological distress than those who are less so. Recent evidence suggests that participation in psychological _____ may give cancer patients an edge in treatment success. It may be that a positive psychological outlook benefits the body's _____ system, the natural line of defense against disease.

Cognitive Development

Does Intelligence Decline in Adulthood?

28. The conclusion that intelligence started to diminish in the mid-20s was based on _____ studies which tested people of different ages at the same point in time. These studies may suffer from _____ effects and may _____ intelligence in older subjects. _____ studies in which the same people are studied periodically over a

span of time reveal that adults tend to show fairly stable and even _____ intelligence test scores until they reach their mid-30s and in some cases up to their 50s. However, _____ effects may account for these results. It is difficult for researchers using this type of study to keep their sample _____, and these studies may _____ intelligence in older subjects.

29. Many researchers believe that there are two kinds of intelligence: _____ intelligence reflects information-processing abilities and situations and _____ intelligence is the store of information, skills, and strategies that people have acquired through education and prior experiences. In general _____ intelligence does show declines with age, but _____ intelligence holds steady and in some cases actually improves.

30. According to Schaie, the broad division of intelligence into fluid and crystallized categories _____ true age-related differences and developments in intelligence. He argues that researchers should instead consider many particular types of _____. Schaie finds that certain abilities such as _____ reasoning, _____ orientation, _____ speed, and _____ memory start a gradual decline at around age 25 and continue to decline through old age. On the other hand, _____ ability tends to increase until the mid-40s, is lower at age 60, and then stays steady throughout the rest of life. _____ ability rises until about the start of middle adulthood and stays fairly steady throughout the rest of the lifespan.

31. Though overall IQ as measured by traditional intelligence tests _____ in middle adulthood, almost all people in middle age show no apparent decline in general _____ competence. During the middle part of the life span, people come to hold some of the most important and _____ positions in society. Salthouse suggests that it is possible that typical measures of cognitive skills tap a different type of cognition than what is required to be successful in particular _____; that the most successful middle-aged adults are not _____ of middle-aged adults in general; that the degree of cognitive ability required for _____ success is simply not that high; or that older people are successful because they have developed specific kinds of _____ and particular _____. Baltes and Baltes claim that older adults use selective _____, the process by which people concentrate on particular skill areas to compensate for losses in other areas.

The Development of Expertise: Separating Experts from Novices

32. _____ is the acquisition of skill or knowledge in a particular area. Expertise develops as people devote _____ and _____ to particular domains. The behavior of experts is more _____, and they are not articulate in _____ how they draw conclusions. They develop better _____ and are more _____ in approaching problems.

Memory: You Must Remember This

33. Most people show only _____ memory losses. Memory is traditionally viewed in terms of _____ sequential components. _____ memory is an initial, momentary storage of information that lasts only an instant. Information then moves into _____ memory which holds it for 15 to 25 seconds. Finally, if the information is _____, it is moved into _____ memory, where it is stored on a relatively permanent basis. Both sensory memory and short-term memory show virtually no _____ during middle adulthood. Long-term memory shows some _____ with age. The initial registering of the information and its storage become less _____ with age.

34. During adulthood, we recall material though the use of _____, organized bodies of information stored in memory. People's schemas serve to _____ their behavior into coherent wholes and help them to _____ social events. Memory schemas influence people's _____ of new information to which they are exposed.

35. _____ are formal strategies for organizing material in ways that make it more likely to be remembered. It is important to get _____ and pay _____. According to the encoding _____ phenomenon, people are most likely to recall information in environments that are _____ to those in which they initially learned. Making _____ images produces better recall. Adults of all ages can improve their memories if they expend more effort in _____ what they want to remember.

CRITICAL THINKING QUESTIONS

To further your mastery of the topics covered in this chapter, write out your answers to the following essay questions in the spaces provided.

1. Do you think a woman of 45 who works hard not to look her age combats or contributes to a cultural bias against middle-aged women? Why?

2. Why isn't the male climacteric given much attention in United States society? What cultural factors might contribute to a lack of awareness and understanding of the changes that men face during this period?

3. Would you rather fly on an airplane with a middle-aged pilot or a young one? Why?

4. Why is the incidence of disabling illness higher in lower SES groups? Are there social-policy implications to this fact?

5. Why do you think women's mortality rate in middle adulthood is lower than men's? Will this situation change as women's societal roles change?

6. Does the effect of psychological attitude on cancer survival suggest that nontraditional healing techniques might have a place in cancer treatment? Why or why not?

7. How could you specifically engage mnemonics to help you synthesize the information that you learned in this chapter?

8. How might crystallized and fluid intelligence work together to help middle-aged people deal with novel situations and problems?

9. How do you explain the apparent discrepancy between declining IQ scores and continuing cognitive competence in middle adulthood?

10. How do memory schemas help people interpret social situations and novel events? How do you think people deal with elements of such situations that do not fit into existing schemas?

PRACTICE TEST – POST TEST

Circle the correct answers for each of the multiple choice questions and check your answers with the Answer Key at the end of this chapter.

1. A common change that middle-aged people experience with their senses is
   a. decline in visual acuity.
   b. increased sensitivity to pain.
   c. increased sensitivity to smell.
   d. reduced ability to hear low frequency sounds.

2. Hearing loss involving high-frequency sounds is more common in
   a. women than in men.
   b. men than in women.
   c. very young men than in middle-aged men.
   d. very young women than in middle-aged women.

3. Mia, a middle-aged woman, has a loss of near vision. This universal change in eyesight is known as
   a. presbyopia.   c. glaucoma.
   b. presbycusis.   d. visual acuity.

4. For the majority of women, menopause starts at around
   a. 35 to 36.   c. 47 or 48.
   b. 40 to 41.   d. 52 or 53.

5. If a man is over 60 years old and complains that he is having problems with urination and needs to urinate frequently at night, what is his likely diagnosis?
   a. colitis   c. enlarged liver
   b. diabetes   d. enlarged prostate gland

6. By the age of 40 what percent of men have enlarged prostates?
   a. 10 percent   c. 50 percent
   b. 30 percent   d. 85 percent

7. What lifestyle factors increase the likelihood of heart disease?
   a. high-fat diet   c. cigarette smoking
   b. lack of exercise   d. All of the answers are true.

8. What components of the Type A pattern are believed to be the central link to coronary heart disease?
   a. achievement and goal-orientation
   b. hostility and anger
   c. patience and competitiveness
   d. competitiveness and time urgency

9. What is the second-leading cause of death in the United States?
   a. cancer
   b. AIDS
   c. homicide
   d. heart disease

10. Cross-sectional studies are to cohort effects as longitudinal studies are to
    a. age effects.
    b. novel effects.
    c. attrition effects.
    d. practice effects.

11. According to Schaie, all of the following abilities start a gradual decline at about age 25, EXCEPT
    a. verbal memory.
    b. numeric ability.
    c. spatial orientation.
    d. inductive reasoning.

12. Short-term memory holds information for
    a. 5 to 10 seconds.
    b. 15 to 25 seconds.
    c. 2 to 5 minutes.
    d. 24 to 48 hours.

13. A mnemonic device exists that enables you to remember information in an environment that is similar to the one in which you initially learned it. What is this called?
    a. rehearsal
    b. method of loci
    c. keyword technique
    d. encoding specificity phenomenon

14. The loss of near vision in middle adulthood is called
    a. presbyopia.
    b. climacteric.
    c. glaucoma.
    d. presbycusis.

15. Most experts regard menopause as
    a. directly linked to depression.
    b. a highly negative experience.
    c. the precursor to severe physical problems.
    d. a normal part of aging.

16. In middle adulthood, people become particularly susceptible to
    a. chronic diseases.
    b. allergies.
    c. infections.
    d. digestive problems.

17. _____ study the relationships among the brain, immune system, and psychological factors.
    a. Gerontologists
    b. Counseling psychologists
    c. Psychoneruoimmunologists
    d. Psychiatrists

18. Stress produces all of the following EXCEPT
    a. elevated blood pressure.
    b. increased compliance with medical advice.
    c. increased hormonal activity.
    d. decreased nutrition.

19. Which of the following was NOT described as an effective strategy for remembering?
    a. verbalize
    b. visualize
    c. rehearsal
    d. get organized

20. The process by which people concentrate on particular skill areas to compensate for losses in other areas is selective
    a. optimization.
    b. compensation.
    c. expertise.
    d. cognition.

ANSWER KEYS

Practice Test – Pretest (with text page numbers)

1.	c 529	6.	d 533	11.	c 548	16.	b 531
2.	a 529	7.	b 535	12.	c 548	17.	b 537
3.	b 530	8.	a 534	13.	d 553	18.	a 536
4.	d 531	9.	c 543	14.	a 553	19.	d 544
5.	a 534	10.	d 545	15.	b 532	20.	c 550

Key Names

1. c   2. b   3. a

Key Vocabulary Terms

1. The female climacteric is the period that marks the transition from being able to bear children to being unable to do so and part of it is menopause, the cessation of menstruation; the male climacteric is the period of physical and psychological change relating to the male reproductive system that occurs during late middle age.

2. Fluid intelligence reflects processing capabilities, reasoning, and memory; crystallized intelligence is the accumulation of information skills, and strategies that people have learned through experience.

3. Type A behavior pattern is characterized by competitiveness, impatience, and tendency towards frustration and aggression; Type B behavior pattern is characterized by noncompetitiveness, patience, and lack of aggression.

8. Passionate, Referential, Expertise, Schemas, Behavior, Y, Osteoporosis, Pattern, Intelligence, Assimilation (Presbyopia)

Programmed Review

1. emotion, self-concepts, physical, satisfaction
2. 20s, 55, spinal column, osteoporosis, bones, calcium
3. weight, fat, obese, exercise, active, strength, 10
4. acuity, lens, retina, transparent
5. presbyopia, depth, distance, three, darkness, glaucoma
6. cilia, eardrum, presbycusis, Men, women, localization
7. increase, simple, Complex, nervous
8. intercourse, erection, orgasm, ejaculated, testosterone
9. vagina, climacteric, children, menopause, pregnancy, estrogen, progesterone
10. climacteric, Menopause, menstrual
11. hot flashes, dizziness, palpitations, joints, one-tenth, half, Perimenopause, African
12. normal, expectations
13. hormone, hot, skin, coronary, bones, stroke, colon, breast

14. climacteric, testosterone, prostate, Erectile
15. 45 and 65, immunities
16. chronic, 40, 50 and 60, Hypertension, chronic, death
17. twice, socioeconomic, illness, dangerous, lower, higher
18. psychoneuroimmunology, physiological, unhealthy, indirect
19. heart, circulatory, Men, women, age
20. genetically, sex, age, fats, cholesterol, exercise, psychological,
21. type A, hostility, polyphasic, angered, hostile, type B, aggression
22. twice, heart, physiologically, circulatory, causes, hostility, anger
23. death, second, genetic, environmental, behavioral
24. radiation, chemotherapy, surgery
25. mammography, 40, positives, negatives
26. emotional, attitude, fighting, denied, social, family
27. optimistic, therapy, immune
28. cross-sectional, cohort, underestimate, Longitudinal, increasing, practice, intact, overestimate
29. fluid, crystallized, fluid, crystallized
30. masks, ability, inductive, spatial, perceptual, verbal, numeric, Verbal
31. drops, cognitive, powerful, occupations, representative, professional, expertise, competencies, optimization
32. Expertise, attention, practice, automatic, explaining, strategies, flexible
33. minimal, three, Sensory, short-term, rehearsed, long-term, weakening, decline, efficient
34. schemas, organize, interpret, recall
35. Mnemonics, organized, attention, specificity, similar, mental, rehearsing

Practice Test - Post Test (with text page numbers)

1. a 530	6. a 535	11. b 549	16. a 537
2. b 531	7. d 541	12. b 552	17. c 540
3. a 530	8. b 542	13. d 553	18. b 540
4. c 533	9. a 543	14. a 530	19. a 553
5. d 535	10. d 547	15. d 533	20. a 550

215

Chapter 16

Social and Personality Development in Middle Adulthood

CHAPTER OUTLINE

◈ Personality Development
  ♦ Two Perspectives on Adult Personality Development: Normative-Crisis versus Life Events
  ♦ Erikson's Stage of Generativity versus Stagnation
  ♦ Stability versus Change in Personality

◈ Relationships: Family and Friends in Middle Age
  ♦ Marriage
  ♦ Family Evolutions: From Full House to Empty Nest
  ♦ Becoming a Grandparent: Who, Me?
  ♦ Family Violence: The Hidden Epidemic

◈ Work and Leisure
  ♦ Work and Careers: Jobs at Midlife
  ♦ Challenges of Work: On-the-Job Dissatisfaction
  ♦ Unemployment: The Dashing of the Dream
  ♦ Switching–and Starting–Careers at Midlife
  ♦ Leisure Time: Life Beyond Work

LEARNING OBJECTIVES

After you have read and studied this chapter, you should be able to answer the following questions.

1. In what ways does personality develop during middle adulthood?
2. Is there continuity in personality development during middle adulthood?
3. What are typical patterns of marriage and divorce in middle adulthood?
4. What changing family situations do middle-aged adults face?
5. What are the causes and characteristics of family violence in the United States?
6. What are the characteristics of work and career in middle adulthood?

PRACTICE TEST - PRETEST

Circle the correct answer for each of the following multiple choice questions and check your answers with the Answer Key at the end of this chapter.

1. In the generativity-versus-stagnation stage, Erikson believed people
   a. develop a sense of competence.
   b. become aware of the uniqueness of self.
   c. consider their contributions to family and society.
   d. develop loving, sexual relationships and close friendships.

2. Levinson theorized that during early adulthood people construct a broad, comprehensive vision of the future. He calls this
   a. The Plan.
   b. The Dream.
   c. Settling Down.
   d. The Blueprint.

3. What approach views personality development in terms of fairly universal stages, tied to a sequence of age-related crises?
   a. stability model
   b. life events model
   c. normative-crisis model
   d. personal growth model

4. Erikson's theory of psychosocial development is a
   a. stability model.
   b. life events model.
   c. normative-crisis model.
   d. personal growth model.

5. If you were to look at a graph of marital satisfaction over time, what shape would it be?
   a. linear incline
   b. linear decline
   c. bell-shaped curve
   d. U-shaped configuration

6. When people have to move back home because they cannot find a job after graduating from college, they are referred to as
   a. yo-yo children.
   b. sandwich children.
   c. boomerang children.
   d. empty nest children.

7. Maxillas is a 56-year-old grandparent , his grandchildren view him as a friend and know that they can count on him for any type of support.   What type of grandparenting has Maxillas adopted?
   a. remote
   b. involved
   c. arbitrator
   d. companionate

8. Why is it easier for middle-aged men to remarry than middle aged women?
   a. marriage gradient
   b. child-care status
   c. attractiveness
   d. employability

9. What is the second stage of marital aggression?
   a. tension-building stage
   b. overreaction stage
   c. loving contrition stage
   d. acute battering incident stage

10. Which stage of violence helps explain why many wives remain with abusive husbands and are the continuing victims of abuse?
    a. overreaction stage
    b. loving contrition stage
    c. tension-building stage
    d. acute battering incident stage

11. _____ satisfaction is related to middle adults' _____ satisfaction.
    a. Martial; job
    b. Job; family
    c. Family, peer
    d. Sex, martial

12. Research indicates that every time the unemployment rate goes up one percent, there is a rise in
    a. crime.
    b. suicide.
    c. homicide.
    d. spousal abuse.

13. Vaillant suggested that an important period during middle adulthood is
    a. keeping the meaning versus rigidity.
    b. generativity versus stagnation.
    c. transformations of development.
    d. life events versus normative crises.

14. Which of the following is an accurate statement concerning Levinson's theory?
    a.   He found that men and women go through a similar dream process.
    b.   His original study was based solely on women.
    c.   Women suffer conflicts between career and family.
    d.   He failed to generalize his findings adequately.

15. Who suggested that there is substantial change in personality over time?
    a.   Gould and Freud
    b.   Costa and McCrae
    c.   Erikson and Levinson
    d.   Vaillant and Gould

16. Research on subjective well-being has shown that
    a.   there are wide variations in happiness levels.
    b.   only ten percent of people rate themselves as "very happy."
    c.   money does buy happiness.
    1.   men and women rate themselves as equally happy.

17. About one woman in _____ who is in her first marriage will get divorced after the age of 40.
    a.   four   c.   eight
    b.   six   d.   ten

18. Couples in second marriages tend to
    a.   be more romantic.   c.   have more durable marriages.
    b.   be more flexible.   d.   experience less stress.

19. Grandparents who are actively engaged in grandparenting and have influence over their grandchildren's lives are
    a.   companionate.   c.   remote.
    b.   involved.   d.   coparents.

20. The idea that events in one's life determines the course of personality development was suggested by
    a.   Levinson.   c.   Helson.
    b.   Gould.   d.   Erikson.

KEY NAMES

Match each of the following names to the most accurate description and check your answers with the Answer Key at the end of this chapter.

1. ___ Erik Erikson   a. generativity vs. stagnation

2. ___ Roger Gould   b. keeping the meaning versus rigidity

3. ___ Ravenna Helson   c. life events model

4. ___ Daniel Levinson   d. seasons of life

5. ___ George Vaillant   e. transformations

KEY VOCABULARY TERMS

Explain the relationship between the following pairs of terms.

1. Empty nest syndrome, Boomerang children

2. Normative-crisis models; Life events models

3. Generativity vs. stagnation; Sandwich generation

Define the following terms and give a specific example of each.

4. Midlife crisis
5. Cycle-of-violence hypothesis
6. Burnout

PROGRAMMED REVIEW

Fill in the blanks in the following programmed review and check your answers with the Answer Key at the end of this chapter.

Personality Development

1. _____ crisis models see personality development in terms of fairly universal stages, tied to a sequence of _____. They arose at a time when society had fairly rigid and uniform _____ for people. Life _____ models suggest that the timing of particular events in an adult's life determines the course of personality development. Theorists would all agree that middle adulthood is a time of continued psychological _____.

Erikson's Stage of Generativity versus Stagnation

2. Erikson suggests that middle adulthood encompasses the period of _____ versus _____. Generative people strive to play a role in guiding and encouraging _____ generations. Lack of psychological success in this period means that people become _____, focusing on the triviality of their own _____ and feeling that they have made only limited _____ to the world.

3. Vaillant has suggested that an important period during middle adulthood is keeping the _____ versus rigidity. People seek to keep the meaning by developing an _____ of the strengths and weaknesses of others. They are relatively _____; whereas those who are unable to keep the meaning risk becoming _____ and increasingly _____ from others.

4. Gould suggests that adults pass through a series of _____ stages associated with specific _____ periods. Gould suggests that coming to grips with the reality that life is _____ can propel people towards adult _____. _____ research has supported his description of the various stages.

5. According to Levinson _____ of life theory, the early 40s are a period of _____ and _____. During early adulthood, people construct _____, a broad, comprehensive vision of the future. People make, and sometimes discard, _____ choices as they come to grips with their capabilities and ultimately commit to _____ decisions. This process leads to a period in the late 30s of _____ down. At around age 40 or 45, people move into a period called midlife _____, a time of questioning. People begin to focus on the _____ nature of life. This period of assessment may lead to a midlife _____, a stage of uncertainty and indecision brought about by the realization that life is _____. Levinson argued that women generally have greater difficulty than men in the _____ stage.

6. Central to Levinson's model is the concept of midlife _____, a period in the early 40s presumed to be marked by intense _____ turmoil. But evidence for a widespread midlife crisis is _____. The majority of people

regard midlife as a particularly _____ time. Rather than looking forward to the _____, they focus on the _____.

7. The notion of a separate _____ age is clearly a cultural _____. The _____ of particular age ranges differs depending on the culture in which one lives.

Stability versus Change in Personality

8. Theorists such as _____ and _____ suggest that there is a substantial change in personality over time. Yet, an impressive body of research suggests that at least in terms of individual traits, _____ is quite stable and continuous over the life span. Self-concept at age _____ is a good indication of self-concept at age 80. There is evidence that people's traits actually become more _____ as they age.

9. The Big Five personality traits include _____, the degree to which a person is moody, anxious, and self-critical; _____, how outgoing or shy a person is; _____, level of curiosity and interest in new experiences; _____ easy going and helpfulness; and _____, tendency to be organized and responsible. The majority of studies find these traits to be _____ past the age of 30.

10. Women who showed more positive emotional expression in their yearbook photos tended to express higher degrees of _____ and _____. They also tended to show increased competence over time and become more _____, focused, and achievement oriented. They tend to have less negative _____ over time. In addition they were more likely to be married at age _____ and report feeling satisfied with marriage at age _____.

11. Adults' sense of _____ well-being or general _____ remains stable over their lives. This suggests that most people have a _____ for happiness.

Relationships: Family in Middle Age

Marriage

12. The most frequent pattern of satisfaction is the _____ configuration. Marital satisfaction begins to _____ just after the marriage and it continues to _____ until it reaches its _____ point following the births of the couple's children. At that point, satisfaction begins to _____.

13. Middle-aged couples state as a source of satisfaction that their spouse is their best _____ and that they like their spouses as _____. They also tend to view marriage as a long-term _____ and to agree on their aims and goals. Most feel that their spouses have grown more _____ over the course of the marriage. For both men and women, being in agreement about their _____ lives leads to satisfaction.

14. Just as with younger couples, today's _____ rate for middle-aged couples is higher than in earlier decades. Divorce can be especially difficult for _____ in midlife, particularly if they have followed the traditional _____ role.

15. Some _____ percent of people who divorce end up marrying again, usually within 2 to 5 years. They are most likely to marry people who have also been _____.

16. It is harder for _____ to remarry than _____. Less than one-third of women over the age of _____ remarry. The reason stems from the marriage _____. Societal norms push men to marry women who are _____, smaller, and lower in _____. Women have the disadvantage of societal standards regarding physical _____.

17. One motivation to remarry is to avoid the _____ consequences of divorce. Divorced people miss the _____ that marriage provides. Divorced _____ report feeling lonely and experience an increase in physical and mental health problems. Marriage provides clear _____ benefits as well.

18. Older couples tend to be more mature and _____, look at marriage in less _____ terms, and are _____. They show greater _____ in terms of roles and duties and make decisions in a more _____ manner.

19. The divorce rate for second marriages is slightly _____. Second marriages may be subject to _____ that are not present in first marriages, such as the strain of _____ different families.

<u>Family Evolutions: From Full House to Empty Nest</u>

20. For many parents, a major transition that typically occurs during middle adulthood is the _____ of children. The _____ syndrome refers to instances in which parents experience unhappiness, worry, loneliness, and depression from their children's departure from home. Particularly for women who have followed the _____ societal model and stayed home to rear their children, the loss can be difficult. But for most people, the empty nest syndrome is more _____ than reality. Some research suggests that men experience some degree of _____ when their children depart.

21. _____ children typically cite _____ issues as the main reason for returning home. Some also return home after the breakup of a _____. _____ tend to be more sympathetic to children who are unemployed. Both mothers and fathers feel positive about returning children who _____ and _____ to the functioning of the household.

22. The term _____ generation refers to couples who in middle adulthood must fulfill the needs of both their children and their aging parents. This generation occurs because both men and women are _____ later, having _____ at an older age, and there is an increased likelihood that middle-aged parents will have parents that are alive and in need of _____. The care of aging parents can be _____ tricky. There is a significant degree of role _____. The loss of _____ on the part of an elderly parent can be particularly difficult. Even when both husband and wife are in the labor force, middle-aged _____ tend to be more involved in the day-to-day care of aging parents.

<u>Becoming a Grandparent: Who, Me?</u>

23. _____ grandparents are actively engaged in grandparenting and have influence over their grandchildren's lives. They hold clear _____ about the ways their grandchildren should behave. _____ grandparents are more relaxed and act as _____ and buddies to them. The most aloof type of grandparents are _____. They are detached and distant and show little _____ in their grandchildren.

24. Generally, _____ are more interested and experience greater satisfaction than _____. And _____-American grandparents are more apt to be involved with their grandchildren than _____ grandparents. African-American families are more likely to be headed by _____ parents, who often rely substantially on the help of grandparents in everyday child care, and cultural _____ tend to be highly supportive of grandparents taking an active role.

<u>Family Violence: The Hidden Epidemic</u>

25. Some form of violence happens in _____ of all marriages, and more than _____ the women who were murdered in one recent 10-year period were murdered by a partner. Violence occurs across _____ strata, races, _____ groups, and religions. It also occurs across _____.

26. Certain factors increase the likelihood of abuse such as lower _____ status. Child abuse occurs most frequently in _____ environments, in lower _____ levels, in _____ parent families, and in situations with high levels of marital _____. Incest is more likely to occur in _____ families.

27. Marital aggression by a husband typically occurs in _____ stages. The first is the _____ building stage, in which a batterer becomes upset and shows dissatisfaction initially through _____ abuse. The next stage consists of an _____ battering incident. Finally, in some, but not all, cases, the episode moves into the loving _____ stage. Some wives may feel that they are partly at _____ for triggering the aggression. Others remain out of _____ of what their husbands will do to them if they leave or stay with batterers because they have learned that violence is an _____ means of settling disputes.

28. According to the _____ of violence hypothesis, abuse and neglect of children leads them to be predisposed to abusiveness as adults. About _____ of people who were abused or neglected as children abuse their own children as adults, and fully _____ of abusers were not themselves abused as children.

29. Measures to help victims of spousal abuse include teaching husbands and wives that_____ violence is never acceptable, calling the _____, understanding that _____ may have no bearing on future violence, providing _____ for victims of domestic violence, seeking a _____ order, and calling the National _____ Violence Hotline.

30. Wife battering is particularly prevalent in cultures in which women are viewed as _____ to men. According to _____ common law, husbands were allowed to beat their wives. Some experts on abuse suggest that the traditional _____ structure under which women and men function is a root cause of abuse. The more a society differentiates between men and women in terms of _____, the more likely that abuse will occur. Relatively _____ status makes women easy targets of violence. Unusually _____ status may make husbands feel threatened and consequently more likely to behave abusively.

Work and Leisure

Work and Careers: Jobs at Midlife

31. The factors that make a job _____ often undergo a transformation during middle age. Whereas younger adults are more interested in abstract and _____ concerns, such as the opportunity for _____ or the possibility of recognition and approval, middle-aged employees are more concerned with pay, _____ conditions, and specific _____.

32. The older workers are, the _____ overall job satisfaction they experience. Younger adults who are dissatisfied with jobs will _____ them and find new positions. Older workers have fewer _____ to change positions, and consequently may learn to _____ with what they have.

Challenges of Work: On-the-Job Dissatisfaction

33. _____ occurs when highly trained professionals experience dissatisfaction, disillusionment, frustration, and weariness from their jobs. It occurs most often in jobs that involve _____ others and it often strikes those who initially were the most _____ and driven. One of the consequences of burnout is a growing _____ about one's work as well as _____ and lack of _____ about how well one does it. Workers with realistic _____ about what can and cannot be accomplished are able to focus on what is practical and doable. Workers can experience small _____ in their daily work.

Unemployment: The Dashing of a Dream

34. The implications of not being able to find work are as much _____ as they are economic. People who are unemployed frequently suffer from _____ and feel anxious, depressed, and irritable. Their self-confidence may plummet and they may be unable to _____. Unemployed people are less apt to participate in _____ activities, use _____, and _____ than employed people. They are more likely to be late for _____ and even for meals.

35. Middle-aged adults who lose their jobs tend to stay unemployed _____ than younger workers, and people have fewer opportunities for _____ work as they age. Employers may _____ against older job applicants and make it more difficult to obtain new employment.

36. Research finds that older workers show _____ absenteeism than younger ones, hold their jobs _____, are more _____, and are _____ willing to learn new skills.

Switching—and Starting—Careers in Midlife

37. People who change careers in middle adulthood do so because their jobs offer little _____, they have achieved _____ and what was once difficult is now _____, or their jobs have _____ in ways they do not like. Still others are unhappy with the _____ they have achieved. Some are _____ out or feel that they are on the _____. For them, middle age is seen as the last point at which they can make a _____ occupational change. A significant number of people, almost all of them _____, return to the job market after having taken time off to raise children. Some need to find paying work after a _____.

38. Middle-aged people who start new careers may find themselves in _____ positions. Some visionaries suggest that career changes may become the _____, rather than the exception. According to this point of view, _____ advances will occur so rapidly that people will be forced to change dramatically what they do to earn a living.

39. Residents born outside the country now represent close to _____ percent of the population. Most legal and illegal immigrants are doing quite well _____ and actually have _____ family income than native-born Americans. Only a few immigrants come to the United States to get on _____. Nonrefugee immigrants who are old enough to work are _____ likely to be on welfare than native-born U.S. citizens. Immigrants become more _____ as they get older.

Leisure Time: Life Beyond Work

40. Most middle-aged adults have some _____ waking hours per week at their disposal. On average, middle-aged people watch around _____ hours of television each week, and adults in the United States spend some six hours each week _____.

41. Some of the motivation for developing leisure activities during middle adulthood comes from the desire to prepare for _____. Most people report that the _____ of their lives does not appear slower.

CRITICAL THINKING QUESTIONS

To further your mastery of the topics in which chapter, write out your answers to the following essay questions from the text in the spaces provided.

1. How do you think the midlife transition is different for a middle-aged person whose child has just entered adolescence versus a middle-aged person who has just become a parent for the first time?

2. What factors (in women, society, or the study) might account for Levinson's finding that women had more difficulty than men in articulating "The Dream"?

3. In what ways might normative-crisis models of personality development be culture specific?

4. What accounts for the typical U-shaped curve of satisfaction in most marriages?

5. How does the experience of divorce differ for women with outside careers versus women who have stayed home to rear children? How does the marriage gradient affect women with outside careers?

6. Are the phenomena of the empty nest, boomerang children, the sandwich generation, and grandparenting culturally dependent? Why might such phenomena be different in societies where multigenerational families are the norm?

7. How would you develop a campaign to end family and marital violence? What educational tools would you employ? What would be the barriers or constraints to such a program?

8. Why might striving for occupational success be less appealing in middle age than before? What cognitive and personality changes might contribute to this phenomenon?

9. Why do you think immigrants' ambition and achievements are widely underestimated? Does the occurrence of conspicuous negative examples play a role (as it does in perceptions of the midlife crisis and stormy adolescence)?

10. Have you known of a middle-aged person who has experienced a midlife crisis? How was his or her experience the same or different from that described in chapter? Was his or her resolution of the "crisis" successful?

Circle the correct answer for each of the following multiple choice questions and check your answers with the Answer Key at the end of this chapter.

1. If a person does not successfully complete the generativity-versus-stagnation stage, the result would be
    a. trivialization of one's activities.
    b. fear of relationships with others.
    c. regret over lost opportunities in life.
    d. inability to identify appropriate roles in life.

2. During Levinson's midlife transition, people confront the knowledge that
    a. their children no longer need them.
    b. their employer does not need them any longer.
    c. they will make only a finite amount of money in their life.
    d. they will be unable to accomplish all of their aims before they die.

3. The particular events in an adult's life, rather than age per se, is suggested as the determinant of the course of personality development by which theory?
    a. stability model
    b. life events model
    c. normative-crisis model
    d. personal growth model

4. Kyle was the last sibling in his family to move out of his parents' home on his own. What period in the family life cycle is occurring?
    a. kinkeeper
    b. empty nest
    c. role reversal
    d. launching adolescents

5. Couples who in middle adulthood must fulfill the needs of both their children and their aging parents are known as the
    a. yo-yo parents.
    b. sandwich generation.
    c. boomerang parents.
    d. empty nest parents.

6. What percent of marriages in the U.S. are characterized by continuing, severe violence?
    a. 2 percent
    b. 5 percent
    c. 10 percent
    d. 15 percent

7. The cycle-of-violence hypothesis states that abuse and neglect of children lead them to be
    a. victims in adult life.
    b. insecure and withdrawn adults.
    c. more sympathetic to others as adults.
    d. predisposed to abusiveness as adults.

8. Alexis is an aloof grandparent who sees her grandchildren on only very rare occasions. She knows little of what is happening in their lives and makes little attempt to get involved. What type of grandparenting is Alexis displaying?
    a. morbid
    b. remote
    c. defensive
    d. uninvolved

9. Spousal abuse occurs in what percent of all marriages?
    a. 2 percent
    b. 10 percent
    c. 20 percent
    d. 25 percent

10. A worker complains that she feels physically and emotionally exhausted from her work. She is probably experiencing
    a. burnout.
    b. role strain.
    c. role conflict.
    d. professional obsolescence.

11. Middle-aged people average about how much TV each week?
    a. 10 hours
    b. 15 hours
    c. 25 hours
    d. 40 hours

12. Who proposed that people experience developmental transformations?
    a. Erikson
    b. Vaillant
    c. Levinson
    d. Gould

13. Research on midlife crisis indicates that
    a. it is a widespread phenomenon.
    b. the majority of people regard midlife as stressful.
    c. people in midlife focus on the present.
    d. most middle-aged people feel older than they really are.

14. The Big Five personality traits include all of the following EXCEPT
    a. neuroticism.
    b. aggressiveness.
    c. openness.
    d. conscientiousness.

15. Middle-age couples cite all of the following sources of satisfaction EXCEPT
    a. their spouse is their best friend.
    b. their marriage was a long term commitment.
    c. their sexual activity has increased.
    d. their spouse has grown more interesting.

16. What percent of divorced people remarry?
    a. 5-10 percent
    b. 25-30 percent
    c. 45-50 percent
    d. 75-80 percent

17. The care of aging parents
    a. involves a significant degree of role reversal.
    b. is usually equally shared among siblings.
    c. usually falls to the oldest son.
    d. is most likely to create severe conflicts.

18. Which segment of society is NOT affected by family violence?
    a. religious families
    b. single-parent families
    c. affluent families
    d. All types of families are affected.

19. According to a growing body of research, adult's _____ remains stable over time.
    a. marital satisfaction
    b. friendships
    c. subjective well-being
    d. job satisfaction

20. Which of the following is NOT suggested as a way to deal with spousal abuse?
    a. fighting back
    b. calling the police
    c. seek a safe haven
    d. seek a restraining order

ANSWER KEYS

Practice Test – Pretest (with text page numbers)

1.	c 561	6.	c 573	11.	d 570	16.	d 568
2.	b 562	7.	d 574	12.	b 580	17.	c 570
3.	c 561	8.	a 571	13.	a 562	18.	b 571
4.	c 561	9.	d 576	14.	c 563	19.	b 574
5.	d 570	10.	b 576	15.	c 567	20.	c 561

Key Names

1. a   2. e   3. c   4. d   5. b

Key Vocabulary Terms

1. The empty nest syndrome is the experience that relates to parents' feelings of unhappiness, worry, loneliness, and depression resulting from their children's departure from home; and this syndrome may be relieved by boomerang children who are young adults who return, after leaving home for some period, to live in the homes of their middle-aged parents.

2. Normative-crisis models approach personality development as based on universal stages, tied to a sequence of age-related crises; life events models approach personality development as based on the timing of particular events in an adult's life, rather than age per se.

3. Generativity versus stagnation is Erikson's stage during middle adulthood in which people consider their contributions to family and society; sandwich generation includes couples who in middle adulthood must fulfill the needs of both their children and their aging parents, something which produces a feeling of generativity.

Programmed Review

1. Normative, age-related, roles, events, growth
2. generativity, stagnation, future, stagnant, activity, contributions
3. meaning, acceptance, content, rigid, isolated
4. seven, age, finite, maturity, Little
5. transition, crisis, dreams, career, long-term, settling, transition, finite, crisis, finite, dream
6. crisis, psychological, lacking, rewarding, future, present
7. middle, construction, significance
8. Erikson, Levinson, personality, 30, ingrained
9. neuroticism, extraversion, openness, agreeableness, conscientiousness, stable
10. affiliation, competence, organized, emotionality, 27, 52
11. subjective, happiness, set point
12. U-shaped, decline, fall, lowest, grow
13. friend, people, commitment, interesting, sex
14. divorce, women, female
15. 75 to 80, divorced
16. women, men, 40, gradient, younger, status, attractiveness
17. social, companionship, men, economic
18. realistic, romantic, cautious, flexibility, participatory
19. higher, stresses, blending
20. departure, empty nest, traditional, myth, loss
21. Boomerang, economic, marriage, Mothers, work, contribute
22. sandwich, marrying, children, care, psychologically, reversal, independence, women,
23. Involved, expectations, Companionate, supporters, remote, interest
24. grandmothers, grandfathers, African, white, single, norms
25. one-fourth, half, social, ethnic, genders

26. socioeconomic, stressful, socioeconomic, single, conflict, affluent
27. three, tension, verbal, acute, contrition, fault, fear, acceptable
28. cycle, one-third, two-thirds
29. physical, police, remorse, shelters, restraining, Domestic
30. inferior, English, power, status, low, high
31. satisfying, future-oriented, advancement, working, policies,
32. more, quit, opportunities, live
33. Burnout, helping, idealistic, cynicism, indifference, concern, expectations, victories
34. psychological, insomnia, concentrate, community, libraries, read, appointments
35. longer, gratifying, discriminate
36. less, longer, reliable, more
37. challenge, mastery, routine, changed, status, burned, treadmill, meaningful, women, divorce
38. entry-level, rule, technological
39. 10, financially, higher, welfare, less, productive
40. 70, 15, socializing
41. retirement, pace

Practice Test – Post Test (with text page numbers)

1.	a	561	6.	d	575	11.	b	584	16.	d 571
2.	d	562	7.	d	576	12.	d	562	17.	a 573
3.	b	561	8.	b	574	13.	c	562	18.	d 576
4.	b	572	9.	d	575	14.	b	566	19.	c 568
5.	b	573	10.	a	580	15.	c	570	20.	a 577

Chapter 17

Physical and Cognitive Development in Late Adulthood

CHAPTER OUTLINE

◆ Physical Development in Late Adulthood
- Aging: Myth and Reality
- Physical Transitions in Older People
- Slowing Reaction Time
- The Senses: Sight, Sound, Taste, and Smell

◆ Health and Wellness in Late Adulthood
- Health Problems in Older People: Physical and Psychological Disorders
- Wellness in Late Adulthood: The Relationship Between Aging and Illness
- Sexuality in Old age: Use It or Lose It
- Approaches to Aging: Why is Death Inevitable?
- Postponing Aging: Can Scientists Find the Fountain of Youth?

◆ Cognitive Development in Late Adulthood
- Intelligence in Older People
- Recent Conclusions about the Nature of Intelligence in Older People
- Memory: Remembrance of Things Past–and Present
- Learning in Later Life: Never Too Late to Learn

LEARNING OBJECTIVES

After you have read and studied this chapter, you should be able to answer the following questions.

1. What is it like to grow old in the United States today?
2. What sorts of physical changes occur in old age?
3. How are the senses affected by aging?
4. What is the general state of health of older people, and to what disorders are they susceptible?
5. Can wellness and sexuality be maintained in old age?
6. How long can people expect to live, and why do they die?
7. How well do older people function intellectually?
8. Do people lose their memories in old age?

PRACTICE TEST – PRETEST

Circle the correct answers for the following multiple choice questions and check your answers with the Answer Key at the end of this chapter.

1. Specialists who study aging are called
    a. ontologists.
    b. thanatologists.
    c. gerontologists.
    d. endocrinologists.

2. The fastest-growing segment of the U.S. population is the
    a. oldest-old.
    b. young-old.
    c. middle-old.
    d. middle-adulthood.

3. Prejudice and discrimination directed at older people is called
    a. bigotry.
    b. ageism.
    c. senescence.
    d. gerontologism.

4. The fact that Ty's pleasant memories are more likely recalled than his unpleasant memories reflects the
    a. denial principle.
    b. positive outlook principle.
    c. Pollyanna principle.
    d. general compensation principle.

5. Hearing loss is found in what percent of people over the age of 75?
    a. 25 percent
    b. 50 percent
    c. 75 percent
    d. 100 percent

6. Hypertension is also known as
    a. hypotension.
    b. osteoporosis.
    c. atherosclerosis.
    d. high blood pressure.

7. Psychological problems are seen in what percent of people over the age of 65?
    a. 15-25 percent
    b. 45-50 percent
    c. 75 percent
    d. 100 percent

8. A progressive brain disorder that produces loss of memory and confusion is called
    a. Hodgkin's disease.
    b. Alzheimer's disease.
    c. Parkinson's disease.
    d. Huntington's disease.

9. What is the primary determinant of whether an elderly person will engage in sexual activity?
    a. susceptibility to cultural taboos
    b. adaptation to changes in sexual functioning
    c. good health and previous, regular sexual activity
    d. previous psychologically healthy sexual relationship

10. What theory suggests that our body's DNA genetic code contains a built-in time limit for the reproduction of human cells?
    a. wear-and-tear theory
    b. peripheral slowing hypothesis
    c. generalized slowing hypothesis
    d. genetic preprogramming theory

11. Cross-sectional methods are sometimes used in studying intelligence in older people. This can be a problem because cross-sectional methods do not take into account
    a. cohort effects.
    b. attrition effects.
    c. cognitive effects.
    d. All of these answers are correct.

12. When older people are riding a bike or walking, they are calling upon a form of memory called
   a. sensory memory.
   b. implicit memory.
   c. semantic memory.
   d. autobiographical memory.

13. After a man retired, he noticed that his memory did not seem as good. His decline in memory is probably due to
   a. biological factors.
   b. environmental factors.
   c. information-processing deficits.
   d. All of the answers are correct.

14. About how many people over the age of 85 suffer from dementia?
   a. one-quarter
   b. one-third
   c. one-half
   d. two-thirds

15. Secondary aging is related to all of the following EXCEPT
   a. illness.
   b. health habits.
   c. senescence.
   d. potentially avoidable factors.

16. Which explanation of slower reactions in older people is based on slowing throughout the body?
   a. wear and tear
   b. peripheral slowing hypothesis
   c. generalized slowing hypothesis
   d. genetic preprogramming

17. Biologically, Alzheimer's occurs when production of what protein goes awry?
   a. acetycholine
   b. collagen
   c. dopamine
   d. beta amyloid precursor

18. Which theory of aging encompasses the impact of free radicals?
   a. preprogrammed
   b. wear and tear
   c. generalized slowing
   d. peripheral

19. Which approach to postponing aging includes replacing worn out organs?
   a. bionic
   b. talomere
   c. free radicals
   d. restricting calories

20. Teri has memories of general facts such as simple arithmetic and the names of U.S. presidents which reflects the functioning of her _____ memory.
   a. semantic
   b. episodic
   c. implicit
   d. autobiographical

KEY NAMES

There are no new names in this chapter. Take this opportunity to go back and review the Key Names section in the previous chapters as a review.

KEY VOCABULARY TERMS

Explain the differences between the following pairs of terms.

1. Peripheral slowing hypothesis; General slowing hypothesis

2. Primary aging; Secondary aging

3. Genetic preprogramming theories of aging; Wear-and-tear theories of aging

4. Dementia; Alzheimer's disease

Define the following terms and give a specific example of each

5. Gerontologists
6. Ageism
7. Osteoporosis
8. Life expectancy
9. Plasticity
10. Autobiographical memory

PROGRAMMED REVIEW

Fill in the blanks in the following Programmed Review and check your answers with the Answer Key at the end of this chapter.

Physical Development in Late Adulthood

Aging: Myth and Reality

1. Because people are living longer, late adulthood is actually _____ in length. For demographers, the _____ old are those 65 to 74 years old, the _____ old are between 75 and 84, and the _____ old, age 85 and older, are the fastest growing segment of the population. In the last two decades, the size of this group has nearly _____.

2. _____ is prejudice and discrimination directed at older people, found in widespread _____ attitudes toward older people and the aging process that suggest that older people are in less than full command of their _____ faculties. Elderly individuals seeking jobs may face open _____, or they are sometimes relegated to jobs for which they are _____. Older adults in nursing homes are often the recipients of _____ talk.

3. The ageism directed toward people in late adulthood is, in some ways, a peculiarly 20th century, and _____ cultural phenomenon. People in Asian societies _____ those who have reached old age.

Physical Transitions in Older People

4. Many older persons remain remarkably _____ and _____ fit in later life. _____ aging or _____ involves universal and irreversible changes experienced by all. _____ aging encompasses changes due to thing that are not inevitable.

5. One of the most obvious signs of aging is the _____. The face and other parts of the body become wrinkled as the skin loses _____ and _____, the protein that forms the basic fibers of body tissue.

6. People may become noticeably _____, with some shrinking as much as _____ inches. Although shortening is partially due to changes in _____, the primary cause is that the _____ in the disks of the backbone has become thinner. This is particularly true for women, who are more susceptible than men to _____, or thinning of the bones. Osteoporosis is largely preventable if people's _____ and _____ intake are sufficient in earlier life, and if they have engaged in sufficient _____.

7. Negative stereotypes are particularly potent for _____. In Western cultures there is a _____ standard for appearance, by which women who show signs of aging are judged more _____ than men. As a consequence women are more likely than men to feel compelled to _____ the signs of aging.

8. The _____ becomes smaller and lighter with age. There is a reduction in the flow of _____ within the brain, which also uses less _____ and glucose. The number of _____, or brain cells, declines in some parts of the brain.

9. Because of hardening and shrinking of blood vessels throughout the body, the _____ is forced to work harder. The efficiency of the _____ system declines with age, and the _____ system is less efficient in pushing food

through the system, which produces a higher incidence of _____. Some _____ are produced at lower levels with increasing age. _____ fibers decrease both in size and in amount, and they become less efficient at using _____ from the bloodstream and storing _____.

Slowing Reaction Time

10. According to the _____ slowing hypothesis, overall processing speed declines in the peripheral nervous system. According to the _____ slowing hypothesis, processing in all parts of the nervous system, including the brain, is less efficient.

11. The slowing of reaction time and general processing results in a higher incidence of _____ for elderly persons. They are unable to efficiently receive information from the _____ that may indicate a dangerous situation, their _____ making processes may be slower, and ultimately their ability to _____ themselves from harms' way is impaired. Although it takes older individuals longer to respond, the _____ of time seems to increase with age.

The Senses: Sight, Sound, Taste, and Smell

12. Age-related changes in physical apparatus of the eye lead to a _____ in visual abilities. The _____ becomes less transparent and the _____ shrinks. Even the _____ nerve becomes less efficient in transmitting nerve impulses. Vision for _____ objects becomes less acute, more _____ is needed to see clearly, and it takes longer to _____ from dark to light places and vice versa.

13. _____, cloudy or opaque areas on the lens of the eye that interfere with passing light, frequently develop. Intraocular _____ implants are plastic lenses permanently implanted in the eye. _____ occurs when pressure in the fluid of the eye increases, either because the fluid cannot _____ properly or because too much is produced. The most common cause of blindness in people over the age of 60 is age-related _____ degeneration (AMD).

14. Around _____ percent of adults between 65 and 74 have some degree of hearing loss, and the figure rises to _____ percent among people over age 75. The ability to hear _____ frequencies is particularly affected during old age. Some elderly persons actually find loud noises _____. A hearing loss can particularly harm the _____ lives of older people. Such hearing losses can lead to feelings of _____. Able to catch only fragments of conversations, a hearing impaired adult can easily feel left out and _____.

15. Taste and smell become less _____. There is a decline in the number of _____. The _____ bulbs in the brain begin to shrivel. Because food does not taste as good, people eat less and open the door to _____, and they may oversalt their food, thereby increasing their chances of developing _____.

Health and Wellness in Late Adulthood

16. Most elderly people are in relatively good _____ for most of old age. Surveys conducted in the United States suggest that _____ of people 65 and older rate their health as good.

Health Problems in Older People: Physical and Psychological Disorders

17. The leading causes of death in elderly people are _____, _____, and _____. Most older people have at least one _____, long-term condition. _____, an inflammation of one or more joints, is common. Around one-third of older people have _____, or high blood pressure.

18. One of the more prevalent _____ disorders in the elderly is major _____, due in part to the cumulative _____ they experience with the death of spouses and friends. Some studies suggest that the rate of depression actually may be _____ in late adulthood.

19. Some psychological disorders are produced by combinations of _____ that elderly people may be taking for various medical conditions. Because of changes in _____, a dose of a particular drug may no longer be appropriate. The effects of drug _____ can be subtle.

20. The most common mental disorder of elderly people is _____, a broad category covering several diseases, with symptoms that include declining _____, lessened _____ abilities, and impaired _____.

21. _____ disease is a progressive brain disorder that produces loss of memory and confusion and leads to the deaths of _____ people in the United States each year. The symptoms develop _____ and generally the first sign is unusual _____.

22. Biologically, Alzheimer's disease occurs when production of the protein _____ precursor goes awry. The _____ shrinks, and several areas of the _____ and _____ and _____ lobes show deterioration. Certain _____ die, which leads to a shortage of various neurotransmitters, such as _____.

23. _____ clearly plays a role, with some families showing a much higher incidence of Alzheimer's than others. Scientists are studying certain kinds of _____, dysfunctions of the _____ system, and _____ imbalances that may produce the disease. Other studies have found that lower levels of _____ ability in the early 20s are associated with declines in _____ capabilities due to Alzheimer's much later in life.

24. The most promising drugs are related to the loss of the neurotransmitter _____ that occurs in some forms of Alzheimer's disease. Other drugs being studied include _____ drugs, which may reduce the brain inflammation that occurs in Alzheimer's. In addition, the chemicals in vitamins _____ and _____ are being tested.

25. As victims increasingly lose abilities they must be taken care of _____ per day, and most end up in _____homes. People who care for the victims often become _____victims.

26. Steps to take to help both patient and caregiver include making the patients feel _____ in their home environments, providing _____ for everyday objects, furnishing _____, keeping _____ simple, putting _____ on a schedule, preventing people with the disease from _____, monitoring the use of the _____, providing opportunities for _____, and remembering to take _____ off.

Wellness in Late Adulthood: The Relationship Between Aging and Illness

27. Certain diseases, such as cancer and heart disease, have a clear _____ component. People's _____ may raise or lower their chances of coming down with a disease and _____ well-being also plays a role. _____ factors play an important role in determining people's susceptibility to illness. Having a sense of _____ over one's environment leads to a better psychological state and superior _____ outcomes. The goal of many professionals is to increase the _____ life span of the elderly, that is the amount of time they remain healthy and are able to enjoy their lives.

28. Estimates suggest that between 15 and 50 percent of elderly people do not have adequate _____ and several million experience _____ every day. Some are too _____ to purchase adequate food and some are too _____ to shop or cook for themselves. Others feel little _____ to prepare and eat proper meals. Obtaining sufficient _____ may also prove problematic for older persons

Sexuality in Old Age: Use It or Lose It

29. Factors determining whether an elderly person will engage in sexual activity include good physical and mental _____ and previous _____ sexual activity. _____, the male hormone, declines during adulthood. It takes a longer time and more stimulation for men to get a full _____. The _____ period, the time following an orgasm during which men are unable to become aroused again, may last as long as a day or even several days. Women's _____ become thin and inelastic, and they produce less natural _____.

Approaches to Aging: Why Is Death Inevitable?

30. Genetic _____ theories of aging suggest that our body's DNA genetic code contains a built-in time limit for the reproduction of human cells. _____ theories argue that the mechanical functions of the body simply wear out,

and the body's constant manufacture of _____ to fuel its activities creates by-products. One specific category of by-products that have been related to aging includes free _____. Wear-and-tear theories paint a more _____ view.

31. Life _____ is the average age of death for members of a population; its mean has steadily _____. _____ and _____ conditions and people's _____ conditions are generally better, and many products are _____.

Postponing Aging: Can Scientists Find the Fountain of Youth?

32. _____ are tiny, protective areas at the tip of chromosomes that appear to grow shorter each time a cell divides. When a cell's telomere has just about disappeared, the cell stops _____. Some scientists believe that if telomeres could be _____, age-related problems could be slowed.

33. Reducing free _____ through _____ drugs may help. Free radicals are _____ molecules that are a by-product of normal cell functioning.

34. Researchers have known that laboratory rats who are fed an extremely low _____ diet often live 30 percent longer than better-fed rats. The reason appears to be that fewer free _____ are produced in the hungry rats.

35. Despite significant advances in organ transplantation, transplants frequently fail because the body _____ the foreign tissue. Some researchers suggest that replacement organs can be grown from a recipient's _____ cells, thereby solving the rejection problem. Cells from _____ could be used or _____ organs can completely diseased or damaged ones.

36. Across the industrialized world, _____ live longer than _____ by some 4 to 10 years. This advantage begins just after _____. Although slightly more _____ are conceived, males are more likely to _____ during the prenatal period, infancy, and childhood. For those over 85, there are _____ women still alive for every male.

37. Naturally higher levels of _____ such as estrogen and progesterone in women provide some protection from diseases. Women experience less _____ than men and engage in _____ behavior during their lives. Disparities in _____ well-being of various groups in the United States account for racial and ethnic differences.

Cognitive Development in Late Adulthood

38. Researchers no longer see the cognitive abilities of older people as inevitably _____.

Intelligence in Older People

39. In studying intelligence, cross-sectional methods do not take into account _____ effects. Because some traditional intelligence tests include _____ portions, the slower reaction time of older people might account for their inferior performance. Longitudinal studies raise some fundamental interpretive difficulties because of _____ exposure to the same test.

Recent Conclusions about the Nature of Intelligence in Older People

40. Schaie has employed _____ methods that combine cross-sectional and longitudinal methods by examining several different age groups at a number of points in time. He has found no _____ pattern in adulthood of age-related changes across all intellectual abilities. For the average person, some _____ declines are found in all abilities by age 67, but these declines are _____ until the 80s. Significant individual differences are found in the _____ of change in intelligence, and certain _____ and _____ factors are related to greater or lesser degrees of intellectual decline.

41. Subsequent research shows that cognitive _____ can have lasting effects. The success of training was related to improvements in _____ intelligence and on tasks associated with daily living. Such _____, or modifiability of behavior, suggests that there is nothing fixed about the changes that may occur in intellectual abilities during late adulthood.

42. Cross-cultural research reveals that in societies where older people are held in high _____, people are less likely to show memory losses. Even when memory declines that can directly be traced to aging occur, they are limited primarily to _____ memories, which relate to specific life experiences. Other types of memory, such as _____ memories (general knowledge and facts) and _____ memories (memories about which people are not consciously aware) are largely unaffected by age. _____ memory slips gradually during adulthood until age 70. Information about things that are completely _____ is more difficult to recall.

43. When it comes to _____ memory, memories of information about one's own life, older people are subject to some of the same principles of _____ as younger individuals. Memory recall frequently follows the _____ principle, in which pleasant memories are more likely to be recalled than unpleasant memories. People tend to forget information about their past that is not _____ with the way they currently see themselves.

44. Explanations for apparent changes in memory among older people tend to focus on _____ factors, _____ deficits, and _____ factors.

Learning in Later life: Never Too Late to Learn

45. The _____ program is the largest educational program for people in late adulthood.

CRITICAL THINKING QUESTIONS

To further your understanding of the topics covered in this chapter, write out your answers to the following essay questions in the spaces provided.

1. What are some social implications of an increasing number and proportion of older people in the population?

2. When jobs for all workers are scarce, is it right for elderly people to hold onto their current jobs or even seek new ones?

3. When older people win praise and attention for being vigorous, active, and youthful, is this a message that combats or supports ageism?

4. Should strict examinations for renewal of driver's licenses be imposed on older people? What issues should be taken into consideration?

5. What factors should a family take into account in deciding whether to care for a person with Alzheimer's at home or in a nursing facility?

6. Given that socioeconomic status relates to wellness in old age and to life expectancy, should our society do more to subsidize the lives of the elderly? Why or why not?

7. How might studies be designed to test whether the genetic preprogramming or wear-and-tear theory is more accurate?

8. Are the reasons for the gender gap in life expectancy primarily genetic or cultural? Why?

9. What do you think underlies the root of ageism in U.S. society, preference for younger individuals as opposed to the elderly? How can one personally address and reduce the ageism that they may hold?

10. Could the Pollyanna principle be a genetic or culturally based phenomenon? What might be the social or mental health advantages of such a principle?

PRACTICE TEST - POST TEST

Circle the correct answers for the following multiple choice questions and check your answers with the Answer Key at the end of this chapter.

1. What percent of the U.S. population will be over age 65 by the year 2050?
    a. 10 percent
    b. 15 percent
    c. 20 percent
    d. 25 percent

2. Rose Marie is 80-years-old, and as thus demographers would classify her as the
    a. oldest-old.
    b. young-old.
    c. dying-old.
    d. old-old.

3. If a doctor feels that a patient is a likely candidate for osteoporosis in later life, the doctor prescribes exercise, plus
   a. niacin and vitamin C.
   b. vitamin B.
   c. riboflavin.
   d. calcium and protein.

4. Carlos has believes all old people are senile, mentally deteriorating, and useless. His views reflect
   a. ageism.
   b. cultural norms.
   c. bigotry.
   d. the true state of aging adults.

5. Joe's alcoholism over the course of his life has caused increased deterioration in his physical aging. This phenomenon reflects
   a. primary aging.
   b. secondary aging.
   c. senescence.
   d. senility.

6. Arthritis is experienced by what percent of older people?
   a. 25 percent
   b. 50 percent
   c. 75 percent
   d. 100 percent

7. The awry production of _____ in Mary's old age has caused her to develop a progressive brain disorder that has produced a loss of memory and confusion.
   a. neurotransmitters
   b. alpha hydroxyl protein
   c. calcium
   d. beta amyloid precursor protein

8. Drugs that are currently under study for use in treating Alzheimer's disease show the most promise if they are related to the
   a. brain inflammation that occurs.
   b. dysfunction of the immune system.
   c. loss of the neurotransmitter acetylcholine.
   d. hormone imbalances that may produce the disease.

9. For persons over the age of 70, what percent have sex with their spouses about once per week?
   a. 5 percent
   b. 50 percent
   c. 46 percent
   d. 66 percent

10. What theory of aging compares the human body to a machine that simply breaks down as a result of constant use?
    a. cellular theory
    b. free radicals theory
    c. cross-linkage theory
    d. wear-and-tear theory

11. What happens to the brain as we age?
    a. Most neurotransmitters are increased.
    b. Blood flow is increased.
    c. It becomes smaller and lighter.
    d. It becomes heavier and denser.

12. Even when memory declines can be directly traced to aging, they are limited primarily to
    a. episodic memory.
    b. implicit memory.
    c. semantic memory.
    d. autobiographical memory.

13. What explanation for memory changes in old age views older adults as concentrating less, and having greater difficulty focusing on appropriate stimuli and organizing material in memory?
    a. biological factors
    b. environmental factors
    c. information-processing deficits
    d. wear and tear

14. Negative views of the elderly
    a. prevail in United States society.
    b. were common one hundred years ago.
    c. are common in most Asian societies.
    d. are traditional in Native Americans.

15. Which of the following does NOT affect vision in old age?
    a. The lenses become less transparent.
    c. The optic nerve becomes less efficient.
    b. The pupils widen.
    d. The number of optic cells decreases drastically.

16. Decrease in the sense of taste can be traced to
    a. reduced ability to smell.
    c. hypertension.
    b. increase in taste buds.
    d. Alzheimers disease.

17. Older people pay _____ percent of their total expenditures on health care.
    a. 1
    c. 12
    b. 3
    d. 15

18. By 1990, the average life expectancy had increased to over _____ years.
    a. 47
    c. 75
    b. 68
    d. 80

19. Schaie's study of aging found that
    a. abilities decline uniformly from age 30.
    b. abilities show severe decline by age 67.
    c. significant individual differences are found.
    d. intellectual decline is strictly genetic.

20. Memories about which people are not aware are
    a. semantic.
    c. implicit.
    b. episodic.
    d. autobiographical.

ANSWER KEYS

Practice Test – Pretest (with text page numbers)

1.	c 592	6.	d 602	11.	a 614	16.	c 598
2.	a 593	7.	a 602	12.	b 617	17.	d 603
3.	b 593	8.	b 603	13.	d 603	18.	b 609
4.	c 617	9.	c 607	14.	b 603	19.	a 611
5.	b 600	10.	d 608	15.	c 595	20.	a 617

Key Vocabulary Terms

1. The peripheral slowing hypothesis is the theory that suggests that overall processing speed declines in the peripheral nervous system with increasing age; the general slowing hypothesis is the theory that processing in all parts of the nervous system, including the brain, is less efficient.

2. Primary aging is aging that involves universal and irreversible changes that, due to genetic preprogramming, occur as people get older; secondary aging is change in physical and cognitive functioning due to illness, health habits, and other individual differences, but which are not due to increased age itself and are not inevitable.

3. <u>Genetic preprogramming theories</u> of aging suggest that our body's DNA genetic code contains a built-in time limit for the reproduction of human cells; <u>wear-and-tear theories</u> of aging state that the mechanical functions of the body simply wear out with age.

4. <u>Dementia</u> is the most common mental disorder of the elderly, and covers several diseases, each of which includes serious memory loss accompanied by declines in other mental functioning; <u>Alzheimer's disease,</u> one of the dementias, is a progressive brain disorder that produces loss of memory and confusion.

Programmed Review

1. increasing, young, old, oldest, doubled
2. Ageism, negative, mental, prejudice, overqualified, baby
3. Western, venerate
4. agile, physically, Primary, senescence, Secondary
5. hair, elasticity, collagen
6. shorter, four, posture, cartilage, osteoporosis, calcium, protein, exercise
7. women, double, harshly, hide
8. brain, blood, oxygen, neurons
9. heart, respiratory, digestive, constipation, hormones, Muscle, oxygen, nutrients
10. peripheral, generalized
11. accidents, environment, decision, remove, perception
12. decrease, lens, pupil, optic, distant, light, adjust
13. Cataracts, lens, Glaucoma, drain, macular
14. 30, 50, higher, painful, social, paranoia, lonely
15. discriminating, taste buds, olfactory, malnutrition, hypertension
16. health, three-quarters
17. heart disease, cancer, stroke, chronic, Arthritis, hypertension
18. psychological, depression, losses, lower
19. drugs, metabolism, interactions
20. dementia, memory, intellectual, judgment
21. Alzheimer's, 100,000, gradually, forgetfulness
22. beta amyloid, brain, hippocampus, frontal, temporal, neurons, acetylcholine
23. Genetics, viruses, immune, hormone, linguistic, cognitive
24. acetylcholine, anti-inflammatory, C, E
25. 24, nursing, secondary
26. secure, labels, calendars, clothing, bathing, driving, telephone, exercise, time
27. genetic, lifestyles, economic, Psychological, control, health, active
28. nutrition, hunger, poor, infirm, motivation, exercise
29. health, regular, Testosterone, erection, refractory, vaginas, lubrication
30. preprogramming, Wear-and-tear, energy, radicals, optimistic
31. expectancy, increased, Health, sanitation, working, safer
32. Telomeres, replicating, lengthened
33. radicals, antioxidant, unstable,
34. calorie, radicals
35. rejects, cloned, nonhuman, artificial
36. women, men, conception, males, die, 2.57
37. hormones, stress, healthier, socioeconomic
38. declining
39. cohort, timed, reaction, repeated
40. cross-sequential, uniform, cognitive, minimal, patterns, environmental, cultural
41. training, practical, plasticity
42. esteem, episodic, semantic, implicit, Short-term, unfamiliar
43. autobiographical, recall, Pollyanna, congruent
44. environmental, information-processing, biological
45. Elderhostel

Practice Test - Post Test (with text page numbers)

1.	d	593	6.	b	602	11.	c	597	16.	a	600
2.	d	593	7.	d	603	12.	a	617	17.	c	605
3.	d	596	8.	c	603	13.	c	618	18.	c	609
4.	a	593	9.	d	604	14.	a	612	19.	c	614
5.	b	595	10.	d	609	15.	b	599	20.	c	617

Chapter 18

Social and Personality Development in Late Adulthood

CHAPTER OUTLINE

◈ Personality Development and Successful Aging
- ♦ Continuity and Change in Personality During Late Adulthood
- ♦ Age Stratification Approaches to Late Adulthood
- ♦ Does Age Bring Wisdom?
- ♦ Successful Aging: What Is the Secret?

◈ The Daily Life of Late Adulthood
- ♦ Living Arrangements: The Places and Spaces of Their Lives
- ♦ Financial Issues: The Economics of Late Adulthood
- ♦ Work and Retirement in Late Adulthood

◈ Relationships: Old and New
- ♦ Marriage in the Later Years: Together, Then Alone
- ♦ The Social Networks of Late adulthood
- ♦ Family Relationships: The Ties that Bind
- ♦ Elder Abuse: Relationships Gone Wrong

LEARNING OBJECTIVES

After you have read and studied this chapter, you should be able to answer the following questions.

1. In what ways does personality develop during late adulthood?
2. How do people deal with aging?
3. In what circumstances do older people live and what difficulties do they face?
4. What is it like to retire?
5. How do marriages in late adulthood fare?
6. What happens when an elderly spouse dies?
7. What sorts of relationships are important in late adulthood?

PRACTICE TEST - PRETEST

Circle the correct answer for the following multiple choice questions and check your answers with the Answer Key at the end of this chapter.

1. Ego integrity or despair is viewed as the outcome of a long process of development by what theorist?
   - a. Peck
   - b. Baltes
   - c. Erikson
   - d. Levinson

2. An elderly woman has arthritis, which is progressively getting worse. She finds herself needing to learn to cope with these changes. If she is successful, what developmental task of Peck's theory will she have accomplished?
   a. ego integrity versus despair
   b. ego transcendence versus ego preoccupation
   c. body transcendence versus body preoccupation
   d. redefinition of self versus preoccupation with work-role

3. Franklin now 73 has been forced to retire from the auto plant he worked at all of his life. As he gets on with his life he attempts to redefine himself in ways that relate to work role. If he is successful, what developmental task of Peck's theory will he have accomplished?
   a. ego integrity versus despair
   b. ego transcendence versus ego preoccupation
   c. body transcendence versus body preoccupation
   d. redefinition of self versus preoccupation with work-role

4. Dominique is 63 years old and is beginning to view herself as "old." According to Levinson she is experiencing a
   a. life review.
   b. transition stage.
   c. integrated personality.
   d. selective optimization.

5. What percent of persons over the age of 65 live with other family members?
   a. 33 percent
   b. 66 percent
   c. 75 percent
   d. 80 percent

6. What percent of people spend the last part of their lives in nursing homes?
   a. 5 percent
   b. 16 percent
   c. 25 percent
   d. 40 percent

7. A woman has several relatives with diabetes and believes that she will experience the same problems that they have. When she is diagnosed with diabetes she decides "what's the use," and refuses to follow her doctor's orders regarding diet and exercise. This process that becomes a downward cycle is called
   a. dementia.
   b. depression.
   c. learned helplessness.
   d. selective optimization.

8. Mohammed is in the _____ retirement stage where he is considering his options and becoming engaged in new, more fulfilling activities.
   a. classic
   b. honeymoon
   c. reorientation
   d. positive

9. In comparison to married individuals in late adulthood, never-married individuals report feeling
   a. less lonely.
   b. less healthy.
   c. more lonely.
   d. more healthy.

10. Which of the following statements about gender roles in late adulthood is true?
    a. Husbands' companionship needs tend to be greater than their wives'.
    b. Wives' companionship needs tend to be greater than their husbands'.
    c. Both husbands' and wives' companionship needs are lower than in early adulthood.
    d. Both husbands' and wives' companionships needs are greater than in early adulthood.

11. Gloria Heinemann and Patricia Evans proposed
    a. stages of dying.
    b. stages of retirement.
    c. developmental tasks of old age.
    d. stages of adjustment to widowhood.

12. The physical or psychological mistreatment or neglect of elderly individuals is called
   a. battering.
   c. institutionalism.
   b. elder abuse.
   d. learned helplessness.

13. Elderly people come to grips with their coming death in Peck's stage of
   a. ego integrity versus despair.
   b. life review.
   c. ego transcendence versus ego preoccupation.
   d. reorientation and readjustment.

14. Maynard seems to fear almost everything: being ill, the future, being unable to cope. He is representative of which personality type?
   a. disintegrated and disorganized
   b. passive dependent
   c. defended
   d. integrated

15. The most successful individuals cope comfortably with aging. They are ____ personalities.
   a. disintegrated and disorganized
   b. passive dependent
   c. defended
   d. integrated

16. In cultures that have higher levels of esteem for old age
   a. there is greater heterogeneity.
   b. people have less responsibility as they age.
   c. elderly people have little control over resources.
   d. there is more homogeneity.

17. Research on disengagement theory indicates that
   a. disengagement is always a negative experience.
   b. disengagement is the predominant pattern of aging.
   c. decreased emotional investment can be beneficial.
   d. in non-Western cultures, disengagement is the norm.

18. Mrs. Chen goes to a care facility during week days while her daughter is at work, but is at home evenings and weekends. She goes to a(n)
   a. nursing home.
   b. continuing care community.
   c. adult day-care facility.
   d. skilled nursing facility.

19. The termination phase of retirement
   a. occurs because of major physical deterioration.
   b. is the first stage of retirement.
   c. occurs at age 65 for most people.
   d. is experienced by everyone.

20. What percent of divorces involve women over the age of 60?
   a. 2 percent
   c. 25 percent
   b. 10 percent
   d. 40 percent

KEY NAMES

Match the following names with the most accurate description and check your answers with the Answer Key at the end of this chapter.

1. ___ Baltes and Baltes   a. developmental tasks

2. ___ Robert Butler   b. ego integrity versus despair

3. ___ Costa and McCrae   c. intelligence

4. ___ Erik Erikson   d. life review

5. ___ Daniel Levinson   e. personality types

6. ___ Bernice Neugarten   f. selective optimization with compensation

7. ___ Robert Peck   g. stability of personality

8. ___ Lewis Terman   h. the winter of life

KEY VOCABULARY TERMS

Compare and contrast the following sets of terms.

1. Continuing care community; Adult day-care facilities; Skilled nursing facilities

2. Age stratification theory; Continuity theory

Fill in the blanks for the term for each definition. When complete, the first letter of each term from top to bottom will spell the term for the last definition. (NOTE: some terms may be from previous chapters.)

3. ___ _____   The positive outcome of Erikson's final stage of life, characterized by a process of looking back over one's life, evaluating it, and coming to terms with it.

    ____ _____   The point in life in which people examine and evaluate their lives.

    _____   The period in late adulthood that marks a gradual withdrawal from the world on physical, psychological, and social levels.

    ___ _____   The period in which elderly people must come to grips with their coming death is _____ vs. ego preoccupation.

    _____   ___ of self versus preoccupation with work-role is a time people redefine themselves in ways that do not relate to their work-roles or occupations.

    _____   The theory that successful aging occurs when people maintain interests, activities, and social interactions with which they were involved during middle age.

    ____ _____   ___ versus body preoccupation is a period in which people must learn to cope with and move beyond changes in physical capabilities as a result of aging.

245

_ _ _ _ _ _ _ _ _   A prenatal test in which sound waves are used to scan the pregnant woman's abdomen.

_ _ _ _ _ _   _ _ _ _ _ _ _   Assistance and comfort supplied by another person or a network of caring, interested people.

_ _ _   The rational part of the personality according to Freud.

The physical or psychological mistreatment or neglect of elderly individuals is _ _ _ _ _ _ _ _ _.

Define each of the following terms and give a specific example of each.

4. Selective optimization
5. Institutionalism
6. Wisdom
7. Activity theory
8. Disengagement theory
9. Ego-integrity-versus despair
10. Body transcendence versus body preoccupation

PROGRAMMED REVIEW

Fill in the blanks in the following Programmed Review and check your answers with the Answer Key at the end of this chapter.

Personality Development and Successful Aging

Continuity and Change in Personality During Late Adulthood

1. According to Costa and McCrae, basic personality traits are remarkably ____ across adulthood. Longitudinal investigations have found the personality traits that remain stable to be agreeableness, ____, intellect, ____, and energy. This suggests that there is a fundamental _____ to personality.

2. Erikson's final stage is _____ and is characterized by a process of looking back over one's life, _____ it and coming to terms with it. People who are successful with this stage experience a sense of _____ and _____. Others, who are not successful with this stage, look back on their lives with _____.

3. Peck suggests that personality development in old age is occupied by _____ major developmental tasks. The first is a redefinition of self versus preoccupation with _____, in which people must redefine themselves in ways that do not relate to their work roles or occupations. The second is body _____ versus body _____ where people cope with the physical changes of aging. The third is _____ transcendence versus _____ preoccupation, where they come to grips with their coming death.

4. According to Levinson, people enter late adulthood by passing through a ____ stage that occurs around age 60 to 65. They come to view themselves as entering ____ adulthood, knowing society's ____ about the elderly. Such changes produce a heightened recognition that one is aging, as well as a sense of one's own ____. People in late adulthood can serve as _____ to younger individuals and they may find themselves regarded as _____ elders whose advice is sought and relied upon.

5. Neugarten examined the way people _____ with aging and found four _____ types. Those who are unable to accept aging and experience despair are _____ and _____. Individuals who lead lives filled with fear are _____. Individuals who seek to ward off aging are _____. The most successful individuals who cope comfortably with aging are _____.

6. Life _____, in which people examine and evaluate their lives, is a common theme for most personality theorists who focus on late adulthood. According to Butler, it is triggered by the increasingly obvious prospect of one's _____. Reminiscence may lead to a sense of sharing and _____, a feeling of _____ with others. It can be a source of _____ interaction. Reminiscence may even have cognitive benefits, serving to improve _____ in older people.

7. Age _____ theories suggest that economic resources, power, and privilege are distributed _____ among people at different stages of the life course. Peak earning years are in the _____. Older adults are seen as not _____and in some cases simply _____. These theories help explain why aging is viewed more _____ in less industrialized countries.

8. Conduct toward elderly people in particular cultures is quite _____. Asian societies hold elderly people, particularly members of their own families, in higher _____ than Western cultures tend to. In general, cultures that hold the elderly in high regard are relatively _____ in socioeconomic terms. The roles that people play in those societies entail greater _____ with increasing age, and elderly people control _____ to a relatively large extent. Moreover, roles display _____ throughout the life span and older adults continue to engage in activities that are _____ by society. Cultures in which older adults are held in higher regard tend to be organized around _____ families.

Does Age Bring Wisdom?

9. Wisdom is expert _____ in the practical aspects of life. Some developmentalists argue that wisdom is a trait of _____. While _____ may permit a person to think logically and systematically, wisdom provides an understanding of _____ behavior. Other research has looked at wisdom in terms of the development of theory of _____, the ability to make inferences about others' thoughts, feelings and intentions.

Successful Aging: What Is the Secret?

10. According to _____ theory, late adulthood marks a gradual _____ from the world on physical, psychological, and social levels. On a physical level, elderly people have lower _____ levels and tend to slow down progressively. Psychologically, they begin to _____ from others and on a social level, they engage in less _____ with others. Disengagement theory suggests that withdrawal is a _____ process. The gradual withdrawal of people in late adulthood permits them to become more _____ about their own lives and less _____ by social roles.

11. According to _____ theory, the people who are most likely to be happy in late adulthood are those who are fully _____ and engaged with the world. This theory suggests that successful aging occurs when people maintain the interests and activities they pursued during _____. Successful aging occurs when older adults _____ to inevitable changes in their environments by resisting reductions to their _____environments. However, not every activity will have an equal impact on a person's _____ and _____ with life.

12. According to _____ theory, people need to maintain their desired level of _____in society in order to maximize their sense of _____ and _____. Good _____ and _____ health are important in determining an elderly persons' sense of well-being. Having _____ security is critical and a sense of _____, independence, and personal control is a significant advantage.

13. Baltes and Baltes focus on the selective _____ with _____ model, the process by which people concentrate on particular _____ areas to compensate for losses in other areas.

The Daily Life of Late Adulthood

Living Arrangements: The Places and Spaces of Their Lives

14. Only _____ percent of the elderly live in nursing homes. Roughly _____ of people over the age of 65 live with other members of the family, in most cases their _____. African Americans are more likely than whites to live in _____ families.

15. One of the most recent innovations in living arrangements is the _____ community. Such communities typically offer an environment in which all residents are of _____ age or older and need various levels of care. Residents sign _____ under which the community makes a commitment to provide care at whatever level is needed, starting with occasional home care and then moving into _____ living, in which people live in independent housing but are supported by _____ providers to the extent required. Continuing care ultimately extends all the way to full-time _____ care. Members of such communities tend to be relatively well-off _____.

16. In adult _____ facilities, elderly individuals receive care only during the day, but spend nights and _____ in their own homes. Sometimes these facilities are combined with _____ and _____ day-care programs.

17. The most intensive institutions are _____ facilities, which provide full-time nursing care for people who have _____ illnesses or are recovering from a temporary medical condition. The greater the extent of nursing home care, the greater the _____ required of residents. The loss of _____ brought about by institutional life may lead to difficulties.

18. Elderly people are as susceptible as other members of society to society's _____ about nursing homes and their expectations may be particularly _____. They may see themselves as just marking time until they eventually _____. Although such fears may be exaggerated, they can lead to _____, a psychological state in which people develop apathy, indifference, and a lack of caring about themselves brought on by a sense of learned _____, a belief that one has no control over one's environment. The loss of control experienced by residents of nursing homes and other institutions can have a profound effect on their sense of _____.

Financial Issues: The Economics of Late Adulthood

19. People who reach late adulthood today may experience growing economic _____ as a result of the increasing human life span. Some _____ percent of people age 65 and older live below the poverty line. Women are almost _____ as likely as men to be living in poverty. Minority _____ fare the worst of any category.

20. One source of financial vulnerability for people in late adulthood is the reliance on a _____ income for support. Another important source of financial vulnerability in older adults is rising _____ care costs. The average older person spends close to _____ percent of his or her income for health care costs.

Work and Retirement in Late Adulthood

21. In the late 1970s, mandatory retirement ages were made _____ in almost every profession. Part of broader legislation that makes age _____ illegal, these laws gave most workers the opportunity either to remain in jobs they held previously or to begin working in entirely different fields. There is little evidence to support the idea that older workers' ability to perform their jobs _____. Age discrimination remains a _____ despite laws making it illegal.

22. Whatever the reason they retire, people often pass through a series of retirement _____. Retirement may begin with a _____ period, in which former workers engage in a variety of activities that were previously hindered by full-time work. The next phase may be _____, in which retirees conclude that retirement is not all they thought it would be. The next phase is _____, in which retirees reconsider their options and become engaged in new, more fulfilling activities. If successful, this leads to the retirement _____ stage, in which they come to grips with the realities of retirement and feel fulfilled in this new phase of life. Finally, the last stage is _____. Although some people terminate retirement by going back to _____, termination for most people results from major physical _____. Not everyone passes through all these stages, and the sequence is not _____.

23. Gerontologists suggest that several factors are related to successful retirement including planning ahead _____, considering _____ off from work gradually, exploring _____ before one retires, discussing views of retirement with one's _____, considering where to _____, determining whether to _____ one's current home, and planning to _____ time.

248

Relationships: Old and New

<u>Marriage in the Later Years: Together, Then Alone</u>

24. After the age of 65, the proportion of men who are married is far _____ than that of women. One reason for this disparity is that _____ percent of women outlive their husbands by at least a few years. The marriage _____ works to keep women single even in the later years of life. At the same time, it makes _____ for men much easier. The vast majority of people who are still married in later life report that they are _____ with their marriages.

25. At least _____ percent of divorces in the United States involve women over the age of 60. Often, women who divorce do so because their husbands are _____ or _____. But in the more frequent case of a husband seeking a divorce from his wife, the reason is often that he has found a _____ woman. Often the divorce occurs soon after _____.

26. For many women, marriage has been their primary role and the center of their identities, and they may view divorce as a major ____. For those who have remained single throughout their lives, about ____ percent of the population, late adulthood may bring fewer transitions. Never-married individuals report feeling less _____ than do most people their age, and they have a greater sense of _____.

27. In late adulthood _____ companionship needs tends to be greater than their _____. _____ become more affectionate and less _____. _____ become more assertive and _____.

28. Some caregivers report feeling quite satisfied as a result of fulfilling what they see as their _____ to demonstrate _____ and _____. And some of those who experience emotional distress initially find that the distress _____ as they successfully adapt to the stress of caregiving. In most cases the spouse that provides care is the _____.

29. The death of a _____ leads to profound feelings of loss and often bring about drastic changes in _____ and _____ circumstances. Although initially family and friends provide a great deal of _____, this assistance quickly fades into the background, and newly widowed people are left to make the adjustment to being single on their own. _____ issues are of major concern to many widowed people.

30. According to Heinemann and Evans, the process of adjusting to widowhood encompasses _____ stages. In the first stage, _____, spouses prepare for the eventual death of the partner. The second stage of adjustment to widowhood is _____ and is an immediate reaction to the death of the spouse. The last stage of adjustment is _____. The period begins with the _____ of one's loss and continues with the _____ of roles and the formation of new _____.

<u>The Social Networks of Late Adulthood</u>

31. Because late adulthood may bring with it a gradual loss of _____, the ability to maintain friendships may take on more importance. Friendships may be more _____ than family ties. When a _____ dies, people typically seek out the companionship of _____ to help deal with their loss. The way that adults view ____ determines how vulnerable they are to the death of a friend.

32. _____ support is assistance and comfort supplied by a network of caring interested people. People can provide _____ support by lending a sympathetic ear and providing a sounding board and _____ support by helping with rides or picking up groceries. In Western societies, older adults value relationships in which _____ is possible.

<u>Family Relationships: The Ties that Bind</u>

33. Siblings may provide unusually strong _____ support during late adulthood. Some 75 percent of children live within a _____ minute drive of their parents. _____ tend to be in more frequent contact with their parents than _____. _____ tend to be the recipients of communication more frequently than _____. Because the great

majority of older adults have at least _____ child who lives fairly close, family members still provide significant aid to one another.

34. The bonds between parents and children are sometimes _____, with parents seeking a _____ relationship and children a more _____ one. Parents have a greater _____ stake in close ties, because they see their children as perpetuating their beliefs, values, and standards. Children are motivated to maintain their _____ and live _____ from their parents.

35. Grandmothers tend to be more _____ with their grandchildren than grandfathers. Most young adult grandchildren feel closer to their _____ and most express a preference for their _____ grandmothers. _____ grandparents tend to be more involved with their grandchildren. _____ seem to play a more central role in the lives of African-American children than in the lives of white children. Most _____ do not have close relationships with their great-grandchildren.

Elder Abuse: Relationships Gone Wrong

36. According to some estimates, elder abuse, the _____ or _____ mistreatment or neglect of elderly individuals, may affect _____ people above the age of 60 each year. Elder abuse is most frequently directed at _____ members, particularly elderly _____. Those most at risk are likely to be less _____ and more _____ than the average person, and they are more likely to be living in a _____ home. The best approach to dealing with elder abuse is to _____ it from occurring. Caregivers should take occasional _____.

CRITICAL THINKING QUESTIONS

In order to further your mastery of the topics covered in this chapter, write out your answers to the following essay questions in the spaces provided.

1. How might personality traits account for success or failure in achieving satisfaction through the life review process?

2. Do individuals in age groups other than late adulthood engage in life review? Under what circumstances could it occur at an earlier point in the life span?

3. How might cultural factors affect an older person's likelihood of pursuing either the disengagement strategy or the activity strategy?

4. Do only older people engage in selective optimization with compensation? Might such a strategy be usefully employed by younger people?

5. What policies might a nursing home institute to minimize the chances that its residents will develop institutionalism? Why are such policies relatively uncommon?

6. How does the marriage gradient contribute to the likelihood that a woman will fall into poverty when she reaches old age?

7. From your observations how do most adults prepare for retirement? According to what you have learned from this chapter how should adults prepare for retirement?

8. What are some factors that can combine to make older adulthood a more difficult time for women than for men?

9. What are some ways in which the retirement of a spouse can bring stress to a marriage? Is retirement less stressful in households where both spouses work, or more stressful?

10. Do you think there are cultural differences in the experience of widowhood? If so, what sorts of differences?

PRACTICE TEST – POST TEST

Circle the correct answer for the following multiple choice questions and check your answers with the Answer Key at the end of this chapter.

1. Which of the following is a developmental task of later adulthood, according to Peck's theory?
   a. ego integrity versus despair
   b. the life review
   c. late life transition
   d. redefinition of self versus preoccupation with work-role

2. The point in life in which people examine and evaluate their lives is known as the
   a. life review.
   b. life journey.
   c. life integration.
   d. life evaluation.

3. What theory suggests that successful aging occurs when people maintain the interests, activities, and social interactions with which they were involved during middle age?
   a. change theory
   b. evolving theory
   c. activity theory
   d. integrity theory

4. The model of selective optimization with compensation was proposed by whom?
   a. Peck
   b. Erikson
   c. Levinson
   d. Baltes and Baltes

5. A woman needs full-time nursing care and is placed in a nursing home. She believes that she no longer has control over her environment and she then develops an indifference to life. What psychological reaction is she experiencing?
   a. dementia
   b. life review
   c. institutionalism
   d. selective optimization

6. What percent of people age 65 or older live below the poverty line?
   a. 5 percent
   b. 12 percent
   c. 25 percent
   d. 40 percent

7. Mr. Bond had been looking forward to retirement but now that he is retired it is not what he thought it was going to be. He misses talking to customers and has difficulty keeping busy. What stage of retirement is he in?
   a. termination
   b. reorientation
   c. disenchantment
   d. retirement routine

8. What percent of women outlive their husband by at least a few years?
   a. 30 percent
   b. 50 percent
   c. 70 percent
   d. 90 percent

9. As Lewis approaches his 91st birthday he begins to gain an increasing sense of acceptance of his mortality. He is successfully displaying which developmental task of Peck's theory?
   a. ego integrity versus despair
   b. ego transcendence versus ego preoccupation
   c. body transcendence versus body preoccupation
   d. redefinition of self versus preoccupation with work-role

10. The power structure of marriage in late adulthood changes in what way?
    a. Both men and women become more assertive.
    b. Both men and women become more affiliative.
    c. Men become more assertive and women become more affiliative.
    d. Men become more affiliative and women become more assertive.

11. The adaptation stage of adjusting to widowhood includes all of the following behaviors EXCEPT
    a. reality testing.
    b. reintegration.
    c. formation of new friendships.
    d. reorganizing roles.

12. Research on the Big Five personality traits indicates that
    a. they are remarkably stable across adulthood.
    b. there is no change over time.
    c. only the trait of extroversion changes.
    d. personality is fundamentally discontinuous.

13. Which of the following is NOT one of the Big Five personality traits?
    a. conscientiousness
    b. psychoticism
    c. neuroticism
    d. openness

14. Meredith is disgusted by the thought of aging, and thus she gets face lifts and frequently exercises in an attempt to ward off aging. She represents which personality type?
    a. disintegrated and disorganized
    b. passive-dependent
    c. defended
    d. integrated

15. Age stratification theories help explain why aging is viewed more positively in
    a. highly industrialized societies.
    b. less industrialized societies.
    c. highly diverse and industrialized societies.
    d. agrarian and industrialized societies alike.

16. Wisdom differs from intelligence in that wisdom
    a. has a timeless quality.   c. is related to the here-and-now.
    b. is a trait of the young.   d. can be measured more easily.

17. People need to maintain their desired level of involvement in society to maximize their sense of well-being and self-esteem according to which theory?
    a. disengagement   c. life review
    b. activity   d. continuity

18. Gary has had an extremely difficult time accepting his aging. He now lives in a nursing home and experiences increasing amounts of despair as he ages. He represents which personality type?
    a. disintegrated and disorganized
    b. passive-dependent
    c. defended
    d. integrated

19. What percent of people caring for their spouses are women?
    a. 10 percent   c. 50 percent
    b. 29 percent   d. 75 percent

20. Research on grandparenting indicates that
    a. grandfathers tend to be more involved with grandchildren.
    b. most young adults express a preference for maternal grandmothers over paternal grandmothers.
    c. white grandparents are more involved with grandchildren than are African-American grandparents.
    d. most great-grandparents have very close relationships with great grandchildren.

ANSWER KEYS

Practice Test – Pretest (with text page numbers)

1. c 625	6. a 637	11. d 646	16. d 630
2. c 625	7. c 637	12. b 652	17. c 632
3. d 625	8. c 641	13. c 625	18. c 637
4. b 627	9. a 644	14. b 628	19. a 641
5. b 636	10. a 644	15. d 628	20. a 644

Key Names

1. f	3. g	5. h	7. a
2. d	4. b	6. e	8. c

Key Vocabulary Terms

1. A <u>continuing care community</u> offers an environment in which all the residents are of retirement age or older and need various levels of care; an <u>adult day-care facility</u> provides elderly individuals with care only during the day; a <u>skilled nursing facility</u> provides full-time nursing care for people who have chronic illnesses or are recovering from a temporary medical condition.

2. <u>Age stratification theory</u> is the view that an unequal distribution of economic resources, power, and privilege exists among people at different stages of the lifecourse; <u>continuity theory</u> suggests that people need to maintain their desired level of involvement in society in order to maximize their sense of well-being and self-esteem.

3. Ego integrity, Life review, Disengagement, Ego transcendence, Redefinition, Activity, Body transcendence, Ultrasound, Social support, Ego (Elder abuse)

Programmed Review

1. stable, satisfaction, extroversion, continuity
2. ego integrity versus despair, evaluating, satisfaction, accomplishment, dissatisfaction
3. three, work role, transcendence, preoccupation, ego, ego
4. transition, late, stereotypes, mortality, resources, venerated
5. cope, personality, disintegrated, disorganized, passive-dependent, defended, integrated
6. review, death, mutuality, interconnectedness, social, memory
7. stratification, unequally, 50s, productive, irrelevant, industrialized
8. variable, esteem, homogeneous, responsibility, resources, continuity, valued, extended
9. knowledge, timing, intelligence, wisdom, mind
10. disengagement, withdrawal, energy, withdraw, interaction, mutual, reflective, constrained
11. activity, involved, middle age, adapt, social, happiness, satisfaction
12. continuity, involvement, well-being, physical, mental, financial, autonomy
13. optimization, compensation, skill
14. 5, two-thirds, spouses, multigenerational
15. continuing care, retirement, contracts, assisted, medical, nursing, financially
16. day-care, weekends, infant, child
17. skilled-nursing, chronic, adjustment, independence
18. stereotypes, negative, die, institutionalism, helplessness, well-being
19. pressure, 11, twice, women
20. fixed, health, 20
21. illegal, discrimination, declines, reality
22. stages, honeymoon, disenchantment, reorientation, routine, termination, work, deterioration, universal
23. financially, tapering, interests, partner, live, downsize, volunteer
24. greater, 70, gradient, remarriage, satisfied
25. 2, abusive, alcoholic, younger, retirement
26. failure, 5, lonely, independence
27. husband's, wives, men, women
28. opportunity, love, devotion, declines, wife
29. spouse, economic, social, support, Economic
30. three, preparation, grief and mourning, adaptation, acceptance, reorganization, friendships
31. control, flexible, spouse, friends, friendship
32. Social, emotional, material, reciprocity
33. emotional, 30, Daughters, sons, Mothers, fathers, one
34. asymmetrical, closer, distant, developmental, autonomy, independently,
35. involved, grandmothers, maternal, African-American, Grandfathers, great-grandparents
36. physical, psychological, two million, family, parents, healthy, isolated, caregiver's, prevent, breaks

Practice Test - Post Test (with text page numbers)

1.	d 625	6.	b 638	11.	a 646	16.	a 631
2.	a 625	7.	c 641	12.	a 625	17.	d 634
3.	c 633	8.	c 646	13.	b 625	18.	a 628
4.	d 634	9.	b 627	14.	c 628	19.	d 645
5.	c 637	10.	d 643	15.	b 629	20.	b 651

Chapter 19

Endings: Death and Dying

CHAPTER OUTLINE

◆ Dying and Death across the Life Span
  ♦ Defining Death: Determining the Point at Which Life Ends
  ♦ Death across the Life Span: Causes and Reactions
  ♦ Can Death Education Prepare Us for the Inevitable?

◆ Confronting Death
  ♦ Understanding the Process of Dying: Are There Steps Toward Death?
  ♦ Choosing the Nature of Death: Is DNR the Way to Go?
  ♦ Caring for the Terminally Ill: The Place of Death

◆ Grief and Bereavement
  ♦ Mourning and Funerals: Final Rites
  ♦ Bereavement and Grief: Adjusting to the Death of a Loved One

LEARNING OBJECTIVES

After you have read and studied this chapter, you should be able to answer the following questions.

1. What is death, and what does it mean at different stages of the life span?
2. In what ways do people face the prospect of their own death?
3. How do survivors react to and cope with death?

PRACTICE TEST - PRETEST

Circle the correct answer for each of the following multiple choice questions and check your answers with the Answer Key at the end of this chapter.

1. If someone's death is confirmed by an electroencephalogram reading of electrical brain waves, the death referred to is
   a. local death.
   b. brain death.
   c. somatic death.
   d. functional death.

2. SIDS (sudden infant death syndrome) occurs more often between the ages of
   a. birth and two months.
   b. two and four months.
   c. four and six months.
   d. six and eight months.

3. When children first think of death, they see death as
   a. fun.
   b. painless.
   c. temporary.
   d. unimportant.

4. Many adolescents have a sense of invulnerability which makes the concept of their death very difficult to comprehend. What is the likely source of the sense of invulnerability?
   a. personal creed
   b. personal fable
   c. diminishing cognitive ability
   d. metacognition skills which support assimilation

5. A significant drop in cognitive performance which foreshadows death is referred to as
   a. terminal decline.
   b. denial.
   c. memory loss.
   d. brain death.

6. A patient has developed a sense of hopelessness over her terminal illness, and she especially mourns over the approaching separation from her friends and family. This would coincide with which of Kübler-Ross's five stages of dying?
   a. anger
   b. denial
   c. bargaining
   d. depression

7. A legal document that informs both family and health-care workers of the signer's wish to avoid the use of heroic measures to maintain life in the event of irreversible illness is called a(n)
   a. living will.
   b. donor's will.
   c. interstate will.
   d. holographic will.

8. What do the letters "DNR" represent?
   a. do not recover
   b. do not respond
   c. do not revitalize
   d. do not resuscitate

9. Administering a lethal dose of a drug to hasten the death of a suffering person is an example of
   a. passive euthanasia.
   b. voluntary active euthanasia.
   c. dyathanasia.
   d. rational suicide.

10. The rate of suicide is highest for
    a. children.
    b. adolescents.
    c. young adults.
    d. the elderly.

11. When it comes to grief and bereavement, most people in Western societies,
    a. seek professional help for the death of a loved one.
    b. are surprisingly ill-prepared for the death of a loved one.
    c. become desensitized to death, even the death of a loved one.
    d. are emotionally well-balanced, and readily accept the death of a loved one.

12. What percent of people show relatively deep depression following the loss of a loved one?
    a. 3 to 5 percent
    b. 15 to 30 percent
    c. 50 to 55 percent
    d. 75 to 80 percent

13. People who study death and dying are called
    a. gerontologists.
    b. thanatologists.
    c. mortologists.
    d. pathophysiologists.

14. Why is miscarriage exceptionally difficult for parents?
    a. SIDS is well researched and very preventable.
    b. Parents form bonds with the unborn child.
    c. The level of hormones produced during pregnancy chnage.
    d. Infant mortality rate in the U.S. is rare.

15. Children come to accept the universality of death by _____ years of age.
    a. 4   c. 7
    b. 5   d. 9

16. Wayne is 16 years old. He is most likely to die from
    a. an accident.   c. murder.
    c. suicide.   d. cancer.

17. Maude is 35 years old and has just found out that she is dying. She thinks that it is wrong that she is dying when a criminal her age is not. Maude is in what stage of dying?
    a. denial   c. bargaining
    b. anger   d. depression

18. The final stage of dying according to Kübler-Ross is
    a. anger.   c. bargaining.
    b. denial.   d. acceptance.

19. Which of the following is an accurate statement about hospice care?
    a. Hospice patients die in their own home.
    b. Hospice's goal is to prolong life as much as possible.
    c. No extraordinary or invasive means are used.
    d. Hospice is another form of hospital care.

20. Rebecca is in the first stage of grief and thus will experience all of the following EXCEPT
    a. shock.   c. accommodation.
    b. disbelief.   d. denial.

KEY NAMES

Match the following names to the most accurate description and check your answers with the Answer Key at the end of this chapter.

1. ___ Jack Kevorkian   a. five stages of dying

2. ___ Elizabeth Kübler-Ross   b. suicide machine

3. ___ Edwin Schneidman   c. themes in reactions to dying

KEY VOCABULARY TERMS

Describe the difference among the following pairs of terms.

1. Functional death; Brain death

2. Home care; Hospice care; Palliative care

3. Bereavement; Grief

4. Living wills; Euthanasia

Define the following terms and give a specific example of each.

5. Sudden infant death syndrome (SIDS)
6. Thanatologists

PROGRAMMED REVIEW

Fill in the blanks in the following Programmed Review and check your answers with the Answer Key at the end of this chapter.

Dying and Death across the Life Span

Defining Death: Determining the Point at Which Life Ends

1. _____ death is defined by an absence of heartbeat and breathing. In _____ death, all signs of brain activity, as measured by electrical brain waves, have ceased. When brain death occurs, there is no possibility of restoring brain _____. Some medical experts suggest that a definition of death that relies only on a lack of brain _____ is too broad. The legal definition of death in most localities in the United States relies on the absence of _____ functioning.

Death across the Life Span: Causes and Reactions

2. Despite its economic wealth, the United States has a relatively _____ infant mortality rate. The United States ranks behind _____ other industrialized countries in the proportion of infants who die during the first year of life. The number of parents who experience the death of an infant is substantial, and their reactions may be _____. One of the most common reactions is extreme _____.

3. Another kind of death that is exceptionally difficult to deal with is prenatal death, or _____. Parents typically form _____ bonds with their unborn child.

4. In _____ infant death syndrome, or SIDS, a seemingly healthy baby stops _____ and dies of unexplained causes. Usually occurring between the ages of _____ months, SIDS strikes unexpectedly. Afterwards, parents often feel intense _____, and acquaintances may be suspicious of the _____ cause of death.

5. During childhood, the most frequent cause of death is _____. A substantial number of children in the United States are victims of _____, which have nearly _____ in number since 1960. Death by homicide has become the _____ leading cause of death for children between the ages of 1 and 9.

6. Around the age of 5, children begin to develop a concept of _____. Although they are aware of death before that time, it is usually thought of as a _____ state that involves a _____ in living. Some preschool-age children think of death in terms of _____. Children sometimes leap to the erroneous conclusion that they are somehow _____ for a person's death. Around the age of 5, the finality and _____ of death become better understood. By age 9 they come to accept the _____ of death and its finality. By middle childhood, children also learn about some of the _____ involved with death.

7. In many ways, adolescents' views of death are as _____ as those of younger children. Adolescents develop a personal _____, a set of beliefs that causes them to feel unique and special. Such thinking can lead to quite _____ behavior because of a sense of _____.

8. The most frequent cause of death among adolescents is _____, most often involving _____. Adolescents who learn that they have a terminal illness often feel _____ and _____, that life has been unjust to them. Some adolescents diagnosed with a terminal illness react with total _____ and may find it impossible to accept the seriousness of their illness.

9. In early adulthood, the leading cause of death continues to be _____. By the end of early adulthood, however, _____ becomes a more prevalent cause of death. For those people facing death in early adulthood, several concerns arise such as the desire to develop _____ relationships and express _____, each of which are inhibited if not completely prevented by a terminal illness. Another particular concern during young adulthood involves future _____. Young adults sometimes make poor _____. They are outraged at their plight and feel the world is _____, and they may direct their _____ at care providers and loved ones.

10. For people in middle adulthood, the shock of a life threatening _____ is not so great. They may be able to consider the possibility of death in a fairly _____ manner. Fears about death are often _____ in middle adulthood than at any time previously or even later in life. These fears may lead people to look at life in terms of the number of years they have _____. The most frequent cause of death in middle adulthood is _____ or _____.

11. The prevalence of death in the lives of elderly people makes them _____ anxious about dying than they were at earlier stages of life. By the time they reach late adulthood, people may begin to make _____ for their demise. The _____ decline is a significant drop in performance on cognitive tasks that may foreshadow death.

12. The _____ rate for men climbs steadily during late adulthood and _____ men over the age of _____ have the highest rate. Suicide is often the result of severe _____ or some form of dementia.

13. One particularly salient issue for older adults suffering from a terminal illness is whether their lives still have _____. Elderly people who are dying fear that they are _____ to their family or to society.

14. Even within Western societies, reactions to death and dying are quite _____. Some societies view death as a _____ or as a judgment about one's contributions to the world. Others see death as _____ from an earthly life of travail. Still others view death as the start of an _____ life.

Can Death Education Prepare Us for the Inevitable?

15. _____, people who study death and dying, have suggested that death _____ should be an important component of schooling. We typically give _____ the task of dealing with dying people, and do not talk to _____ about death or allow them to go to funerals for fear of disturbing them. Even those most familiar with death such as _____ workers are uncomfortable talking about the subject. There are several death education programs, which include _____ intervention education, _____ death education, and death education for members of the _____ professions.

Confronting Death

Understanding the Process of Dying: Are There Steps Toward Death?

16. Kübler-Ross developed a stage theory of death and dying, built on extensive _____ with people who were dying and with those who cared for them. Based on her observations, she suggests that people pass through _____ basic stages.

17. In _____ people resist the idea that they are going to die. Many experts view this stage in _____ terms as a _____ mechanism that can permit people to absorb the unwelcome news on their own terms. People pass into the stage of _____ and then to the stage of _____, in which they try to negotiate their way out of death. In some ways, bargaining seems to have _____ consequences. Although death cannot be postponed indefinitely, having a _____ may in fact delay death until then.

18. Eventually people proceed to the _____ stage, realizing that the issue is settled and they cannot bargain their way out of death. In _____ depression, the feelings of sadness are based on events that have already occurred. In _____ depression, people feel sadness over future losses. In the stage of _____, people are fully _____ that death is impending. They have virtually no _____ about the present or future. They have made _____ with themselves, and they may wish to be left _____.

19. Kübler-Ross's theory is largely limited to those who are _____ that they are dying and who die in a relatively _____ fashion. For people who suffer from diseases in which the prognosis is _____ as to when or even if they will die, the theory is not applicable. Not every person passes through every _____, and some people move through the stages in a different _____. The stages are so well known the caregivers have sometimes encouraged patients to work through steps in a prescribed order, without consideration of their _____ needs. Other researchers suggest that _____ plays an important role throughout the process of dying. And there are

substantial differences in people's reactions to _____ death. Schneidman suggests that there are _____ in people's reactions to dying.

Choosing the Nature of Death: Is DNR the Way to Go?

20. The letters DNR written on a patient's medical chart mean do not _____. This issue is related to _____ of terms and concerns about _____ of life. Medical personnel are _____ to carry out the wishes of the terminally ill and their families to suspend aggressive treatment.

21. To gain more control over decisions regarding their death, people are increasingly signing living _____, legal documents that designate the medical treatments they want or do not want, and a specific person, called a health care _____, to act as an individual's representative in making health care decisions.

22. Dr. Kevorkian became well known for his invention and promotion of a _____ machine in a process known as _____ suicide, a death in which a person provides the means for a terminally ill individual to commit suicide. In the _____, it is an acceptable practice for medical personnel to help end their patients' lives.

23. Assisted suicide is one form of _____, the practice of assisting terminally ill people to die more quickly. Popularly known as _____ killing, it involves either actively hastening death (_____ euthanasia) or withholding treatment that might be expected to postpone death (_____ euthanasia).

24. A survey of nurses in intensive care units found that _____ percent had deliberately hastened a patient's death at least once. Euthanasia is controversial because it centers on decisions about who should _____ life. Many opponents argue that the practice is _____ wrong. Others point out that physicians are often _____ in predicting when a person will die. Others say that even if patients ask or beg health care providers to help them die, they may be suffering from a form of deep _____.

Caring for the Terminally Ill: The Place of Death

25. Hospitals are among the least _____ locales in which to face death. Hospitals are typically _____, with staff _____ throughout the day. They are designed for people to get _____ not deal with _____. People frequently die _____. Hospitals typically don't have the resources needed to deal adequately with the _____ requirements of terminal cases.

26. In _____ care, dying people stay in their homes and receive treatment from their families and visiting medical staff. _____ care is meant to provide physical and psychological comfort, not _____. _____ care is provided in institutions devoted to those who are terminally ill.

Grief and Bereavement

Mourning and Funerals: Final Rites

27. The average funeral in the United States costs _____. The nature of funerals is also determined by social _____ and customs. In Western societies, funeral _____ follow a typical pattern. Prior to the funeral, the body is _____ in some way and is dressed in special clothing. Funerals usually include the celebration of a _____ rite, the delivery of a _____, a _____ of some sort, and some _____ period in which relatives and friends visit the mourning family and pay their respects. Military funerals typically include the firing of _____ and a _____ draped over the coffin.

28. Other _____ include funeral rituals of different sorts. In _____, a traditional Hindu practice in India that is now illegal, a widow was expected to throw herself into the fire that consumed her husband's body. In ancient China, _____ were sometimes buried alive with their master's body.

29. _____ is acknowledgement of the objective fact that one has experienced a death, whereas _____ is the emotional response to one's loss.

30. The first stage of adjustment to loss typically entails _____, numbness, disbelief, or outright denial. In the next phase, people begin to confront the death and realize the extent of their _____. They fully experience their _____ and they react to the _____ that the separation from the dead person will be permanent. Finally, people who have lost a loved one reach the _____ stage. They begin to pick up the pieces of their _____, and to construct new _____.

31. There is no evidence that a particular _____ for grieving exists. Those who show the most _____ distress immediately after a death are the most apt to have adjustment difficulties and _____ problems later on.

32. A good deal of evidence suggests that _____ people are particularly at risk of death. Remarriage seems to _____ the risk of death for survivors. People who are already insecure, anxious, or fearful are less able to _____ effectively. People whose relationships were marked by _____ before death are more apt to suffer poor postdeath outcomes than those who were secure in their relationships. Those who were _____ on their partners and who feel more _____ without them, are apt to suffer more after the death. Bereaved people who lack _____ support are more likely to have feelings of loneliness and are at more risk. The _____ of a loved one's death appears to affect the course of grieving.

33. Among the strategies that can help a child cope with grief are being _____, encouraging _____ of grief, reassuring children that they are not to _____ for the death, and understanding that children's _____ may surface in unanticipated ways.

CRITICAL THINKING QUESTIONS

To further your understanding of the topics covered in this chapter, write out your answers to the following essay questions in the spaces provided.

1. Given their developmental level and understanding of death, how do you think preschool children react to the death of a parent?

2. What aspects of their development make terminally ill young adults become concerned about marriage, childbearing, and work?

3. Have you ever had to grieve the loss of something? How was your grief similar or different to the stages described in the text?

4. In what ways do you think older people's sense of worth can be affected, negatively and positively, by family attitudes, caregiver actions, and other environmental influences?

5. Do you think Kübler-Ross's five stages of dying might be subject to cultural influences? Age differences? Why or why not?

6. Do you think assisted suicide should be permissible? What about other forms of euthanasia? Why or why not?

7. Can you think of additional stages, not discussed by Kübler-Ross, that people might experience when dying? How would you test your hypothesis?

8. What cultural beliefs in U.S. society do you think contribute to people's reluctance to think about death?

9. Why do you think the risk of death is so high for people who have recently lost a spouse? Why might remarriage lower the risk?

10. Would you recommend death education for children in elementary school? At what age would you start to deal with the subject of death? Why?

PRACTICE TEST – POST TEST

Circle the correct answer for each of the following multiple choice questions and check your answers with the Answer Key at the end of this chapter.

1. Functional death is defined by a(n)
   a. absence of a brain wave.
   b. inability to think, reason, or feel.
   c. absence of heartbeat and breathing.
   d. failure to respond to external stimuli.

2. The infant mortality rate for those under age 1 in the United States ranks _____ compared to the infant mortality rate for other industrialized countries.
   a. first
   b. second
   c. twelfth
   d. twenty-second

3. At what age do children begin to develop a concept of death?
   a. 2 years
   b. 5 years
   c. 6 years
   d. 7 years

4. Most older patients who are going to die
   a. want to know they are dying, but most doctors prefer not to tell them.
   b. want to know they are dying, and most doctors prefer to tell them.
   c. do not want to know they are dying, but most doctors prefer to tell them.
   d. do not want to know they are dying, and most doctors prefer not to tell them.

5. What is the sequence in the stages of death, according to Kübler-Ross?
   a. anger, denial, bargaining, depression, acceptance
   b. anger, bargaining, depression, denial, acceptance
   c. bargaining, denial, anger, depression, acceptance
   d. denial, anger, bargaining, depression, acceptance

6. One significant criticism of Kübler-Ross's work on dying is that
   a. her data were based on women only.
   b. her data were done from a small sample.
   c. the concept of death is changing, and her conclusions may no longer be valid.
   d. the stages are not universal and do not always occur in the same order.

7. What percentage of terminal patients do not want to be resuscitated?
   a. 21 percent
   b. 33 percent
   c. 41 percent
   d. 51 percent

8. Euthanasia is also known as
   a. death-aid.
   b. mercy killing.
   c. dyathanasia.
   d. rational suicide.

9. In the United States, death occurs most often in
   a. hospices.
   b. hospitals.
   c. the home.
   d. the workplace.

10. When you lose a loved one, the emotional response is called
    a. bereavement.
    b. grief.
    c. coping.
    d. bargaining.

11. Diane's mother is 103 years old and she experiences sadness regarding her mother morality. Diane is experiencing
    a. denial.
    b. acceptance.
    c. preparatory depression.
    d. reactive depression.

12. How much higher than normal is the risk of death in the first year following the loss of a spouse?
    a. 7 times
    b. 17 times
    c. 27 times
    d. 37 times

13. What does the average funeral cost in the United States?
    a. $1,000
    b. $3,000
    c. $7,000
    d. $15,000

14. During childhood, the most frequent cause of death is
    a. accidents.   c. homicide.
    b. SIDS.   d. AIDS.

15. In early adulthood, the leading cause of death is
    a. suicide.   c. homicide.
    b. accidents.   d. AIDS.

16. The feelings of sadness based on events that have already occurred is
    a. reactive depression   c. suttee.
    b. preparatory depression.   d. acceptance.

17. Max has a terminal disease. In his prayers, he promises that he will give time to charitable causes if he is just allowed to live a few years more. Max is in which stage of dying?
    a. denial   c. bargaining
    b. anger   d. depression

18. A health care proxy is
    a. a legal guardian of a terminally ill person's estate.
    b. representative to make health care decisions.
    c. has assisted a loved one in suicide.
    d. is a recipient of passive euthanasia.

19. In India, a traditional Hindu practice which is now illegal dictated that a widow throw herself on her husband's funeral fire. This practice is called
    a. suttee.   c. wake.
    b. shivah.   d. mourning.

20. In order to help a child cope with death, adult caregivers should
    a. explain that the person is just sleeping.
    b. reassure the child that he or she is not to blame.
    c. discourage expressions of grief.
    d. expect the child to react as an adult would

ANSWER KEYS

Practice Test – Pretest (with text page numbers)

1.	b 659	6.	d 668	11.	b 677	16.	a 661
2.	b 659	7.	a 670	12.	b 678	17.	b 677
3.	c 660	8.	d 669	13.	b 665	18.	d 668
4.	b 661	9.	b 661	14.	b. 659	19.	c 674
5.	a 663	10.	d 663	15.	d 660	20.	c 677

Key Names

1. b   2. a   3. c

Key Vocabulary Terms

1. <u>Functional death</u> is the absence of a heartbeat and breathing; <u>brain death</u> is a diagnosis of death based on the cessation of all signs of brain activity, as measured by electrical brain waves.

2. <u>Home care</u> is an alternative to hospitalization in which dying people stay in their homes and receive treatment from their families and visiting medical staff; <u>hospice care</u> is provided for the dying in institutions devoted to

those who are terminally ill; <u>palliative care</u> is meant to provide physical and psychological comfort but not a cure.

3. <u>Bereavement</u> is acknowledgement of the objective fact that one has experienced a death; <u>grief</u> is the emotional response to one's loss.

4. <u>Living wills</u> are legal documents designating what medical treatments people want or do not want if they cannot express their wishes; <u>euthanasia</u> is the practice of assisting people who are terminally ill to die more quickly and may be included in a living will.

Programmed Review

1. Functional, brain, functioning, waves, brain
2. high, 22, profound, depression
3. miscarriage, psychological
4. sudden, breathing, 2 and 4, guilt, "true"
5. accidents, homicides, tripled, fourth
6. death, temporary, reduction, sleep, responsible, irreversibility, universality, customs
7. unrealistic, fable, risky, invulnerability
8. accidents, motor vehicles, angry, cheated, denial
9. accidents, disease, intimate, sexuality, planning, patients, unfair, anger
10. disease, realistic, greater, remaining, heart attack, stroke
11. less, preparations, terminal
12. suicide, white, 85, depression
13. value, burdens
14. diverse, punishment, redemption, eternal
15. Thanatologists, education, hospital, children, emergency, crisis, routine, helping
16. interviews, five
17. denial, positive, defense, anger, bargaining, positive, goal
18. depression, reactive, preparatory, acceptance, aware, feelings, peace, alone
19. aware, leisurely, ambiguous, step, sequence, individual, anxiety, impending, themes
20. resuscitate, differentiation, quality, reluctant
21. wills, proxy
22. suicide, assisted, Netherlands
23. euthanasia, mercy, voluntary active, passive
24. 20, control, morally, inaccurate, depression
25. desirable, impersonal, rotating, better, dying, alone, emotional
26. home, Palliative, cure, Hospice
27. $7,000, norms, rituals, prepared, religious, eulogy, procession, formal, weapons, flag
28. cultures, suttee, servants
29. Bereavement, grief
30. shock, loss, grief, reality, accommodation, lives, identities
31. timetable, intense, health
32. widowed, lower, cope, ambivalence, dependent, vulnerable, social, suddenness
33. honest, expressions, blame, grief

Practice Test - Post Test (with text page numbers)

1. c 659	6. d 668	11. c 668	16. a 668
2. d 659	7. b 670	12. a 678	17. c 667
3. b 660	8. b 671	13. c 676	18. b 670
4. a 663	9. b 672	14. a 660	19. a 677
5. d 667	10. b 677	15. b 661	20. b 660